water

A TURBULENT HISTORY

Stephen Halliday

SUTTON PUBLISHING

First published in 2004 by
Sutton Publishing Limited
Phoenix Mill · Thrupp · Stroud
Gloucestershire · GL5 2BU

British Library Cataloguing in Publication Data
A catalogue record for this book is available from the British Library.

ISBN 0-7509-3300-3

Fifty per cent of the author's royalties on this book will be paid
to WaterAid Trading Limited which gives all of its taxable
profits to WaterAid, registered charity number 288701.
WaterAid is the UK's only major charity dedicated exclusively
to the provision of safe domestic water, sanitation and hygiene
education to the world's poorest people. WaterAid, Prince
Consort House, 27–29 Albert Embankment, London SE1 7UB;
www.wateraid.org.uk.

Typeset in 10.5/15 pt Photina MT.
Typesetting and origination by
Sutton Publishing Limited.
Printed and bound in England by
J.H. Haynes & Co. Ltd, Sparkford.

CONTENTS

LIST OF ILLUSTRATIONS

PROLOGUE
'WATER, WATER, EVERYWHERE'

Water, along with air, is the commodity most essential to human life. There is no shortage of it in the world, though most of it is in the wrong place or in the wrong form. Some seventy per cent of the world's surface is covered by oceans. They hold about 97 per cent of the world's water but their briny contents, unless expensively treated, are useless for drinking or irrigation. Some of the world's heaviest precipitation is to be found in the tropical forests of Brazil, the icy wastes of Siberia and the semi-Arctic regions of northern Canada and Alaska where few people live.[1] This explains why a further 2 per cent of water is in the form of ice sheets or permanent snow cover. Indeed, fresh water, in the form of rainfall, rarely occurs where the need is greatest. Of all the continents, Asia has the highest availability of fresh water but the lowest usable quantity per capita because much of its water is in sparsely inhabited mountain regions where few of its vast population make their homes. Australia, the world's driest continent, has the highest availability per capita because of its relatively small population. Yet in the Australian capital territory, Canberra, the shortage of fresh water has led the government to adopt schemes whereby 'grey water', from bathing and from domestic appliances, is recycled for irrigation in order to conserve drinking water supplies.[2]

'NOR ANY DROP TO DRINK'

Abundance of water in populated areas is no guarantee of its usefulness. Bangladesh, served by 230 rivers, is one of the wettest places on earth, yet of the 6.3 million people who live in the capital, Dhaka, less than half live in dwellings connected to a regular water supply.[3] Those who are connected receive a supply on average only 7 hours a day. Paradoxically, safe water supplies are often rendered dangerous during the monsoon season of summer and early autumn when disastrous floods cause inadequate sewage systems to overflow into water supplies. The majority of the city's population who live in shanty towns, with no title to the land they occupy, are often the victims of 'waterlords' who control access to wells and springs on their land. Lack of effective drainage can mean that the rains which bring life to Bangladesh's paddy fields sometimes wash them away.

In Great Britain, a land well supplied with fresh water sources, treatment and supply facilities, we rarely think about where our water comes from or how we use it. In many developing countries the availability of water is a source of continuous anxiety. It has been estimated that one-sixth of the world's population have to travel 1km or more to collect water which is often of doubtful quality. About half the world's population lacks access to *safe* water free from diseases and a greater proportion is without adequate sanitation.[4] A London family spends about 0.22 per cent of its income on treated water whereas a family in Accra, Ghana, spends 22 per cent on water whose quality may not be guaranteed – a hundred times greater outlay for a more doubtful benefit.[5] The consequences are social as well as economic. In much of Africa and Asia, water-gathering is the task of women and children, so the sight of a five-year-old child with a container of water balanced on her head is a familiar one. The child would be better off at school. The consequences extend to health and mortality. Five million people, most of them children, die each year from waterborne diseases like typhoid and cholera. To these must be added the countless millions who contract disabling diseases like polio and river blindness.

Our own ancestors in Great Britain suffered similar anxieties. The availability of an apparently reliable water supply determined where they lived and how they spent their daily lives or met their deaths. Until the nineteenth century, water was, for many, a precious commodity which was gathered from wells by women and children, bought from water carriers or, for a wealthy minority, piped into their homes. It was carefully conserved and recycled. Water that was drunk would end up in a cesspool from which it would be collected and sold as fertiliser. Water used for cooking would be kept for washing clothes or cleaning the home and used for such purposes several times before being surreptitiously dumped in the street sewers which were supposed to be used only for conducting rainwater to the rivers. Occasionally, water brought death into the home, as during the great cholera epidemics of the nineteenth century which carried off almost 40,000 citizens of London alone.

TAKEN FOR GRANTED

This volume considers the way in which water has become a part of our daily lives that we take for granted. Sir Hugh Myddleton (*c.* 1560–1631) constructed the New River in the reign of James I to give Londoners an assured supply of clean drinking water, an office it still performs. Others followed the example he set. In the same reign the Dutchman, Cornelius Vermuyden (*c.* 1593–1677), created some of England's richest agricultural land by draining the swamps of East Anglia and gave Canvey Island its first defences against the sea. The Duke of Bridgewater (1736–1803), the 'Canal Duke', began the process of transforming Britain's transport system: a necessary component of the Industrial Revolution which made Britain the workshop of the world. The Duke was followed by the inventors who turned Britain's principal sources of power for industry from the waterwheel to those based on water in another form – the steam engine. Thomas Newcomen (1663–1729), James Watt (1736–1819), Robert Stephenson (1803–59) and others each contributed to the process which created the economy on which we have come to depend.

In the nineteenth century, as Britain faced the possibility of foreign invasion, water was used to defend the kingdom as William Pitt the Younger (1759–1806) authorised the construction of the Royal Military Canal which, like the inland waterway network, has now become an attraction for visitors. A more enduring threat to the life of the nation was ended by great engineers like Sir Joseph Bazalgette (1819–91) who, by beginning the process of constructing a modern system of sanitation, ensured that supplies of drinking water ceased to be contaminated by deadly cholera and typhoid, diseases that caused such alarm to the population of Europe that his methods were adopted by other European cities. Bazalgette himself designed the sewerage of Budapest in 1869; at the same time the English engineer William Lindley installed a similar design for Hamburg; and Bazalgette's contemporary Eugene Belgrand was simultaneously at work in Paris.

There were also gentler influences. The landscape of the Lake District was not only the home of William Wordsworth (1770–1850) but the inspiration for some of his finest poetry and for the work of many other writers who chose to make their homes there. Beau Nash (1674–1762) turned the process of 'taking the waters' at Bath into a fashionable as well as a therapeutic experience, while at Malvern, Dr James Gully (1808–83), later disgraced, was as adept at making money from distinguished patients like Charles Darwin as he was at offering 'water cures'. Less affluent citizens had the Prince Regent, later George IV

(1762–1830), to thank for establishing Brighton as a resort for sea bathing, a model quickly followed by hundreds of other resorts offering the traditional seaside holiday.

In all these ways water has affected our lives, usually for the better. Perhaps after reading this volume we will value it more and be more sympathetic to the needs of those who still endure a daily struggle to obtain a commodity which we take for granted.

A 5-year old African girl fetches water for her family. See WaterAid website at WaterAid.org; 27–9 Albert Embankment, London SE1 7UB. (*WaterAid/Caroline Penn*)

1
WATER FOR DRINKING

Sir Hugh Myddleton, the New River and Clean Water

Let every man beware of all waters the which be standing, and be putrified
with froth.

> A Compendious Regimen or Dyetary of Health, c. *1545*

Fresh and fair New River Water! None of your pipe sludge!

> *The cry of water-carriers in seventeenth-century London*
> *advertising New River water*

A dilute solution of animal and vegetable substances in a state of
putrefaction.

> *A description of London's water in 1827*

HIDDEN RIVERS AND ELM PIPES

In 1603 in his *Survey of London*, John Stow wrote in flattering terms of the
quality of London's water, recording twelve conduits bringing water to the city
and claiming that 'they had in every street and lane of the City divers wells and
fresh springs'. Even as Stow wrote these words his complacency was becoming
ill-advised and within a few years Sir Hugh Myddleton (*c.* 1560–1631)[1] had
embarked upon the greatest engineering project of his age to remedy serious
deficiencies in the supply of water to the capital. As Stow recorded, the city's
water had traditionally been drawn from its network of springs, wells and
rivers, most of which still flow beneath the streets of the capital. The most

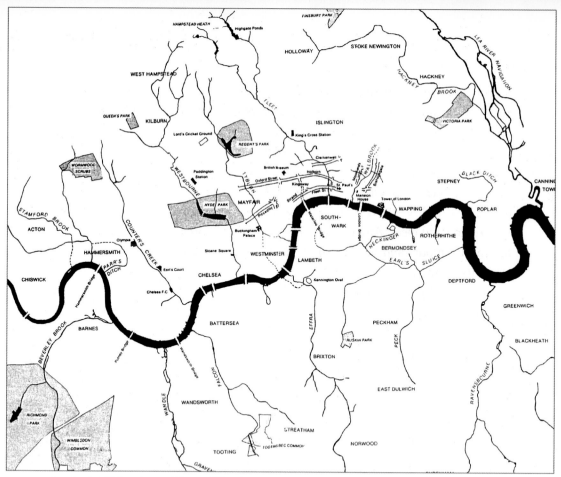

London's hidden rivers. (*Thames Water*)

important of those within the city walls was the Walbrook, which rises in Islington and enters the Thames near Cannon Street station. According to John Stow the Walbrook remained 'a fair brook of sweet water' for two hundred years after the Norman conquest, but by the reign of Edward I it had become little more than an open sewer and within twenty years its approaches to the Thames were mostly covered by streets and buildings. Other sources of water remained in use including the Fleet, a substantial river which was navigable as far as Oldbourne (Holborn) and which enters the Thames beneath Blackfriars bridge. Outside the boundary of the city itself, other rivers serve the capital. In Westminster the Tyburn, also known as the Kings Scholars Pond, rises on Hampstead Heath, surfaces as the lake in Regent's Park, flows beneath Buckingham Palace and enters the Thames near the Houses of Parliament. The Westbourne, like the Fleet and the Tyburn, rises on Hampstead Heath, surfaces in the Serpentine in Hyde Park, crosses Sloane Square underground station in a culvert just above the trains and enters the Thames at Chelsea. South of the Thames, rivers such as the Falconbrook, the Effra, the Neckringer and the

Ravensbourne served the much sparser populations of Battersea, Lambeth, Southwark and Bermondsey. Most of these rivers are completely covered over. Some, like the Shoreditch, are lost without trace (see map).

An earlier chronicler, William Fitzstephens, who worked as secretary to Thomas à Becket, recorded some of the springs and wells which supplied drinking water to Londoners. He wrote in his biography of Becket that 'there are also round about London most excellent wells whose waters are sweet, wholesome and clear. Among these Holywell, Clerkenwell and St Clement's well are most famous, and are visited by thicker throngs and greater multitudes of students from the schools and the young men of the City who go out on summer evenings to take the air.'[2] Clerkenwell has given its name to a district of London; Holywell is preserved in a street name north of Liverpool Street station; and Clement's Lane is near the Monument. Some, like Sadler's Wells,

Entrance to the Fleet river, 1756. (*Thames Water*)

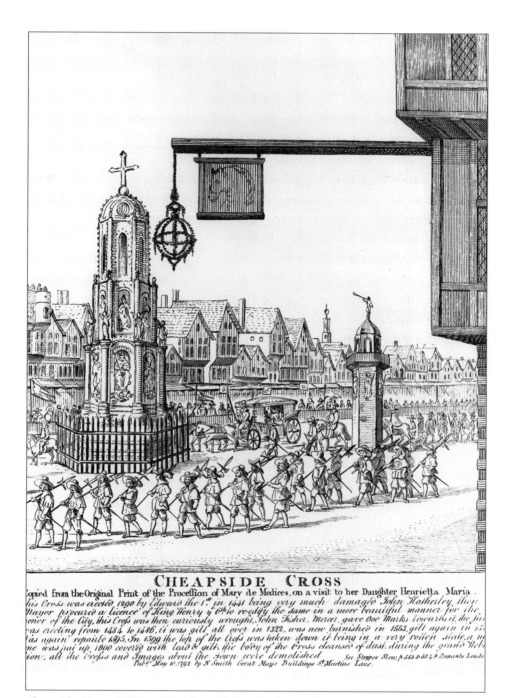

CHEAPSIDE CROSS

opied from the Original Print of the Proceffion of Mary de Medices, on a visit to her Daughter Henrietta Maria. his Crofs was erected 1290 by Edward the 1ft in 1441 being very much damaged John Hatherley then Mayor procured a licence of King Henry y 6th to re-edify the same in a more beautiful manner for the oner of the City, this Crofs was then curiously wrought. John Fisher, Mercer, gave 600 Marks towards it, the fu as erecting from 1484 to 1486, it was gilt all over in 1522, was new burnished in 1553 gilt again in 15 as again repaire 1595. In 1599 the top of the Crofs was taken down it being in a very rotten state, a n ne was put up, 1600 covered with lead & gilt, the body of the Cross cleansed of dust, during the grand Reb ion, all the Croffs and Images about the town were demolished   See Strypes Stow p 553 & 554 & Pennants Londo

Pub.d May 10.1792 by N Smith Great Mays Buildings St Martins Lane.

Cheapside Cross, 1798, with Gilbert de Sandford's conduit of 1236 visible in the background. *(Corporation of London)*

became fashionable spas with supposedly curative powers. Many of these sources remained in use until well into the nineteenth century. By the thirteenth century the city's natural supplies of water were inadequate for its needs so, in the words of Stow 'the citizens were forced to seek waters abroad'. In 1236, King Henry III 'for the profit of the City and the good of the whole realm thither repairing . . . granted to the citizens and their successors liberty to convey water from the town of Tyburn by pipes of lead into their city'. Gilbert de Sandford, a man otherwise unknown to history, allowed water to be conducted to the city from springs on land in his fief of Tyburn at Mary le Bourne (Marylebone). This was achieved by constructing a lead pipe from Tyburn along Oxford Street and Holborn, terminating at the Great Conduit in Cheapside, a prominent city landmark seen in pictures of Cheapside until the nineteenth century. The pipe was financed by French merchants from Amiens who were currying favour with the authorities because they wanted to enter the flourishing London wool market.[3] From the conduit water was carried beneath the streets in pipes made of elm and from them lead pipes bore the water into the houses of the well-to-do via connections known as 'quills'. These householders, together with tradesmen, paid for the water. The less wealthy citizens drew the water themselves, free of charge, or paid water carriers to do so for them, conveying the water in vessels known as 'tankards'. These were of a specified capacity and certified as such by the city authorities just as they certified weights and measures. In the centuries that followed, other conduits were constructed, their locations preserved in street names like Conduit Street, off Regent Street and Lamb's Conduit Passage in Holborn. The conduits themselves, like the wells referred to by William Fitzstephen in the twelfth century, became gathering places where citizens drew water and stayed to socialise with their fellow citizens, rather like public houses in later centuries. Another similarity to the pub lay in the fisticuffs that arose at the conduit at closing time. Conduits were normally open from early morning until about 11 a.m. and then from about 1 p.m. to 6 p.m. As closing

ANCIENT WATER CARRIER.

Medieval water carrier. (*Thames Water*)

time approached, tempers could rise as anxious citizens elbowed one another aside in their attempts to fill their 'tankards' before the conduit closed. The concept of the orderly queue was some centuries distant and magistrates were kept busy by the mayhem which occasionally resulted. In the centuries that followed, the city's supplies were further supplemented by similar enterprises, the Abbot of Westminster allowing the city to draw water from the Abbey's manor of Paddington in 1439.

In 1594, a mining engineer called Bevis Bulmer leased Broken Wharf, just east of the site of the Millennium Bridge, where he built London's first water tower, 120ft high. A horse-driven chain pump drew water from the river and pumped it to the tower from which it was distributed to premises throughout the city. It remained a prominent feature of the city skyline until the middle of the eighteenth century. In 1582 a Dutchman (possibly a German) called Peter Morice had leased from the City the first arch of London Bridge for £25 10s a year for five hundred years. Within the arch Morice constructed a waterwheel which drove a pump through which Thames water was distributed to premises

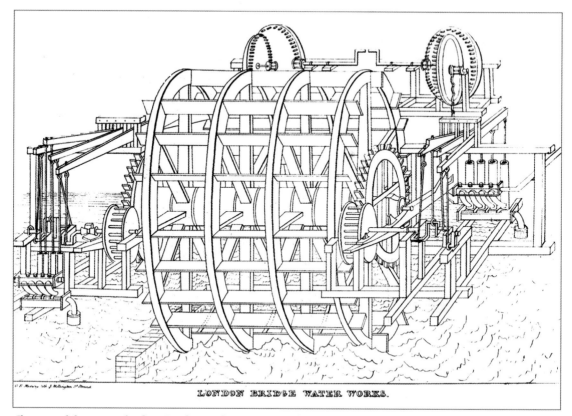

LONDON BRIDGE WATER WORKS.

Close-up of the waterwheel on London Bridge, *c.* 1750. (*Thames Water*)

in the City. The idea of pumped water was so novel that he was obliged to persuade the city fathers of the viability of his scheme by pumping a jet of water over St Magnus's church, adjacent to London Bridge.[4] The enterprise was so profitable that in 1701 Morice's descendant was able to sell it for the enormous sum of £38,000.[5] The wheel continued in use until 1822, when the demolition of the old London Bridge eliminated the waterwheel. By this time the water it was drawing from the river was seriously polluted by London's sewage. The organisation which bought out Morice's enterprise in 1701 was the New River Company.

THE NEW RIVER IS BORN

By the reign of Henry VIII it had become clear that London's sanitation and water supply needed further attention. The 1531 Bill of Sewers set up eight commissions of sewers whose duties included those of ensuring that streams and other watercourses were kept clean and free-flowing. At this time a number of theories emerged on the qualities to be sought in water. One of the writers most generous with his advice was Andrew Boorde who, having abandoned his calling as a Carthusian monk, travelled around Europe. Undeterred by the failure of a premature attempt to introduce rhubarb, with its health-giving properties, into England from Spain he compiled a book called *A Compendious Regimen or Dyetary of Health* in which he advised his fellow citizens: 'The best water is rainwater, so be it that it be clean and purely taken. Next to it is running water, the which doth swiftly run from the east unto the west on stones or pebbles . . . let every man beware of all waters the which be standing and which be putrified with froth.'

In 1543 the London Water Act empowered the city to supplement its supplies by drawing water from Hampstead Heath, paying an annual rental of a pound of pepper. No one stepped forward with the money required to build the necessary channels to bring the water to the city. The deadlock was not broken until 1604 when a former army captain called Edmund Colthurst was granted letters patent by James I to bring water from the vicinity of Ware, in Hertfordshire, to the capital. The water issued from chalk springs which rose from the southern slope of the Chilterns near the hamlets of Chadwell and Great Amwell. Colthurst planned to bring it to the vicinity of Sadler's Wells in London. Colthurst's moment of glory was brief. The following year, 1605, the Lord Mayor and the Court of Common Council secured the passage of the New River Act 'for bringing a fresh streame of running water to the North part of the City of London'.[6] This effectively supplanted Colthurst's scheme, despite the fact that Colthurst had already excavated about three miles of the river at a cost to himself of £200. Colthurst, in a final attempt to retain control of his brainchild, offered the City two-thirds of the shares in the New River Company if they would contribute £2,400 but the city fathers were not prepared to invest any hard cash in the scheme.[7] One of the Members of Parliament who sat on the committee which considered the Act was the MP for Denbighshire, Hugh Myddleton.

Hugh Myddleton

Hugh Myddleton was born in about 1560, the sixth son of Richard Myddleton, a modestly prosperous Denbighshire landowner. Hugh Myddleton made a considerable fortune from mining lead, copper and silver in Cardiganshire which he sold in London. By 1592 he was a liveryman of the company of Goldsmiths and was elected Prime Warden of that wealthy and influential body in 1610. He was a friend of Sir Walter Raleigh and may have invested in some of Raleigh's overseas adventures, few of which yielded good returns. Myddleton

may have traded in the tobacco which Raleigh had brought back from Virginia. Myddleton and Raleigh were reputed to have promoted the sale of the novelty by smoking it publicly while sitting and chatting outside Myddleton's house in Bassishaw Street, near Basinghall Street in the heart of the city: this despite King James's disapproval of the new substance as expressed in his *Blast Against Tobacco*.[8] In 1603 Myddleton was elected MP for Denbighshire, a position he held through-out the reign of James I.

In 1609 the city authorities, having secured the passage of the New River Act, delegated responsibility for the construction work to Myddleton, who had offered to finance it himself. It is not entirely clear why the city fathers chose Myddleton in preference to Colthurst but it is likely that

Sir Hugh Myddleton. *(Thames Water)*

Myddleton's greater wealth was a factor. The city had shown its reluctance to invest in Colthurst's scheme and, as has been seen, other sources of finance had also proved disappointing.[9] The Aldermen probably had greater confidence in the ability of Myddleton to finance the project from his own resources. Myddleton and Colthurst remained on friendly terms and Colthurst became an investor in what was now Myddleton's river.

Constructing the New River

Work began, at Myddleton's expense, in 1609. Carpenters were paid 1*s* 4*d* a day (about 7p) and labourers were paid 10*d* (4p) unless they were working in water in which case they were paid 1*s* (5p). These were quite generous wages for the period and up to a hundred men were employed at any one time. In the early phases of the work the builders used an 'Ingen', a plough drawn by a dozen horses, to loosen the soil before digging it out but this was abandoned after the first year so presumably it was not a success. The cost of the work was made greater by the lengthy route which the river had to take. The distance from Amwell to New River Head, adjacent to Sadler's Wells, is about twenty miles as the crow flies. However, New River Head is only 18ft lower than the source at Great Amwell, so the need to maintain a steady downhill gradient for the flowing water required the channel to follow a line close to the 100ft contour whose deviations made it necessary to create a channel approximately forty miles in length. In later centuries further engineering works were undertaken to straighten some of the more extravagant bends including the 'Enfield Loop' whose elimination shortened the river by some three miles. In October 1940 the three pipes which had been installed to bypass the loop were destroyed by German bombs and the water supply to London, some 46 million gallons a day, was thereby lost. Within 24 hours the army had excavated and re-opened the seventeenth-century loop and restored the water supply.[10]

Throughout its length the New River is approximately 10ft wide and 4ft deep. The chalk through which much of it runs is porous so the river bed was sealed with clay which was 'puddled' (trampled) into the bed to make it impervious to water. A peculiarity of the New River Act meant that Myddleton, as the owner of the company, did not own the river bed itself. The Act had granted way-leave over the lands through which the river passed but while the water belonged to Hugh Myddleton the river bed remained the property of the landowners on either side. If this device was intended to placate the landowners it did not succeed. In 1610, as the river advanced towards London, a group of landowners, worried that their fields would be drained of water by the river, or alternatively flooded by it, tried to have the Act repealed. The city authorities successfully lobbied the chancellor of the exchequer (whose name was Julius Caesar) to prevent this. At about the same time a warrant was issued against 'a seditious fellow who persuaded ye water bearers of London to petition his Majesty against the New River'.[11]

In 1612, as the river reached Cheshunt, near the half-way point on its journey to London, Myddleton's finances became overstretched and work temporarily ceased. Now the King came to the rescue. In May 1612, in a display of financial acumen most uncharacteristic of that impecunious monarch, James I agreed to pay £6,347 4s 11d into the struggling enterprise in return for half the profits that it generated: in effect the King was buying a half share in the company. On the same day, in an understandable effort to safeguard his new investment against further troubles from predatory landowners, His Majesty issued a command that no one was to 'molest, inquiet, trouble or hinder the said Hugh Myddleton' in the completion of the

Sir Hugh Myddleton's New River Head, 1665. In the background is the medieval St Paul's Cathedral a year before its destruction in the Great Fire. (*Thames Water*).

work. As work progressed, the King made further contributions to maintain his half-share until, in 1615, it amounted to £9,262 9s 6d.[12]

With royal support on the financial and legal fronts, work now proceeded smoothly to its conclusion, though some engineering obstacles remained. To cross Salmons Brook at Bush Hill, south of Enfield, a lead trough was constructed, 666ft long, mounted on a timber frame. The frame was later replaced by a bank of clay. In 1619 the course of the river was shortened by building a similar aqueduct 462ft long, to carry it across the Hackney Brook at Highbury. The river was carried in a lead-lined wooden trough which became known as the 'boarded river'. The wooden frames which carried these structures were replaced in the eighteenth century by more durable clay embankments.

A great occasion

The terminus of the river, New River Head, was the scene of the official opening ceremony on Michaelmas day, 29 September 1613 when, in the presence of the Lord Mayor and his immediate successor Sir Thomas Myddleton (Hugh's brother) the sluices were opened and the water from the river flowed into the 'inner pond' which had been built as a reservoir. The outlet pipe from the pond to the cistern was 18ft from its top. When the accumulation of dirt in the river caused sludge to approach the outlet pipe, the pond was emptied and cleaned. Despite this rather crude approach to hygiene, the New River Company enjoyed one of the best records for water cleanliness of all the London water companies and its record in furnishing a safe supply remained good throughout the cholera epidemics of the nineteenth century. The process of cleaning was aided after 1709 when a second reservoir pond was built above the first, the water being pumped by a windmill which can be seen on contemporary prints. Since the bed of the river itself technically remained the property of the adjacent landowners, the extensive grounds and premises at New River Head were the only property that the company owned. The New River was the longest channel carrying drinking water in Europe.

The water was distributed to streets and houses via a network of elm pipes which were sunk into the ground. With a maximum diameter of 7in, one end was 'sharpened' to fit into the next pipe, the same technology as had been used to distribute water from the Cheapside conduit four centuries earlier. The elm pipes were not replaced by iron pipes until the early nineteenth century. New River Head is 80ft above the Thames so it was possible to distribute the water throughout the city by gravity without the need for any pumping. One of the first to pay 5s (25p) to be connected to the supply was the father of the poet John Milton who then paid 6s 8d (33p) a quarter for the continuing supply to him as a 'tenant' of the company. Not everyone was as prompt as Mr Milton in recognising the benefits offered by the New River. By March 1614 only 384 properties[13] were connected, one of these being Myddleton's own house in Bassishaw Street which, presumably because of its size, paid £2 a year. However, this reluctance to pay for the supply did not deter a number of 'lewd and ill-disposed people' (in the words of the Privy Council) from drawing water illegally, vandalising the pipes and using the river to dispose of sewage and dead dogs. There was some prejudice against the idea of piped water, much of it encouraged by the water-carriers whose livelihood was threatened by it. Some of them, however, drew water from the company's cistern and announced themselves with the cry 'Fresh and fair New River Water! None of your pipe sludge!'[14] When freezing temperatures seemed likely to interrupt the supply, the pipes, where exposed, were covered with horse manure though this did not provide sufficient insulation when the Thames itself froze, as recorded by John Evelyn.[15]

By 1619 the number of such 'tenants' had reached one thousand, at which point the river struggled to cope with demand. In 1620 the supply of water was augmented by damming the River Lea and diverting some of its water to the New River. This enraged the bargemen on the Lea who believed that a drop in water levels on the river would endanger their livelihoods, so they destroyed the dam. This dispute rumbled on for fifty years, throughout the period of the Civil War until, in 1670, Charles II appointed Christopher Wren to investigate the bargemen's complaints. Wren concluded that the New River had no adverse effect on the navigability of the Lea and the dam remained in place. The company must have had some anxious moments during Wren's inquiry since the removal of the dam would have had serious consequences for its business. Its directors were certainly very conscious of the need for thrifty use of water. It was the New River Company which first installed cistern overflow pipes above the doors of tenants' houses so that their customers would have an incentive to stem the loss of water.[16] In 1738 an Act limited the company to the extraction of 22.5 million gallons of water a day and in 1770 a marble gauge was installed to measure the extraction rate. The gauge remains in place though no longer in use.

The company was involved in a controversy over the Great Fire of London in 1666. It was popularly believed that the fire had been started deliberately by Roman Catholics – a belief that was disgracefully reflected in the inscription on the Monument until it was removed in the nineteenth century at the insistence of a public-spirited solicitor called Charles Pearson. A source of this baseless rumour was a story that a member (shareholder) of the New River Company, referred to as 'one Grant, a papist', had turned off the water supply at New River Head during the fire. In reality Grant did not become a member of the company until after the fire but this did not prevent the story, or the inscription, from becoming firmly established. A similar alarm occurred in 1803 during a panic over the possibility of invasion by France supported by Irish Catholics. The Lord Mayor was worried that the New River Company had too many Irish employees who might shut off the water supply in the event of fire. The company dutifully provided details of their employees to the authorities.[17]

A new company

In the meantime Myddleton had restructured the company. In 1619 it was incorporated under the cumbersome title 'The Governor and Company of the New River brought from Chadwell and Amwell to London' and Myddleton issued shares in the company.[18] Half of the company, referred to as 'the King's moiety' remained in the ownership of the King. The other 'moiety' was divided into thirty-six shares which were owned by twenty-nine people, known as 'adventurers' – what we would now call venture capitalists. Four of the shares were owned by Edmund Colthurst, whose idea the New River had originally been. One authority has estimated that the shares were valued at £289 each at the time of incorporation.[19] All the authority, however, remained with Myddleton during his lifetime. He was appointed the 'governor' of the company and in his lifetime he retained all the executive powers associated with his position as the representative, or 'deputy' of the city under the terms of the original Act. He never transferred these powers to the company as a corporate body, a curious anomaly which was made possible by the then primitive state of company law. Hugh Myddleton was paid the very generous salary of £800 per annum. James I seems to have been a contented proprietor, receiving a payment of £433 2s 7d at Michaelmas, 1622.[20] Perhaps it was while inspecting his new investment that he inadvertently fell into the New River while riding in Theobalds Park in 1622. This experience did not alter his opinion of Myddleton for in the same year he conferred a baronetcy on his fellow entrepreneur who thus became Sir Hugh. The citation praised the new baronet for 'bringing to the City of London, with excessive charge and greater difficulty, a new cutt or river of fresh water, to the great benefit and inestimable preservation thereof'. Baronetcies, effectively hereditary knighthoods, had been devised by the King as a money-raising measure so the honour was all the more remarkable for the fact that the new baronet did not have to pay the King for his title. Bevis Bulmer had also received a knighthood from James in 1604 – perhaps a reflection of the importance that water was assuming in the life of the growing city.

A dividend of £11 19s 1d per share was paid in 1633 and thereafter dividends were paid annually. This was not enough for James's son, Charles I. Always short of money as a result of his endless disputes with Parliament, Charles agreed in 1630 to sell his shares back to Hugh Myddleton. In return Myddleton, on behalf of the company, agreed to pay £500 per annum to the Crown. This arrangement was known as the 'Crown Clog' and was challenged by the Metropolitan Water Board after it bought out the company in 1904, but in 1911 the House of Lords ruled that it remained an obligation of the board. It remained so until 1956 when the board bought out the Crown's interest for a payment of £8,230. In 1631 Sir Hugh Myddleton died and was buried in the church of St Matthew, Friday Street where he had been churchwarden. The church, just to the south of St Paul's cathedral, was destroyed in the Great Fire of 1666 and subsequently rebuilt by Wren, but Myddleton's tomb was lost. At his death he still owned all thirty-six of the King's shares. These carried no votes in the affairs of the company but since by this time he also owned twenty-six of the thirty-six adventurers' shares, he was effectively the owner of the company as well as its governor. The King's shares, however, did entitle the owner to vote in Parliamentary elections in both Hertfordshire and Middlesex, the two counties through which the river passed. The shares passed to Hugh's son, Sir William Myddleton, and thence to his grandson, also Sir Hugh, who sold fourteen of the King's shares for £7,000 free of the 'Crown Clog' which the Myddletons continued to pay. He kept the adventurers' shares, some of which remained in the Myddleton family until the New River Company was taken over by the Metropolitan Water Board in 1904. Hugh's granddaughter Elizabeth, who inherited four shares, married a man called John Grene (or Green) who commissioned Grinling Gibbons (1648–1720) to design the magnificent oaken room at Cistern House, New River Head. The shares steadily increased in value as dividends began to be paid regularly from the 1630s. By 1737 each share was valued at £5,250. By 1700 the annual dividend on each share was over £200 and by 1794 it had passed £430, representing an excellent investment for Sir Hugh's descendants. By 1901, shortly before the company passed into public ownership, it was estimated that the adventurers' shares were worth £125,000 and the King's shares £120,000,[21] the lower value reflecting their non-voting status.

COMPETITION

For half a century the company faced very little competition. In May 1664, the King received a petition from two entrepreneurs for authority to supply water to buildings in the vicinity of Piccadilly and the royal precinct of St James from a waterworks on the present site of Charing Cross station. Their joint-stock company (one of the first) was to be called the York Buildings Company because of its proximity to the buildings of that name to the south of the Strand. The waterworks was erected in 1675 and its huge tower remained a feature of the area into the nineteenth century, though the company itself enjoyed a chequered history. In 1720, at the time of the speculative frenzy known as the 'South Sea Bubble', a controlling interest in the company was acquired by a group of speculators. They used it as a vehicle for purchasing property confiscated from supporters of the 'Old Pretender' (father of 'Bonnie Prince Charlie') in the insurrection of 1715. In this way they bought up sequestered estates in Scotland and cashed in on the forestry, coal and iron reserve they contained, though with little benefit to the rest of the shareholders. A contemporary rhyme advised:

River Thames, looking west, showing York Buildings and York Buildings Waterworks, *c. 1700. (Corporation of London)*

> You that are blessed with wealth by your creator
> And want to drown your money in Thames Water,
> Buy but York Buildings and the Cistern there
> Will sink more pence than any fool can spare.

The company did have a more praiseworthy claim to distinction. In 1725 the company's horse-driven pump was replaced by Newcomen's 'atmospheric' steam engine. This was the first such engine installed in London and was described by an excited press as 'the famous and useful engine for raising water by fire'. It was probably installed on the premises by Thomas Newcomen himself but only survived for five years. The cost of coal for the comparatively inefficient engine was such that, in 1831, the engine was shut down and the horses resumed their work.[22]

In 1722 a more conventional organisation, the Chelsea Company, began to supply customers in Westminster from an intake close to the present site of Chelsea Bridge and this was followed by the Lambeth and Vauxhall companies south of the river. It was not until 1806 that the New River faced direct competition in the form of the East London Company, which also drew water from the River Lea. A fierce battle ensued between the two companies, each approaching the customers of the other in an attempt to persuade them to change suppliers, every switch requiring the roadways to be dug up. In 1807 the directors of the New River accused the East London Company of damaging its pipes and a price war ensued which slashed the profits of both companies. The East London directors complained that, if things carried on as they were, water would soon be as cheap as beer! In 1815, the year of a more memorable battle, the two companies signed a peace treaty which one writer has described as being 'as decisive as the battle of Waterloo'.[23] London was divided into spheres of interest and each agreed to stay away from the other's territory. Similar agreements were made with other competitors north of the river, the West Middlesex (drawing from the Thames at Hammersmith) and the Grand Junction Company drawing from the rivers Colne and Brent. Prices rose and customers complained. A contemporary writer estimated that the value of each share rose to £14,000 at this time.[24]

POLLUTION

The New River flowed very slowly, a process which helped to ensure that sediment was deposited on the river bed long before it reached New River

Head. Screens were installed at intervals of a few miles to remove flotsam and weeds and 'walksmen' were employed to patrol the river, clean the screens and cut out excessive weed growth. For these reasons the New River remained a reasonably clean supplier of water, though in 1810 a meeting at a tavern in Canonbury registered complaints about people who used the New River for bathing, washing clothes and as a receptacle for household waste. However, the company became caught up in a much sharper controversy about the quality and price of water, a controversy over which it had no control. Householders had long been forbidden to connect their drains to the public sewers, since the latter were supposedly reserved for the disposal of rainwater to the Thames. In 1815 the prohibition on connecting house drains and cesspools to the public sewers had been lifted so from that date an ever-swelling flood of sewage had been flowing into the Thames, still the capital's principal source of drinking water.[25] In 1827 a campaigner called John Wright published an inflammatory pamphlet whose cumbersome title tells all that needs to be known about its contents: 'The Dolphin, or Grand Junction Nuisance Proving that Several Thousand Families in Westminster and its Suburbs are Supplied with Water in a State Offensive to the Sight, Disgusting

Chelsea waterworks, *c.* 1830, the intake worryingly close to the Ranelagh sewer to the right of the picture. (*Thames Water*)

Sir Francis Burdett (1770–1844) A seasoned agitator, Sir Francis Burdett wisely married into the wealthy Coutts banking family which gave him a degree of financial independence to pursue the causes that he embraced. He campaigned against the wars with revolutionary France, the suspension of habeas corpus and the treatment of 'political' prisoners in prisons. So effective was his activity in this area that he was barred from visiting any prisons. He was elected MP for Middlesex in 1802 and deprived of his seat after objections from opponents. Despite swearing to have nothing more to do with politics he returned as MP for Westminster in 1807 after a duel with a rival whose candidature he had originally promoted. In 1809 he was committed to the Tower of London for supposedly infringing Parliamentary privilege and later gaoled for three months for agitation in connection with the Peterloo massacre of 1819 when a peaceful assembly in Manchester had been charged by cavalry on the orders of magistrates. He also advocated Catholic emancipation and Parliamentary reform but once these had been achieved, in 1829 and 1832 respectively, Burdett decided that things had gone too far. His reactionary views then caused him to be rejected by his Westminster constituents whereupon he was adopted by a Tory constituency in Wiltshire. His daughter Angela Burdett-Coutts was also a reformer and is credited with the establishment of drinking fountains in London to encourage temperance.

---

to the Imagination and Destructive to Health'. The pamphlet described the Grand Junction's water as 'a dilute solution of animal and vegetable substances in a state of putrefaction'.[26] Wright distributed thousands of copies of the pamphlet in Westminster and dedicated it to the campaigning MP Sir Francis Burdett who raised the matter in Parliament, declaring that: 'the water taken from the River Thames at Chelsea, being charged with the contents of the great common sewers, ought no longer to be taken up by any of the water companies'.[27] Burdett suggested, for the first time, that public ownership of the companies was the only solution to London's water problems. The time for this novel idea had not yet come. Instead, the government of the day appointed a Royal Commission, the first of many which wrestled with the problem over the decades which followed.

In 1828 the distinguished engineer Thomas Telford, aged seventy-one, was appointed to consider the problem, assisted by a chemist and by Dr Roget, a physician better known for his *Thesaurus*. The committee concluded that the Thames was no longer a safe source of drinking water and proposed that water be brought from the River Wandle in Surrey and from the Ver in Hertfordshire. The New River was identified as a supplier of safe water and Telford suggested that it be permitted to draw more water from the Lea and from wells on the Chiltern slopes. The cost of these measures was estimated, with confident precision, as amounting to £1,177,840 16*s* 5*d*. No suggestions were forthcoming as to how this huge sum might be raised. In the years that followed a number of increasingly extravagant schemes were put forward. A Royal Commission of 1866 listened to an engineer called Bateman who proposed to bring water 180 miles from Wales to a reservoir at Stanmore whence it would flow by gravity to buildings throughout the capital. The commissioners were not convinced, fearing that over such a long route the supply would be vulnerable to sabotage by an enemy. They came to the same conclusion about an even more ambitious scheme to bring water from Ullswater, Thirlmere and Haweswater in the Lake District.

TWO GREAT WATER ENGINEERS

In the meantime some more practical steps were being taken to clean up the existing water supply. In 1823 an engineer called James Simpson (1799–1869) succeeded his father Thomas as engineer to both the Chelsea and Lambeth water companies. In 1828 he built for the Chelsea company the world's first 'slow sand filter bed'. This consisted of a 2ft-deep layer of fine sand beneath which were further layers of sea shells, gravel and bricks. At the bottom were pipes with small holes. Water was released onto the filter and made its way through the sand, the top inch of which filtered out impurities. The shells were designed to prevent the sand being washed into the pipes. The water then made its way through the gravel and bricks until it entered the pipes from which it passed to the reservoirs, cleansed of 95 per cent of its impurities. Virtually all the pollutants were trapped in the top inch of the sand layer which would regularly be removed and replaced with fresh sand. Simpson regarded his novel device as a physical filter, which it was. It was not for many years that advances in chemistry and biology by scientists like Sir Edward Frankland (1825–99) revealed that the bacteria in the bed made it a biological filter as well. Filter beds which are recognisably descended from Simpson's are still used. Simpson also persuaded both the companies he served to remove their reservoirs to Seething Wells, near Kingston upon Thames. There, in 1852, he

Le Petit Trianon pumping station, Hyde Park, Thomas Hawksley's only monument in London. *(S. Halliday)*

installed sand filter beds which ensured that the companies' water supplies were as safe as science could then make them. In both respects he anticipated the Metropolis Water Act of 1852 which required that, by 1856, all companies should move their water intakes to a point above Teddington weir, the upper limit of the tidal river. Beyond that point London's sewage could not pollute the upper reaches of the river. The Act also followed Simpson's example in requiring filtration.

Simpson's most notable rival as a water engineer was Thomas Hawksley (1807–93) a man with whom he had some serious disagreements. Hawksley was born in Nottingham, apprenticed to an architect, and became engineer to the Nottingham water company. He was an advocate of the 'constant supply' of water under pressure to all users, a process that Simpson regarded as unduly costly. Simpson favoured an arrangement whereby water was made available at certain times and withheld at others, arguing that the rudimentary state of taps, valves and other plumbing apparatus would ensure that constant supply would lead to constant wastage. Simpson and Hawksley came into conflict in 1845 when they were both asked to enquire into the state of Liverpool's water supply.[28] Hawksley pointed out that the constant supply system that he had pioneered in Nottingham was suited to Liverpool, then the second largest town in Great Britain. As usual Hawksley supported his arguments with an overwhelming mass of evidence. His obituary recorded that 'His appearance in a case was heralded by the introduction of piles of statistics and other data which he had sent before him . . . out came a mass of figures which appalled the opposing counsel and made the younger members of the committee groan in secret.'[29] It fell to the arbitrator, the famous railway engineer Robert Stephenson, to decide the matter and he supported Hawksley's scheme, though Hawksley followed Simpson's model in installing slow sand filter beds which are still in use. Hawksley was later appointed as engineer to the scheme which, in 1881, began to bring water to Liverpool from Lake Vyrnwy in Wales. Hawksley's engineering practice, like that of many nineteenth-century engineers, was based in Great George Street, close to the Institution of Civil Engineers. His only surviving memorial in London is the little pumping station at the north end of the Serpentine, thought by some to be modelled on the *Petit Trianon* at Versailles.

PUBLIC OWNERSHIP

Advocates of public ownership redoubled their efforts after the failure of the Royal Commission of 1866 but a series of further inquiries and commissions which examined their proposals over the next twenty years came to nothing. Paradoxically, the completion of Sir Joseph Bazalgette's system of main drainage in the 1870s may have set back the campaigners.[30] By protecting London from its own sewage and eliminating cholera epidemics for ever, Bazalgette made the problem of water supply less urgent. In the 1870s Disraeli asked a civil engineer called E.J. Smith to value the companies with a view to buying them out but the Conservative government's heart was not in it and nothing resulted. In 1878 Bazalgette's employers, the Metropolitan Board of Works, which since 1856 had been responsible for public services throughout the capital, put forward a proposal to buy out the companies but the necessary legislation to create compulsory purchase powers foundered. A Bill promoted by the City of London in 1884 to conserve water supplies by metering them was denounced by Lord Randolph Churchill as 'the wildest Socialistic doctrine'.

In 1889 the London County Council (LCC) replaced the Metropolitan Board of Works. It had wider powers than the board and in 1895 it presented to Parliament bills which would have enabled it to buy out the London water companies. The companies showed that they were masters of procrastination and yet another Royal Commission was appointed. The LCC conducted its own guerrilla campaign against the companies. It drew attention to any failures by companies to maintain a continuous supply – a problem which particularly afflicted the much criticised East London Company in the long hot summers of the 1890s. The LCC also did what it could to obstruct rate increases in an attempt to drive down the companies' profits, demoralise the shareholders and make the companies cheaper to buy when the time came.

Their moment came in 1902 with the passage of the Metropolis Water Act. This created the Metropolitan Water Board whose members were appointed by local authorities, including the LCC, and which bought out the existing

Sir Hugh Myddleton's memorial, Amwell. *(S. Halliday)*

companies. The new body paid £6,534,000 to the shareholders of the New River, Sir Hugh Myddleton's descendants being among them. Since 1946 the New River has terminated at Stoke Newington whose water treatment works continue to supply water to London. In 1974 the Thames Water Authority replaced the Metropolitan Water Board and its responsibilities passed on to Thames Water Plc in 1989. At Stoke Newington the New River now feeds water to the Thames Water Ring Main, a 50-mile 'water tunnel' which encircles London 40m beneath the surface and supplies treated water to the whole of the capital. New River Head still functions as a water treatment works, though it now treats water from south of the Thames.

The New River Company technically continues to exist. Its property assets at New River Head were transferred to London Merchant Securities which continues to own 100,000 sq. ft of air-conditioned office space at Myddleton Place, off Rosebery Avenue. Grinling Gibbons's famous oak room has also been preserved. When the Metropolitan Water Board built a new headquarters in 1920, the panelling was removed from Cistern House, together with the fine plaster ceiling, and installed in the new building. It has recently been converted into luxury flats but the oak room remains open to visitors.

Sir Hugh Myddleton continues to be commemorated in the vicinity of New River Head in Myddleton Square, Myddleton Street and Myddleton Passage as well as in many suburban streets near the New River. A statue of him stands on Islington Green and he is also celebrated in a commemorative stone in the basin of the Amwell spring at the start of the New River, bearing the following inscription:

> Sacred to the memory of
> Sir Hugh Myddleton, Bart.,
> Whose successful care,
> Aided by the patronage of his king,
> Conveyed this stream to London:
> An immortal work
> Since men cannot more nearly
> Imitate the Deity
> Than in Bestowing Health.

LONDON WATER COMPANIES

Many of the London water companies which followed the New River had very short lives. For example the *Somerset House Waterworks*, near the present site of Temple underground station, was founded in 1655 and lasted little more than ten years before disappearing from history. *Marchant's Waterworks*, founded in 1696, supplied water to the dwellings near the present site of Tottenham Court Road underground station. This likewise vanished together with the windmill which pumped its water, its memory being preserved only by Windmill Street, off Tottenham Court Road. The following companies were the principal ones serving London, listed in chronological order. After 1852 those companies which drew water from the tidal Thames moved their intakes to other sources. The Metropolitan Water Board, created by Act of Parliament in 1902, took over the responsibilities of all these companies.

Shadwell Waterworks: 1669; disappeared in the early nineteenth century when its site was required for the London docks.

Hampstead Water Company: 1692; bought by the New River company in 1856; drew water from Hampstead ponds.

Ravensbourne Water Company: 1701; drew water from the Ravensbourne (Thames tributary); bought by the Kent water company (see below).

Bankside Waterworks: 1720; founded to supply the Anchor Brewery of Henry Thrale (friend of Dr Johnson) on the site now occupied by the Anchor public house; drew from the Thames.

Chelsea Water Company: 1722; drew from the Thames.

West Ham Water Company: 1743; drew from the River Lee; bought out by the East London water company.

Southwark Water Company: 1783; drew from the Thames; its polluted water was the subject of mocking cartoons by George Cruikshank.

Lambeth Water Company: 1785; drew from the Thames but was one of the first to move its intake above the tidal limit, to Seething Wells, Surbiton.

South London Water Company: 1804; drew from the Thames at Vauxhall Creek.

West Middlesex Water Company: 1806; drew from the Thames at Hammersmith.

East London Water Company: 1806; drew water from the River Lee.

Kent Water Company: 1809 drew from the Thames.

Grand Junction Water Company: 1811; offshoot of the Grand Junction Canal company; drew water from rivers Colne and Brent.

Southwark and Vauxhall Water Company: 1845; drew from the Thames.

2
TOO MUCH WATER

Sir Cornelius Vermuyden and the Draining of the Fens

The inhabitants of the Isle of Axholme did about Michaelmas in the year 1645 tumultuously throw down a great part of the Banks and filled up the Ditches, putting Cattle into the Corn and Pastures of those that had been Adventurers for the draining.

> *A contemporary description of the hostility shown towards*
> *the fen drainage projects by the local population*

Many have burned their fingers in these waters, and instead of draining the fens emptied their own estates.

> *A contemporary description of the financial misfortunes*
> *which attended investors in fen drainage*

Sir Cornelius was an incubus, a nightmare, an obnoxious foreigner.

> *A distinctly partisan description by the barrister who was secretary*
> *in the nineteenth century to the Bedford Level Corporation*

POPHAM'S EAU TO WHORES' REST

An examination of the Ordnance Survey maps covering the area between the Isle of Ely and the Wash reveals a dense network of blue lines far outnumbering the roads. They represent the drains, dykes and artificial channels which, over a period of two thousand years, have been added to the landscape to prevent the natural watercourses from flooding the rich agricultural land through which they pass. They give the landscape its own strange nomenclature with names like Popham's Eau, Morton's Leam, Soham Lode, Eau Brink Cut and even Whores' Rest. In the medieval and Tudor periods Ely and other small communities on higher ground would become islands after spells of heavy rain. Writing early in the eighth century, the Venerable Bede recorded that 'the country of Ely is on every side encompassed by water and by marsh'. The watery environment is determined by the topography of the area.

The fens themselves cover an area of about 1,300 square miles in the counties of Cambridgeshire, Northamptonshire, Norfolk and Suffolk. However, the rivers that pass through the fens come from farther afield including the counties of Essex and Bedfordshire, so the fens actually drain an area of about 6,000 square miles. This huge volume of water has to reach the Wash through an area which once, about 8,000 years ago, alternated between an inland lake and low-lying dry land as sea levels rose and fell. Among the survivals of this period are the 'bog oaks' (in fact, trees of many species) which flourished during the drier centuries and are occasionally unearthed by ploughing. The rivers meander uncertainly and circuitously through the peat bogs, slowly circumventing the occasional hillocks of more substantial clay on which small towns like Ely stand. Silt, carried in on the swift flood tides from the Wash, causes river estuaries to become blocked so that a town like Wisbech, which was once a coastal community, is now ten miles inland on the River Nene. The problem is compounded by the fact that the ebb tides into the Wash are normally longer and slower than the incoming flood tides, so the sea is less effective in carrying away silt than it is in depositing it. The result is a landscape of rich agricultural land which has long been vulnerable to disastrous floods. These are caused by heavy rainfall in the catchment area or by exceptionally strong spring tides. The Anglo-Saxon word '*ey*' meant 'island' and this accounts for the number of communities whose name ends in this suffix: Thorney, Ramsey, Whittlesey and others are revealed by a glance at the map. Fenmen were referred to as 'yellow bellies' because of their supposed resemblance to frogs or, more prosaically, 'slodgers'. One tradition even held that they had webbed feet.

The Romans appear to have been the first to recognise the agricultural potential of the rich silt and peat because there is some evidence that they constructed the 'Carrdyke' between Ramsey and Lincoln, though it is not clear whether this was for drainage or navigational purposes. There is also evidence of the existence of a substantial causeway built by the Romans between Denver, near the present site of Downham Market, and Peterborough. When the

Ely Cathedral, queen of the Fens on the 'Island of Eels'. *(Stephen Halliday)*

Domesday Book was compiled in 1086 a few settlements are recorded on higher ground but during the Middle Ages the area became popular with religious communities. These were established at Peterborough, Ramsey, Thorney, Denny and Crowland. Early in the twelfth century, within fifty years of the Domesday Book, William of Malmesbury recorded that apple trees and vineyards flourished at Thorney Abbey, and later in the Middle Ages huge flocks of sheep, more than a thousand in number, made the area prosperous. Eels, a nutritious delicacy, were particularly abundant. Ely means 'island of eels' and the monks of Ramsey Abbey paid 4,000 eels annually to their neighbours at Peterborough in return for the right to take stone from their quarry.

The monks were good husbandmen and such efforts as were made at this time to manage the fenland waters were made by the religious communities. One of the most remarkable is still in use. This is 'Morton's Leam'. John Morton (*c.* 1420–1500) is usually remembered as Cardinal Morton, chief minister to Henry VII, but his work in the fens dates from the time when he was Bishop of Ely in 1480. Morton's Leam runs about 10 miles from Peterborough to Guyhirn and was designed to straighten and quicken the flow of the River Nene to Wisbech and the Wash. With some recent modifications Morton's Leam still serves this purpose. Sir William Dugdale, in his *History of Imbanking*, written in 1662, suggested that the dissolution of the religious houses by Henry VIII was

William Russell, Duke of Bedford, who employed Vermuyden to drain the fens. (*National Portrait Gallery*)

possibly the principal reason for the decline of the area in the later Tudor period as upkeep of the dykes was neglected.[1] In the late sixteenth century a number of other schemes were proposed. In 1593 a man called Humphrey Bradley, who lived in the Low Countries but was of English descent, proposed to Elizabeth I's minister Lord Burghley a scheme for draining the fens, the money to be advanced by 'certain gentlemen of wealth'. Much of the reclaimed ground would revert to the Crown. Nothing came of this proposal but the successful schemes of the future would depend upon two attributes which were imported from the Low Countries. The first was the experience of drainage work which was to be found there; the second was the '*ondernemimg*' or co-operative venture. This concept was well established in the Low Countries and enabled several wealthy individuals to subscribe to a common enterprise: in effect to become shareholders.

It was during Elizabeth I's campaign in support of the Low Countries against Philip II that Sir William Russell was sent to the country to act as governor of Flushing. Russell was impressed by the extent and quality of the drainage works that he observed there and invited three Dutchmen to his estate at Thorney, near Peterborough, to advise him on drainage works. There was no immediate result from their visit but it marked the beginning of the Russell family's long and historic involvement in the drainage of the fens. William Russell's son Francis, fourth Earl of Bedford, began the process which led to the creation of the 'Bedford Level' and the Bedford Level Corporation which managed them from 1634.

CORNELIUS VERMUYDEN

Cornelius Vermuyden was born in about 1593 on the Dutch island of Tholen which, at the time, was the home of the Roosevelt family who emigrated to America in 1649. Cornelius's family had been involved in land drainage work on Tholen since the fourteenth century and by the early seventeenth century he had some useful connections in London. A cousin and a brother-in-law both served as ambassadors to King James I and a friend from Tholen had been engaged on drainage works on Canvey Island in the Thames estuary.[2] It was probably as a result of these connections that, in 1621, he was called upon by James I to repair a breach in the bank of the Thames at Dagenham that had caused severe flooding. There was some dispute about the quality of his repair work and a further difficulty over the payment of his workmen but these matters must have been resolved since James I granted Vermuyden some of the reclaimed land and later asked him to drain Windsor Park.

Cornelius displayed considerable adeptness during the troubles of the English Civil War and managed, at different times, to work both with Charles I and with Oliver Cromwell who was himself a man of the fens. Cornelius contracted with the King to carry out drainage works which should have enriched them both and were for that reason opposed by Cromwell, the local Member of Parliament. He then continued the work under the auspices of the Commonwealth and was asked by Cromwell to travel to the Low Countries to negotiate a defensive pact with his native country.[3] He aroused the animosity of contemporaries and later chroniclers. His plans for draining the fens provoked riots and a historian of his work, far from celebrating him, described him as 'an obnoxious foreigner'.[4] There is some evidence that the Cornelius Vermuyden who commanded a troop of horse on the Parliamentary side at the battle of Marston Moor was his eldest son who certainly became a Fellow of the Royal Society during the reign of Charles II and a member of the Bedford Level Corporation, managing the fens, in 1645. The strife and changes of regime which characterised the seventeenth century did not affect the fortunes of this highly adaptable family.

The Isle of Axholme and Hatfield Chase

The Isle of Axholme and Hatfield Chase in Lincolnshire and South Yorkshire had long been Crown land though few monarchs had hunted there. Its topography was similar to that of the fens with rivers like the Don, the Trent and the Idle meandering around some isolated tracts of high ground whose limits could not be satisfactorily marked owing to the tendency of boundary posts to sink or be washed away. As in the southern fens it seems probable that the Romans undertook some drainage work since Bycarrs Dyke near Doncaster is similar to Carrdyke near Lincoln.[5] The remoteness of the area also discouraged royal visits, a fact of which the local residents took full advantage. If the king neglected to hunt the abundant deer then they would perform this office for him. It was claimed that 'the inhabitants dined on venison more frequently than mutton'.[6] James I, whose disagreements with Parliament over taxation ensured that he was always susceptible to any suggestions that the royal revenue could be increased, was impressed when Vermuyden told him that the area could be drained and yield a handsome revenue. James died before he could engage the services of the enterprising Dutchman but his successor, Charles I, made an agreement with Vermuyden in May, 1626. Approximately 75,000 acres was to be drained, of which one-third would be allocated to the 'Participants' as the investors in the enterprise were to be called. All but two of the Participants were the family and Dutch friends of Vermuyden. According to the agreement Vermuyden would 'do his best endeavour to drain and lay dry the said drowned and surrounded grounds as to make the same fit for tillage and pasture'.[7]

The work proceeded, much of it being carried out by Dutch and French Protestants who were fleeing from persecution on the continent: an influx of refugees which created its own problems. However, there were more pressing matters to disturb the local residents. Vermuyden's new channels diverted some water to the River Don which overflowed its banks and flooded the communities of Fishlake, Snaith and Sykehouse which had previously occupied dry land. The same fate overtook the village of Epworth further south. These calamities provoked riots, especially when, in 1628, it was proposed to grant the participants their share of the reclaimed land. The problems were greatly complicated by the fact that a fourteenth-century owner of much of the Isle of Axholme had assigned rights of common to local residents and undertaken not to 'improve' the land to their disadvantage. This was exactly what Vermuyden, on the King's authority, had now done. Sir William Dugdale, writing in 1662, reported that the annual rental of the land had increased from 6*d* per acre in its waterlogged state to 10*s* an acre when drained[8] and a grateful King duly conferred a knighthood on Vermuyden in January 1629. The local residents whose rights had been infringed were less impressed, so Sir Cornelius and his colleagues were summoned to appear before Thomas, Viscount Wentworth, president of the Council for the North, at Pontefract in August 1630.

Wentworth, who was later executed for his support for the King, on this occasion supported the rights of the commoners. He declared that 'the ancient rights and privileges of the inhabitants of Hatfield Manor were to be restored and maintained whereby those inhabitants should have the right to dig turf and fell timber'. Wentworth ordered the construction of a further relief channel running from Snaith to Goole which is still known as the Dutch River. This decision prompted Vermuyden to sell the land that he had been allocated in the area but it was not the end of his troubles. In 1633 he was indicted for his failure to pay his share of the cost of the Dutch River.[9]

Nor was it the end of the local strife. The residents wanted to exercise their long-established practices of illegally hunting deer and catching ducks and fish as well as gathering fuel, so in the decades that followed no opportunity was missed to damage or destroy Vermuyden's drainage works or harass his workforce. In 1642, as the Civil War gathered pace, the approach of a Royalist force to the Isle of Axholme prompted the residents to display a previously undetected enthusiasm for the Parliamentary cause. On the pretext that they wanted to deny the Isle to the King's supporters, they destroyed locks, dams and inhabitants and flooded much of the reclaimed area, declaring that they 'would not rest until all the reclaimed areas of land were again under water or till the foreigners should be constrained to swim away'.[10] Further disturbances followed three years later when 'the inhabitants of the Isle of Axholme did about Michaelmas in the year 1645 tumultuously throw down a great part of the Banks and filled up the Ditches, putting Cattle into the Corn and Pastures of those that had been Adventurers for the drayning . . . the Inhabitants were forced to swim away like Ducks'.[11] Local Justices of the Peace usually supported the residents against the 'foreigners' and the prominent Parliamentarian, John Lilburne, in an arrangement that smacked of self-interest rather than principle, agreed to support the rights of the residents in Parliament in return for the granting of 2,000 acres of reclaimed land that had been abandoned by the despairing Participants. Vermuyden had little success in gaining official support in the face of this lawlessness. On one occasion, as he hastened from London to deal with a disturbance, the postmaster at Royston refused to supply him with horses despite the royal commission that Vermuyden brandished at him.[12]

'Foreigners'

The antagonism directed against the 'drayners' was not based solely on economic interests. There was an element of xenophobia. Certainly the residents who depended on fishing, snaring ducks and the illegal pursuit of venison were hostile to any venture that would make these activities more risky or less profitable. As observed above, all but two of the 'Participants' in Vermuyden's enterprise were Dutch. Moreover, in the face of the unwillingness of the resident population to become involved in the unpopular drainage work, the great majority of his workforce were Dutch, Walloons or French. The last were Huguenots fleeing from persecution in France, a substantial number of whom settled in Hatfield Chase and the Isle of Axholme.[13] They brought with them their religious practices, building a chapel at Sandtoft on the Isle of Axholme where the minister preached each Sunday in English and French. This caused some alarm to the local bishop who did not welcome the foreign Protestants with their unorthodox practices and it became a focal point for the hostility of the local populace. It was attacked several times during the Civil War as part of a general campaign against the drainage works and the refugees. The only serious attempt to defend either the drainage works or the hated foreigners was made by a local Justice of the Peace called Reading who, in September 1655, raised a force of twenty men and fought thirty-one skirmishes with the local hooligans.[14] Reading died in 1716, allegedly at the age of one hundred, 'fifty of which he had spent in danger of personal violence'.[15] The church was finally destroyed in 1688, after which the refugees, according to one authority 'returned to their native country after seeing the fruits of their labours here continually destroyed by malevolent commoners'.[16] This is an overstatement. The Participants may have been disappointed with the results of their investments but most of the refugees either remained in the area, intermarrying with the resident population, or made their way south to Vermuyden's next, much more ambitious project.

The Bedford Level

In 1629 the newly knighted Sir Cornelius had proposed to Charles I a far more ambitious scheme than any previously undertaken: the draining of the Great Fen of East Anglia. In the face of hostility to the Dutchman himself Charles entrusted the work to Francis, Earl of Bedford, the son of Sir William Russell who had first examined the possibility of draining his estates at Thorney in the previous century.[17] Francis was made the 'undertaker' to the scheme with responsibility for raising the necessary resources and executing the work. The 'Lynn Law', in effect a commission promulgated in King's Lynn in January 1630, specified that 'Francis, Earl of Bedford would do his best endeavour at his own charge to drain the said marsh, waste, fenny and surrounding grounds in such manner as they shall be fit for meadow, or pasture, or arable'. The work was to be completed in six years and Bedford's reward would be 95,000 acres of the drained land – about a third of the total area, as in Axholme. Taxes on 40,000 of the acres would be devoted to the upkeep of the drained land. The agreement did not specify what 'draining' meant and this was to cause difficulties in the years ahead.

Bedford, whose resources were substantial though not inexhaustible, took into partnership thirteen fellow 'Adventurers', described as 'men of rank and fortune'. Each of them subscribed £500 at the start of the venture on the understanding that there would be calls for further contributions. If any Adventurer failed to meet such a call, then he would forfeit his share in the venture though he could invite other investors to join him, thereby increasing the number of Adventurers: a process rather like selling some of one's shares in a public company. In this way the number of Adventurers eventually exceeded two hundred. It has been estimated that Francis himself invested over £90,000 in the scheme.[18] A stretch of land east of Peterborough is still labelled as 'Adventurers Land' on the Ordnance Survey map. Unlike Vermuyden's 'Participants' in Axholme, the Adventurers were English though this did not entirely eliminate the xenophobia that had plagued the earlier venture.

Vermuyden was not the only contender for the post of engineer. Another Dutchman called Jan Westerdyke put forward a plan for building up the banks of the rivers in the area – principally the Nene, the Great Ouse, the Cam (or Granta), the Lark and the Wissey. This would increase their capacity and reduce the likelihood of their overflowing and 'drowning' the surrounding country. The disadvantage of this plan was that the length of the slow, winding rivers amounted to several hundred miles, so the embankments would have had to be of a similar length and therefore very costly. Moreover, there was a very limited supply of suitable material for embanking within the fens themselves. The abundant peat would shrink as soon as it dried out and the supplies of the right material, clay, were limited, so materials would have to be brought from outside the fens, further adding to the cost. Vermuyden's plan was, in effect, to bypass the existing rivers by cutting new, straight channels into which the river water would be diverted. Instead of travelling 50 miles along a winding course with a very shallow fall, the flood waters of the Great Ouse would travel 20 miles, falling at more than twice the rate and at greater speed. Embankments would still be needed but less than half those required for Westerdyke's scheme. For these reasons Vermuyden's plan was preferred.

A nineteenth-century historian of the Bedford Level called Samuel Wells, who was also secretary to the Bedford Level Corporation, explained that 'unfortunately' Cornelius Vermuyden 'to whom the country had always shown the greatest aversion' was appointed by the Earl as engineer to the scheme. The reasons for Wells's hostility to Vermuyden are not clear. Vermuyden certainly drove a hard bargain, eventually agreeing that he would undertake the work in return for the allocation of 4,000 of the reclaimed acres. The plan he implemented also had some weaknesses which had to be rectified in the centuries that followed but that was hardly surprising given the scale and difficulty of the undertaking. Some of those weaknesses proved costly to the always strained finances of the corporation which, for over two centuries, struggled to maintain Vermuyden's works. It may be that Wells, as secretary to the corporation, bore the brunt of these struggles and thereby became resentful towards the man he thought had caused them. Whatever the reason, Wells's two-volume history of the Bedford Level never loses an opportunity to criticise the man who created it. At one point Wells describes Vermuyden as 'an incubus, a nightmare'.[19]

The drainage is completed?

Over the next six years Vermuyden completed about sixty miles of new drainage channels in accordance with this plan. The most remarkable was the 'Old Bedford River' which carried the floodwaters of the Great Ouse from Earith in Huntingdonshire to Denver in Norfolk, a distance of twenty-one miles in a dead straight line. A sluice was erected at Earith to admit the floodwaters when required, leaving the normal course of the river, more than twice that length, to take the remaining water via Ely. Vermuyden re-cut the medieval 'Morton's Leam' and also wanted to create a channel further to the east to intercept the headwaters of the Little Ouse, the Lark and the Wissey as they descended from higher ground. This would prevent the flooding of the area north of Ely. Shortage of funds prevented him from doing this but his foresight in the matter was recognised when the work was finally executed in 1964 in the form of the Great Ouse Cut-off Channel.

In 1838 the straightness of the Bedford River attracted the attention of an eccentric gentleman called Samuel Rowbotham who used it in a curious scientific experiment. For nine months he lodged in a hut on the edge of the river and aligned identical floats on the river. If the earth was, as he believed, flat then the tops of the floats, over a distance of 6 miles, would exactly align. If the earth was a sphere then the more distant floats would appear to fall away. The earth remained obstinately spherical in the face of Rowbotham's experiments as it did in the face of a similar experiment by a Lady Blount in 1904.

The drainage engineers were no more popular in East Anglia than they had been in Axholme. In the words of Samuel Smiles, 'difficult though it was to deal with the unreclaimed bogs, the unreclaimed "fen-slodgers" were still more impracticable'.[20] The fact that the area was more sparsely populated mitigated the strength of the hostility but made it difficult to recruit a labour force. For this reason the refugees who left Sandtoft in the face of local hostility[21] were particularly welcomed, not only by Vermuyden but also by the Bishop of Ely who invited the newcomers to adopt the disused chapel of Thorney Abbey as their place of worship in 1652. They also used the church of St John the Baptist at Parson Drove near Wisbech where

Thorney Abbey, home to a congregation of Dutch Protestants from 1652. *(Stephen Halliday)*

their unfamiliar ceremonies provoked the censure of Samuel Pepys whose relatives lived nearby. Pepys referred to Parson Drove as 'a heathen place'.[22] The baptismal registers of these churches record many foreign names at this time, one of them being that of De la Pryme whose descendant, George Pryme, became the first professor of political economy (economics) at Cambridge in 1828 and was MP for Cambridge for 10 years from 1832.

The newcomers did not suffer as much violence in East Anglia as they had at Axholme but the drainage works attracted the same degree of xenophobia. The local population, known as *Gyrwas*, a Saxon word for 'Water People', were reluctant to forfeit their fishing and duck snaring in order to generate profits for the Adventurers. A petition entitled 'The Anti-Projector', referring to the plans to turn marsh into arable and pasture land asked 'What is coleseed and rape? They are but Dutch commodities and trash and trumpery', while a tract called 'The Drayner Confirmed', referring to the Dutch, asked 'must we give place to our most ancient and dangerous enemies?' A contemporary poem called 'The Powte's [sea-lamprey's] Complaint' was more subtle:[23]

> Behold the great design which they do now determine,
> Will make our bodies pine, a prey to crows and vermin;
> For they do mean all fens to drain and waters overmaster,
> All will be dry and we must die 'cause Essex cows want pasture.

In 1637 at St Ives a court adjudged that the drainage had been satisfactorily completed and that the Adventurers should receive their 95,000 acres. This immediately provoked a storm of controversy since it was claimed by some residents that Vermuyden's system had only completed half the task required. All he had done was to turn marshes into 'summer ground' in which it was possible to grow crops or graze livestock in summer before autumn rains restored them to their watery condition. Since the original agreement with Francis, Earl of Bedford, had simply specified that he should 'drain the said marsh', it was open to debate whether it was enough to have drained it for half the year. The King therefore summoned another court which sat at Huntingdon the following year, 1638, at which the decision of the earlier court was annulled and Charles announced that he would assume the role of 'undertaker' himself and finish the job. The Earl of Bedford and the Adventurers would receive 40,000 acres as their share for the unfinished drainage but the King, as ever short of money in his battles with Parliament, would reap most of the rewards for finishing the work. In the process he proposed to build 'an eminent town in the midst of the Level, at a little place called Manea, and have it called Charlemont'.[24] A fragment of the work carried out for this latter venture may be seen in the small village of Manea. It takes the form of a square mound on which, it is assumed, a palace was to be built.

Oliver Cromwell

Politics now intervened. Oliver Cromwell, the local MP, who was already prominent in the struggle with the King over the right to levy taxes without the consent of Parliament, saw the King's interest in the drainage as a way of raising money for the royal exchequer. He therefore opposed the plan, taking his stand, as others had done, on the rights of commoners. He undertook 'to hold the drainers in suit of law for five years and that in the meantime they should enjoy every part of their common'.[25] Over the chaotic years of the Civil War that now followed, very little progress was made with the drainage work. Parliament remained suspicious of the King's interest in the matter and on 25 January 1641, the year before the dispute with the King became a war, the Long Parliament decided 'Sir Cornelius Vermuyden shall be forthwith summoned to attend this House, to give an Account by what Authority he goeth on with his Works in the Fens'.[26]

Cromwell's enthusiasm for the rights of the commoners did not long survive Parliament's victory in the Civil War. Vermuyden had managed to remain on good terms with the Parliamentarians, possibly through his son's service in their army and, as we have seen, Cromwell evidently used him as an envoy to the Dutch republic.[27] The Earl of Bedford had died in 1649, of smallpox, and his son and heir William, later the first Duke, had survived the Civil War by judiciously changing sides at opportune moments. It was therefore no surprise when the new Earl was appointed to revive the drainage project in 1649. This was done under the 'Pretended Act' of that year, so called because all acts passed during the Commonwealth and Protectorate were deemed to be invalid. Once again, 95,000 acres of the drained land was to be allocated to the Adventurers, as in the earlier scheme.

This 'Act for the Drainage of the Great Level of the Fens' prompted Vermuyden to present his 'Discourse Touching the Drainage of the Great Fennes', a plan which he had first produced for Charles I when the King appointed himself 'undertaker' for the project but which Vermuyden was happy to offer to the new masters of the Commonwealth.[28] It is similar in conception to his earlier plan but broader in scale, proposing additional channels in order to make the drained land free of flooding in winter. It thus overcame the objection that his earlier scheme had created only 'summer ground'. He divided the area to be drained into three sections whose names have survived to this day. The first, north of Morton's Leam, he called the North Level. The area between Morton's Leam and the Bedford River he called the Middle Level. The area to the south he called the South Level. Collectively they remain known as the Bedford Level. He continued to argue that the drainage should be effected by creating new channels rather than embanking old rivers (as Westerdyke had advocated) which would have involved deepening the channels of these rivers and throwing up embankments on either side: 'I find it best to lead most of the rivers about another way.'[29]

As with the earlier plans, Vermuyden was not without rival contenders for the post of engineer.[30] A man called Andrewes Burrell, who had been one of the 'Adventurers' in the original scheme[31] produced a nineteen-page denunciation of Vermuyden's new plan entitled 'Exceptions against Sir Cornelius Virmuden's [*sic*] Discourse for the Draining of the great Fennes'.[32] He complained that Vermuyden's plan 'misinformed and abused in regard it wanteth all the essential parts of a design' and that 'Sir Cornelius Virmuden's discourse is contrived in a mystical way' which was intended to confuse its readers. His own plan, which this reader at least had the greatest difficulty in understanding, appeared to favour deepening and embanking the existing rivers. Given the meandering courses of rivers in this flat country, this would, like Westerdyke's scheme, have involved creating many more miles of embankments than were required by the straight channels of Vermuyden's proposal.

Despite its allegedly 'mystical' properties, Vermuyden's plan was chosen though this did not preclude another bout of tough bargaining with the Adventurers. Vermuyden wanted 4,000 acres of land for himself, plus a fee of £1,000 for completing the work. The Adventurers wanted to pay out the money in instalments as the work was done. They also wanted to be sure that Vermuyden would not take advantage of an opportunity to sell off his 4,000 acres at an early stage before any deficiencies in his plan became evident. Vermuyden demurred and for three weeks in December 1649, was supplanted as engineer by one of the Adventurers, Sir Edward Partridge. It is not clear what alternative plans, if any, Partridge had. Perhaps it was a bluff. On 1 January 1650 agreement was finally reached. Vermuyden was reinstated as engineer. His fee was to be paid in three annual instalments and 2,000 of his 4,000 acres were to be held in trust for seven years.

Vermuyden's second phase of drainage works involved the cutting of further channels, of which the most conspicuous is the 'New Bedford River', also known as the 'Hundred Foot Drain'. It runs parallel to the Old Bedford River throughout its length and, as well as providing additional drainage capacity in itself, it created a 'wash' for flood waters in times of very heavy rainfall. The 'wash' is the low-lying area between the Old Bedford River and the New Bedford River which can be flooded when required. The area to the north of the old river is protected by a high embankment as is the area to the south of the new river. By this means, exceptional floodwaters are released into a 5,000-acre flood plain where they can do no harm.

The resident population of the fens was no more enthusiastic about the new drainage works than it had been about the old. The refugees from Sandtoft

New Bedford River. *(Stephen Halliday)*

therefore had to be supplemented by less conventional methods of recruitment. The first 'recruits' were Scotsmen taken prisoner following Cromwell's victory at the battle of Dunbar in September 1650. One hundred and sixteen of them were marched by a Corporal Foster to Earith, where they were provided with coarse woollen suits to protect them against the chilling winds of the fens and were set to work digging the New Bedford River.[33] Eventually about 2,000 Scottish prisoners worked on the fen drainage, the redoubtable Corporal Foster receiving a payment of £2 for his services. In 1653 the Scottish prisoners were joined in the work by 500 Dutch sailors who had been captured in the victory of Robert Blake, the Commonwealth's admiral, over Maarten Tromp. Without these reluctant immigrants, the work would certainly have taken much longer, though many of them, particularly the Scots, eventually settled in the area and worked the reclaimed land.

The financial returns for the Adventurers were doubtful. It has been estimated that the cost of the drainage eventually amounted to about half a million pounds,[34] an unimaginably large sum at the time which put intolerable strains on the resources of many of the original Adventurers. Some of the reclaimed land, rich agricultural terrain, was later bought by colleges of Cambridge University whose contemporary historian, Thomas Fuller, wrote in 1665 that[35] 'Many have burned their fingers in these waters, and instead of draining the fens emptied their own estates.' The curious mixed metaphor does not alter the fact that, for many of the Adventurers, the drainage was a poor investment. Many failed to meet the 'calls' for additional investment and sold on their shares. Vermuyden himself was referred to as a bankrupt in a suit in the Chancery court in 1655, though he survived until 1677, his death being recorded in that year at St Margaret's, Westminster.[36]

The Corporation

Responsibility for maintaining the drainage system was vested in the Bedford Level Corporation which was established by Act of Parliament in 1663 with the official title 'The Society of Conservators of the Fens'. The 'members' of the corporation were the owners of 83,000 of the reclaimed acres – the remaining 12,000 having been given to the Crown. Anyone with more than 100 acres could vote for the governing body which consisted of twenty 'conservators', six 'bailiffs' and a governor, the last office being held by the Duke of Bedford. The corporation acted as a kind of local government in the Levels with powers to raise rather inadequate taxes, to require owners to carry out necessary works and, where necessary, to confiscate the lands of those who neglected their responsibilities. The corporation remained in existence until 1920 but in the meantime many drainage boards had been created to control tributary rivers which were outside the authority of the corporation. The first was the Haddenham Board, south of Ely, in 1727, and there were eventually scores of boards whose relationship with the corporation was not always clear. Some boards did not resist the temptation to drain their own lands by passing on their watery problems to the lands of their neighbours. This confusing situation was a reflection of the fact that the corporation never had enough money to do what was required of it. Local residents, much of whose land had not been reclaimed because it had always been on dry ground, felt the need to elect their own commissioners to look after their interests. In 1920 the corporation was dissolved and replaced by the Ouse Drainage Board whose responsibilities eventually passed to Anglian Water.

Problems: the land shrinks

Problems with Vermuyden's scheme were evident within a few years of its completion: indeed it could be argued that it has never been completed since it has been supplemented and modified until the present time. Many references have already been made to the hostility of residents, particularly those who enjoyed rights of common, to the drainage of their lands. As late as 1867 the drainage commissioners at Lakenheath in Suffolk advertised a £20 reward for information about those responsible for damaging an embankment in order to flood the surrounding land.[37] However, more pressing than the activities of a few local hooligans were the objections of those who pointed to the effects of the drainage upon navigation. Vermuyden had built a sluice (a water gate) at Denver where the New Bedford River, the Old Bedford River and the Great Ouse converged, the intention being to channel the waters in such a way as to 'scour' the bed of the Ouse and keep it clear for navigation. It appeared to have had the opposite effect and complaints were heard from King's Lynn and Cambridge that the rivers, and especially the outfalls to the sea, were becoming impassable. There was therefore general rejoicing when the Denver sluice was destroyed in a storm in 1713. Opposition to its reconstruction was so effective that it was not rebuilt until 1750. A further problem arose from the shrinkage of the peat.

Peat can hold as much as 95 per cent of its bulk in water, so when the wetlands were drained the peat began to shrink. In places the level of the land fell by 8ft in thirty years, leaving the fields below the level of the embanked channels and of the natural river courses. This in turn led to disastrous floods and left some houses, which may still be seen, with their doors marooned 8ft above the ground.[38] There was a particularly disastrous inundation in 1796 when some of the most fertile land in Britain remained 'drowned' throughout the summer. Two measures were adopted to manage this problem. First, the channels, and some of the rivers, were embanked to a higher level than previously so that the water levels could rise higher without the danger of flooding. The alternative would have been to dredge the rivers and thus lower their beds but this would have reduced the already inadequate fall of most of the rivers and made the situation worse. The only material suitable for building strong embankments was clay so the reserves of this material were worked by men known as 'Gault gangs' or 'bankers' and taken by barge to the embankments. The principal source was the Roswell pit at Ely which was excavated to such an extent that the resulting reservoir has become a home for Ely sailing club. The work was well paid and in 1886 the commissioners for the 'Burnt Fen' district near Ely were scandalised to learn that members of one gang were earning as much as 32*s* 6*d* (£1.62) a week.[39] This was slightly more than a London bricklayer, so they renegotiated their contract with the gang.

Having raised the levels of the rivers and their embankments above the surrounding fields the local landowners now had to devise a method of raising the water from the dykes that drained the fields into the drainage channels. The method used was the 'scoop windmill'. This is a conventional windmill

Wicken Fen scoop mill. *(Stephen Halliday)*

attached to a device like a waterwheel which is set into the channel at the point where the water is to be raised from one level to another. Radiating from the wheel are a series of paddles, set at an angle, which 'scoop' the water from one level to another. The mills were manned from October to April by keepers who lived in their basements with their families and were responsible for operating them when necessary. As the danger of floods passed with the coming of spring, the keepers emerged from their watery, troglodytic existence and farmed the nearby fields. The usefulness of the scoop mills was limited by the fact that floods were not always accompanied by the necessary wind; also by the limited power of the scoop wheels which could not drive a paddle much more than a foot in length. It was therefore necessary to have banks of mills to raise the water the 8 or 10ft that was often necessary. At one time there were 750 scoop mills in the fens, of which one survives at Wicken fen.

'THE POWER OF STEAM SHE SAID SHALL BE EMPLOYED'

By 1817 wind began to give way to steam when, for the first time, a steam engine was attached to a scoop wheel at Sutton St Edmund near Wisbech. The new form of power enabled much larger scoop wheels to be used, necessitating fewer of them. The largest propelled the scoop wheel on the New Bedford ('Hundred Foot') River in 1881 with its diameter of 50ft, ten times that of the wind scoops, and its arrival was celebrated by a piece of doggerel which is still inscribed on the pumping station:

> These Fens have oft times been by Water drowned,
> Science a remedy in Water found,
> The power of STEAM she said shall be employed
> And the destroyer by itself destroyed.

Initially local turf was used as fuel for the steam engines but after 1830, as coal became cheaper with the opening up of the canal and railway systems, this became the preferred fuel. Scoops were also being replaced by conventional pumps. In 1852, Whittlesey, near Peterborough, saw the installation of a sophisticated centrifugal pump which had been one of the star exhibits of modern technology at the Great Exhibition the previous year.

'LORD ORFORD'S VOYAGE ROUND THE FENS IN 1774'

Some idea of the condition of the fens in the century after Vermuyden's death may be gained from a remarkable journal of a voyage around them by boat in 1774. George Walpole, 3rd Earl of Orford, was the grandson of Britain's first prime minister, Sir Robert Walpole, and occupied the magnificent Houghton Hall east of King's Lynn. In July 1774, with a retinue of friends, mistress and servants, Orford set out on a twenty-day tour of the fens in five fenland lighters accompanied by four skiffs. The fen lighters were shallow-bottomed barges which were normally used for conveying farm produce on the network of waterways established by the drainage system. On this occasion they were adapted for the comfort of the earl and his companions. The skiffs were used for recreational purposes: sailing, fishing and shooting wildfowl occur frequently in the journal of the voyage which was kept by the earl and two of his fellows. The flotilla left Lakenheath on 16 July 1774, pulled by a horse called Hippopotamus and travelled by river and channel to and around Peterborough, the trip ending on 6 August.

There are frequent references to other craft on the waterways carrying agricultural produce to market, though the earl's party was sufficiently unusual to arouse the curious stares of residents, bullocks and a cat. Some of them were recorded as suffering from 'ague, the reigning disorder in these parts'.[40] The companions' attitude to the needs of other users seems to have been exceedingly casual since the *Journal* records that 'we were obliged to break up four Bridges, which were not high enough for our vessels'.[41] The party had no difficulty in catching fresh fish, on which they dined almost every day. Pike, perch, eels and 'salted jacks' (young salted pike) were especially abundant. The journals comment frequently on the richness of the land, Orford himself writing that 'the pastures on each side are exceedingly rich, and feed numbers of large cattle, and produce large quantities of hay'.[42] He noted that a new kind of wheat 'from Barbary' (North Africa) was being grown in the fens which yielded heavier crops but he also commented on some less pleasant features of the area including that of plucking geese while alive: 'the inhuman custom of plucking the latter for their down prevails and had just been put into execution, their feathers being mostly bloody'. The journal recorded, in unflattering terms, the survival of a Dutch settlement at Outwell, near Wisbech. Having commented on 'the ugliness of the inhabitants', the *Journal* attributes this feature to 'a Dutch colony which, we were informed, had settled here at the time of the [1688] Revolution'.[43] Nevertheless it is clear that by the late eighteenth century the fens were beginning to enjoy the prosperity that Vermuyden, Bedford and the Adventurers had sought.

THE WORK NEVER ENDS

The work of improving the drainage, dredging the channels and clearing the outfalls as the Ouse and the Nene approach the sea has never been completed and never will be. Moreover the dry weather which is characteristic of the summer presents problems of its own. In 1688 the inhabitants of Little Downham named part of the surrounding land 'Downham Dry Grounds', 'which in ye summer are burnt up for want of water'.[44] Peat, when dry, is highly flammable. This is a useful quality when it is being used as a cheap fuel for scoop engines but a hazard in hot weather. A second problem, caused when the peat dries out in the spring, is the 'fen blow' which occurs when dry peat dust is lifted by strong winds into the fenland equivalent of a sandstorm, obscuring vision and penetrating buildings and motor car engines.[45] They can also lift newly sown seed with the peat and deposit it in adjacent fields where it is not supposed to be. Modern irrigation methods have overcome the worst effects of this phenomenon.

Drainage, however, remains the greatest challenge as it has always been and some of the most eminent engineers of their times have been recruited to deal with the endless problems. An additional channel on the Ouse as it approached Ely was proposed in 1720 but the Bedford Level Corporation, short of funds as ever, did not feel able to take on the work. It had to wait 100 years before it was finally built, as the 'Eau Brink Cut', in 1820 at the suggestion of Thomas Telford, the most eminent engineer of the age. In 1764 and again in 1776 John Smeaton, builder of the Eddystone lighthouse and of early canal works, recommended some additional works in Lincolnshire but the local inhabitants insisted that the money should be found by the descendants of 'the Participants' rather than from their taxes so nothing was done.[46] John Rennie and his son Sir John Rennie, creators of London Bridge and of docks and canals, advised on new works, as did the celebrated railway engineer Robert Stephenson. Only Brunel and Bazalgette seem to have escaped and they were probably too busy! The fens also retained their reputation as a thoroughly unhealthy place with a particular tendency to bring on ague, a malarial fever characterised by alternating shivering and sweating. Samuel Smiles recorded that 'When Dr Whalley, was presented by the Bishop of Ely to the rectory of Hagworthingham-in-the-Fens it was with the singular proviso that he was not to reside in it, as the air was fatal to any but a native.'[47] Absentee clergymen were not unusual in the eighteenth and nineteenth centuries but this was not usually on the recommendation of their bishops. Thomas Whalley held the benefice for fifty-six years from 1772 to 1828 while living much of the time in the more benign climate of the continent.[48]

Some of the works that were undertaken appear to have been encouraged in part by the prospect of providing work for those who would otherwise have been paupers in the parish workhouse. Thus Woodhouse Marsh Cut on the River Nene north of Wisbech became known as 'Pauper's Cut' because it was built in the 1820s by men of the district who had been thrown on the poor rate. Likewise in 1929 a new pumping station was built at St Germans, south of King's Lynn, recruiting men from areas of high unemployment. They were accommodated in huts, each holding twenty-eight men, and paid 36s (£1.80) for a 48-hour week, 10s being charged for food. Each man was expected to take a hot bath once a week. The commissioners who insisted on this unfamiliar luxury for unemployed men noted that 'unless something of this nature is done the camp bedding etc. is liable to become unclean'.[49]

Works for more conventional reasons followed in the years after the Second World War. In 1953 the floods that affected much of southern

Denver Sluice, ingeniously designed so that natural river flows can be reversed to avoid flooding. *(Stephen Halliday)*

England were particularly devastating in the fens and this prompted a series of measures which, after many delays, were completed in the period 1955–71. The Great Ouse Cut-off Channel, completed in 1964, intercepts the headwaters of the Wissey, the Lark and the Little Ouse and conducts them to Denver, thereby preventing them from swelling the Great Ouse north of Ely. As noted above, Vermuyden had wanted to include this in his earlier scheme but shortage of money had not allowed.[50] Denver sluice was redesigned so that the flow of the cut-off channel can be reversed by channelling water into it from the Ouse itself. The water then makes its way to the River Stour in Essex whence it can be diverted to reservoirs at Abberton, near Colchester and Hanningfield, near Chelmsford: a creative solution to water surplus in one area and shortage in another.[51]

'Corn and Pasture, Fat Sheep and Fat Oxen'

The drainage works did eventually achieve their aim of turning the waterlogged fens into rich agricultural land though it was not until the nineteenth century, almost two hundred years after Vermuyden, that steam power and improved agricultural methods enabled something like the land's potential riches to be realised. Early crops included oats, wheat, rye and coleseed, the last later known as oilseed rape which yielded 'colza' oil for lamps. These were preferred to the older tallow lamps as giving a better light and they were extensively used from the middle of the nineteenth century by railway companies who provided a ready outlet for this profitable crop. At one time Wisbech alone had seven mills devoted to the production of colza oil. Hemp was another major crop at this time, its strong fibres being used to make ropes for sailing ships. The railway stations at Ely and Littleport built quays to receive the farm produce that began its journey on barges before transferring to goods trains for onward carriage to the town of March which became an important railway junction with a huge marshalling yard. There the railwaymen assembled the trucks into trains for London, the Midlands and the North as well as local destinations like Cambridge and Peterborough.

In the early eighteenth century Daniel Defoe in *A Tour Through England and Wales* commented on the huge numbers of geese that were raised in the fens and then driven, in droves of a thousand or more, to markets in London. Nor was the trade in fish eliminated by the drainage. The natural rivers and artificial channels were filled with the fish that had previously been dispersed over acres of flooded fields so in many cases it was easier to find and catch them. Tench, pike, perch and especially eels were caught and transported to market in barrels whose water was drained and replaced at each overnight stop so that the fish arrived reasonably fresh. By 1830, in his *Rural Rides*, William Cobbett was recording that though Ely was 'a miserable little town', it was surrounded by 'this beautiful and most productive part of the country' and that the fenland was 'a country of rich arable land and grass fields and of beautiful meadows'. It was from this time that it attracted purchasers from Cambridge colleges, some of which continue to hold agricultural land. By 1850 Bedford lands which had earned rents of £650 in 1800 had seen that figure grow to £4,000.[52]

The area suffered from the depression which affected agriculture in the period between the wars but when the Second World War began and Britain's normal sources of food were cut off, the area again attracted the interest of the government which paid for improved roads to enable local produce to be brought more easily to the cities. The fens are particularly well supplied with flat, straight roads along which motorists are tempted to speed but which are also used for the purpose for which they were designed. Tractors pulling trailers loaded with potatoes, celery, carrots, onions and other market garden produce share the roads with combine harvesters which have been gathering the local crops of sugar beet and cereal. The fens remain one of the most prosperous agricultural regions in Europe, as Cornelius Vermuyden promised they would be three and a half centuries ago.

The Forgotten Fen

One area which was never drained by Vermuyden or any of his successors lies midway between Ely and Newmarket. This is Wicken Fen, an area now amounting to 800 acres which in 1899 became the National Trust's first nature reserve and is designated a Site of Special Scientific Interest. It is home to more than 200 bird species, over 1,000 species of butterfly and moth and 1,400 species of beetle. The fen accommodates Britain's oldest birdwatcher's hide. The young Charles Darwin spent much of his time here collecting the beetles when, as an undergraduate at nearby Cambridge University, he should have been studying theology. The site is now the subject of more official scrutiny by the university's scientists as a rare example of natural fenland which has evaded the intensive cultivation which followed Vermuyden's great scheme. Moreover English Nature has plans to re-create the Great Fen which lies east of the A1(M) between Peterborough and Huntingdon. In 2004 the process of flooding 7,500 acres between Woodwalton Fen and Holme Fen will begin as ditches and drains are blocked and habitats are created for birds like snipe and bittern in the hope that they will return to the area which they once populated in large numbers. Threatened plants such as the rare fen violet will be planted and reeds will be planted for thatching. At present the fen thatchers import most of their raw material from Poland. Perhaps the ghost of Cornelius Vermuyden will look on as English Nature's engineers reverse the process over which he laboured almost four hundred years ago.[53]

Postscript: The Sea Strikes Back

The sea has not always been a passive recipient of the land water despatched to its briny depths by engineers like Cornelius Vermuyden. The high-water level at London Bridge has risen by about 30in each century owing to the melting of the polar ice cap and to the fact that the British Isles are tilting towards Europe at a rate of about 12in per century. In addition, surge tides, bodies of water driven down the North Sea by strong northerly winds, present a particular threat to the low-lying areas of the east coast which Vermuyden drained. The vulnerability of the communities of this coast, especially the Thames estuary, is well illustrated by the fate of Canvey Island. This community of 4,000 acres in the vicinity of Southend appears on an early second-century map of Ptolemy of Alexandria[54] and by 1577 it had taken the name *Canwaie Iles* in the *Description of England* by an Essex clergyman, the Revd William Harrison. At this time it was not so much an island as a series of islets whose appearance above water depended upon the state of the tide. Despite this uncertain existence it was home to 4,000 sheep who produced ewes' milk for the local markets and for the capital. In 1622 the islands became a part of the drainage projects of England's eastern landscape. Cornelius Vermuyden himself executed some of the work, responsibility for which lay with a fellow Dutchman, Joas Croppenburgh. Croppenburgh was granted 471 acres of ground on Canvey Island as payment for walling in 3,600 acres. His sea defences survived the numerous floods of the following 330 years, though they were frequently overtopped. To this day Canvey Island is home to a Cornelius Vermuyden School, and a 'Dutch Cottage' which the Dutch 'bankers' used while engaged on the embanking work is now a museum.

The substantial Dutch community which remained on the island after the work had been completed did not protect Canvey Island from a raid by Dutch seamen during the wars of 1667 though most of the dangers associated with the area concerned poor health rather than foreign enemies. The island's damp

Dutch Cottage, Canvey Island, home to Dutch 'bankers' in 1618, now a museum. *(Stephen Halliday)*

climate had a reputation for promoting 'ague' which we have already observed in the fens and which carried off many of its residents. According to Daniel Defoe's account in his *Tour of the Eastern Counties*, published in 1724, women were particularly vulnerable to this condition. This accounted for his report that some men on the island had had as many as fifteen wives, their mortality being attributed to the dreaded 'ague'. To the dangers of illness were added those of frequent flooding which simply overflowed Croppenburgh's sturdy but inadequate wall. A series of disastrous floods in the mid-eighteenth century led to the establishment, in 1792, of a Canvey Island Commission whose task was to maintain and strengthen the sea walls but, lacking both authority and finance, little was achieved by this body.

It says much for the island's reputation for good arable soil that, in the 1841 census, the population of this remote community was as high as 477, mostly engaged in cereal farming. The island also became a centre for sporting activities of doubtful legality which were best pursued at a safe distance from the authorities in the capital. It was particularly favoured as the venue for bare-knuckle fighting. Thus on 22 September 1857 it was the scene of a bout between Nat Langham and 'Big Ben' Caunt who fought each other to a standstill over sixty rounds and then shook hands, the match being declared a draw. The following year 'Big Ben' retired and, according to some accounts, gave his name to the great bell in the Parliamentary clock which was commissioned in the same year.[55]

An alarming fate

In 1881 one-third of the island was flooded but three years later it was threatened with a more alarming fate. During the time that Sir Joseph Bazalgette was building London's sewers, to clean up the River Thames, he was besieged with ideas for improving the system that he was designing.[56] Many of these were wildly eccentric, to which category we must assign a plan by a solicitor called Thomas Ellis to pump London's sewage to the summit of Hampstead Heath and let it flow in all directions. In the 1880s, by which time the areas close to Bazalgette's outfall works at Plumstead and Barking were becoming inhabited, there were renewed calls for London's sewage to be taken further downstream, well beyond the metropolis's residential area. A company had been formed in 1865 called the 'Metropolitan Sewage and Essex Reclamation Company' whose intention was to collect the northern sewage at Barking and convey it, via a 'sewage canal' to low-lying parts of Essex which would thereby become reclaimed and highly fertile land. The company foundered through lack of finance but in 1886 attention was turned to Canvey Island as a suitable receptacle for London sewage, as shown by a prescient article in the *Pall Mall Gazette*:[57] 'Canvey Island may claim whatever credit belongs to the fact that it is as clearly designed for the treatment of London sewage as the belt of chalk under the English Channel was created by providence for the creation of the channel Tunnel.' The Channel Tunnel had to wait for another century but the threat to Canvey Island passed when Bazalgette built two treatment works at Barking and Crossness and ceased the practice of discharging untreated sewage into the Thames.

After escaping its fate as the receptacle for London's sewage, Canvey Island now entered upon a period of prosperity as rail links from London to Southend made the island accessible to people from the east end of London. In the early years of the twentieth century an entrepreneur called Hester promoted Canvey Island as 'Little Holland', a seaside holiday home for working people. The island acquired a holiday hostel for working girls and a Winter Gardens like the best spas. Indeed one advertisement described it as 'Holland-in-England: A unique health resort. The far end of the island confronts the German Ocean, [North Sea], commanding a fine view of the shipping continually passing.'[58]

By the time of the 1921 census the resident population had reached 1,795 and this was further boosted with the opening of the first bridge in 1931 so that residents no longer had to use a ferry or causeway, the latter frequently flooded. By 1938 there were over 4,000 buildings on the island, many of them holiday bungalows for Londoners. Many of these became the principal dwellings of their owners when war broke out and bombing drove people out of the capital, though Canvey Island itself was one of the first places to be bombed in the Blitz. After the war it became the home of one of the early holiday camps, situated at Thorney Bay on the island's south coast. The island now seemed well protected from floods and the sympathy the islanders in their bungalows now felt for beleaguered communities is demonstrated by the generosity they showed for the inhabitants of Lynmouth, Devon, for whom they collected money when Lynmouth was badly affected by floods in August 1952. They would soon be devastated themselves.

The 1953 floods

On Saturday 31 January 1953, there was a strong east wind and an exceptionally high tide was expected as the islanders gathered to open a War

Memorial Hall in honour of fifty-seven islanders who had been killed in the Second World War. In the days that followed, the island was to lose an even greater number of its inhabitants to the floods that were advancing from the North Sea. At 2 a.m. the following day, Sunday, the incoming flood breached the eastern seawalls and Frank Griffith, head of the island's retained fire brigade, fired maroons and sounded the air-raid sirens to warn of the impending disaster. The Canvey Island Council's engineer now organised the wholesale evacuation of the island. Eight thousand residents left the island but two thousand decided to remain in their homes. The emergency services, with much assistance from the military, returned to the island with sandbags and other defences and set up the headquarters of 'Operation King Canute' at a public house named the Red Cow, subsequently renamed 'King Canute'. MPs particularly commended the work of 164 Borstal boys who had voluntarily helped the stricken islanders.[59] By the following Wednesday, 4 February, the flood defences had been restored and the water was receding but the devastation was appalling. Fifty-eight people had died, some whole families being lost. The War Memorial Hall, opened four days earlier, was wrecked as were many bungalows. Other east coast communities were flooded in an area extending from King's Lynn, from which 1,000 inhabitants were evacuated, to the Thames estuary but none as badly as Canvey Island.[60] Of the 839 breaches in 310 miles of seawall in Essex, 51 breaches had occurred in the island's perimeter walls and it accounted for almost half the county's fatalities.

On Monday 2 February the Prime Minister, Winston Churchill, declared in his orotund phraseology that 'the disaster which has fallen upon the habitants [*sic*] of Canvey Island seems to me to be a most grievous one. Our hearts go out to them, as will our help, in their hour of need' while the local MP, Bernard Braine, claimed, not quite appropriately, that 'Canvey Island will rise again'.[61] The island remained at its modest elevation but steps were now taken to strengthen its defences against the sea. Not everyone agreed with this policy. The humorous writer and *Punch* contributor A.P. Herbert suggested that Canvey Island should be sacrificed to save London, becoming part of a flood plain to protect the capital from future disasters. Other counsels prevailed. The Lord Mayor of London opened a fund for the islanders which received contributions from US airforce personnel serving in Britain and from Mr Andrei Gromyko on behalf of Stalin's Soviet Union. Not wishing to be left out, Chairman Mao sent £15,000, supposedly collected from some Chinese peasants who knew what it was like to be flooded by the Yangstse.[62] By May

1954, fifteen months after the floods, the Queen was able to inspect the new and much more substantial seawalls: 350,000 concrete blocks, supported by steel piling and reinforced with half a million cubic yards of clay.

The Thames Barrier

Canvey Island was now secure but the floods drew attention to the vulnerability of the Thames estuary and, in particular, the danger posed to London itself by surge tides. The committee which enquired into the Canvey Island floods recommended that a barrier be erected across the Thames which could be raised at times of danger to prevent flood waters from inundating the capital. In the 1950s and 1960s the Port of London, east of Tower Bridge, still received huge tonnages of shipping in large cargo vessels and all attempts to design a barrier which would allow these vessels to pass in safety met with failure. The gradual run-down of the London docks in the 1970s and the transfer of shipping to the container port of Tilbury changed all this.[63] It was now possible to build a barrier further upstream with openings for shipping no wider than Tower Bridge itself. Work on building the Thames Barrier began in

Thames barrier. (Stephen Halliday)

1974 and occupied as many as 4,000 men and women in its construction. It was officially opened by the Queen in May 1984. Nine reinforced concrete piers, sheathed in steel hoods, divide the river into ten lanes, each protected by a steel gate. Six of the lanes are used by shipping. In addition, river walls to the east provide further protection. Each of the gates, when fully raised, is as high as a five-storey building and since its opening the barrier has been raised more than sixty times as a precaution against flooding. The Thames Barrier, like Wickham Fen and the Great Fen, has become a visitors' attraction. Its visitor and education centre, open throughout the year, attracts tens of thousands of visitors who arrive by boat from Tower Pier and Greenwich, especially during the planned monthly raising of the barrier to test the mechanism. Cornelius Vermuyden himself would be impressed.

3

THE INLAND WATERWAYS AND THE INDUSTRIAL REVOLUTION

His Grace the Duke of Bridgewater, in whose praise it would be unpardonable to be silent who, at an age too often spent in dissipation by our young nobility, applied his attention to useful objects.

> A General History of Inland Navigation, *John Phillips, 1792*

Beware of Public Companies but particularly of the Grand Junction Canal Company.

> The Tocsin sounded, or a Libel extraordinary, *by Augustus Cove, an aggrieved customer of the Grand Junction Canal Company, 1813*

A sense of immediate danger was conveyed by the canal – the menace of insulting words from strange, brutal canal workers with blackened faces like miners, with their gypsy wives and ragged children.

> A Sort of Life, *by Graham Greene, describing his experience of the Grand Junction Canal in Berkhamsted during his childhood*

THE DUKE

Francis Egerton (1736–1803), the third (and last) Duke of Bridgewater, was a living symbol of the distinction between the aristocracies of France and England in the eighteenth century. While his French contemporaries were hanging about Versailles, helping Louis XV to dress, arguing about precedence and successfully resisting attempts to tax their lands, Francis Egerton was to be seen on his wharves on the River Mersey. Clad in a brown worsted suit made

Sir Francis Egerton, 3rd Duke of Bridgewater.
(National Portrait Gallery)

by the tailor that supplied clothing to his coal miners, the Duke would supervise the unloading of barges transporting coal from his Worsley pits and its onward carriage to the factories and householders of Liverpool. In times of shortage he ensured that the poorer citizens were supplied before the richer ones. Many of his aristocratic contemporaries regarded him as eccentric while some of his family found him embarrassing. Both groups envied the wealth that his enterprise had created.

The Duke was descended from Thomas Egerton who was created the 1st Lord Ellesmere by Elizabeth I and became Lord Chancellor in 1604, shortly after the accession of James I. The new lord took his title from the family estate of Ellesmere in Shropshire, though he made his home at Ashridge, near Berkhamsted in Hertfordshire. Ashridge had been a monastic foundation, created in the thirteenth century by Edmund, Earl of Cornwall, grandson of King John. It was one of the casualties of the dissolution of the monasteries by Henry VIII and it became a home for the King's children. The future Edward VI, Queen Mary and Elizabeth all lived there before they ascended the throne. Following the death of Elizabeth, the estate was acquired by the new Lord Chancellor, Thomas Egerton, 1st Baron Ellesmere. Thomas's son became the 1st Earl of Bridgewater, the title being taken from another of the family's estates near that town in Somerset. The town dropped the 'e' from its name to become Bridgwater but the earls kept theirs. The family were better at acquiring lands than they were at producing heirs. Brothers succeeded brothers who had failed to produce healthy sons but this did not prevent them from acquiring properties through judicious marriages to wealthy brides. By the time the 4th Earl, Scroop Egerton, had become the 1st Duke of Bridgewater in 1720 he had acquired estates in twelve counties.[1] One of these was the Worsley estate on Walkden Moor north of Manchester. Scroop had eight sons and three daughters by two marriages but only two of the boys survived the tuberculosis that carried off their brothers in childhood. One, John, succeeded as the 2nd duke in 1745 but died childless within three years. He was succeeded by his only surviving brother, the 11-year-old Francis, in 1748: the 'Canal Duke'.

Francis endured a turbulent relationship with his mother Rachel. Within a few months of her husband's death the 49-year-old widowed duchess married a man aged 26. The incongruous couple embarked on a life of entertainment and jollity in London society while Francis was despatched to Eton and encouraged to live with his cousin Samuel Egerton, MP for Cheshire, in Samuel's home at Tatton, a good distance from his neglectful mother. This did not bring peace. At one point Francis had to enlist the assistance of the Duke of Bedford, his uncle by marriage, to extract from his mother a sum of money to pay for his school fees. In 1756 cousin Samuel, who had taken over the administration of the young Duke's estates until he became an adult, provided the money to send him on a grand tour. The Duke of Bedford found a suitable travelling companion in Robert Wood, a classical scholar and traveller whose stoicism was to be severely tested during the forthcoming visit to France, Switzerland and Italy. In his early reports to the Duke of Bedford Robert Wood confined his criticisms to descriptions of his charge's unwillingness to engage in serious reading but the tone changed abruptly when Wood wrote begging to be released from his responsibilities, explaining that he was becoming increasingly concerned at the Duke's taste for 'the worst company'. Some idea of the degree of Wood's distress may be gained from his protestation that, if the Duke insisted on holding him to the full length of his contract, he would expect 'three hundred pounds a year during my life from the time I leave his Grace . . . and this I must say I shall expect as an act of Justice, not of generosity'.[2]

Wood calmed down, remained at his post and decided to try a new tactic. A week after his resignation letter he wrote, 'I grew convinced that the most effectual service I could render him was to give him a taste, if possible, for the company of women of fashion.'[3] If this solicitude reflected anxieties about the Duke's sexuality then the seventeen-year-old Francis soon resolved them, though not with the decorum that the scholarly Wood had intended. He took an actress as a mistress and 'hired a country house by means of the lowest Scoundrell in ye town who became his companion and *Intendant des Plaisirs*'.[4] A further offer of resignation was withdrawn and a calmer period followed during which the Duke and his increasingly anxious companion visited Switzerland.

Le Canal du Midi

Upon returning to France in the autumn of 1752 Francis began to show a previously undetected interest in engineering. He expressed a wish to see the Languedoc canal. It is possible that his interest in this distinctly unaristocratic feature of southern France was prompted by conversations with his late father. Before his death Scroop had been approached by some Lancashire businessmen who wanted his support in making navigable Worsley Brook, a small stream close to Scroop's coal workings at Walkden, near Bolton. This would have enabled the coal from Worsley to be transported by water to the growing city of Manchester. An Act to permit these improvements to Worsley Brook was passed in 1737, the year after Francis's birth. Nothing came of the scheme but the potential advantages to the Duke's coal workings were obvious and, as he approached his majority and the prospect of inheriting the Worsley mines, Francis suddenly discovered an interest in canals.

The Languedoc canal, now called *Le Canal du Midi*, had been constructed during the reign of Louis XIV by the Baron de Bonrepos. It was 150 miles in length and had been conceived by a tax collector called Riquet as a means of joining the economies of the Atlantic and the Mediterranean. It linked the Mediterranean at Sète with Toulouse, from where craft could proceed to the Atlantic ocean via the River Garonne, thereby saving the long journey round Spain via the straits of Gibraltar. It had taken 12,000 men nineteen years to build and was one of the wonders of Europe as well as being a valuable military and commercial facility. It had all the features of later canals: aqueducts across valleys and rivers; tunnels through hills; reservoirs at the summit fed by mountain streams; and over a hundred locks. No structure on this scale existed in Britain. The canal made such an impression on the young Duke that Wood was able to report that his charge had started to attend a course on 'Experimental Philosophy' which we would call engineering.[5] Some anxious weeks followed when Francis appears to have succumbed to the tuberculosis which had carried off so many of his siblings. He recovered and returned to England where his long-suffering companion, Robert Wood, was rewarded with a seat in Parliament for the Duke of Bedford's pocket borough of Brackley in Northamptonshire.

Early canals

Canals were to be found in England long before the third Duke of Bridgewater was born, though they were very different in character and purpose from those he was to build. As observed in an earlier chapter, canals had been built by the Romans and later by Cornelius Vermuyden in the fen country of East Anglia and Lincolnshire, though these were primarily used for drainage and only incidentally for navigation.[6] In the twelfth century the earls of Devon had built a weir across the River Exe which prevented boats of any size from reaching Exeter. The purpose of the weir was to regulate the flow of water in the river for those of the earls' tenants who relied on waterwheels to drive their mills. The protests of the marooned citizens of Exeter were unavailing until the reign of Elizabeth I when a short canal was built to bypass the obstruction. This canal used locks with 'mitre' designs for the gates: a 'V' shape in which the point of the V pointed upstream, thus ensuring that the pressure of the water kept the lock gates closed. This design, attributed by some to Leonardo da Vinci, was later to be widely adopted and is still in use. The Aire and Calder river navigation had been completed in 1704 between Goole, Leeds and Wakefield, carrying coal, cloth, agricultural produce and other materials between those towns. In Lancashire itself the Sankey Canal Company obtained an Act of Parliament in 1755 which authorised its promoters to render navigable the Sankey Brook, a stream which linked the River Mersey to St Helens. By 1771 it was carrying almost 90,000 tons of coal a year from St Helens to Liverpool and Cheshire as well as slate, limestone, agricultural produce and glass from the works at St Helens.[7] In 1734 an attempt had been made to enable boats to reach the wharves of the growing city of Manchester via the Mersey and the Irwell but the scheme was never a great success. At times of low rainfall the volume of water in the Irwell was too low to enable any but the smallest craft to reach Manchester. The sight of bargees struggling to haul their craft through shallows, the hulls scraping along the bed of the river, was a familiar and depressing one. This did not prevent the 'river navigation' proprietors, led by the local Stanley family, from opposing the efforts of the 'canal faction', led by the Duke of Bridgewater, to provide a channel navigable at all seasons.

The Bridgewater canal

On 25 November 1758 the 22-year-old Duke presented to Parliament a petition for an act which would allow him to construct a navigable waterway from his mines at Worsley, up on Walkden Moor, to Manchester, 7 miles distant. This would become the first Bridgewater canal, a name it retains. The Duke estimated that this would enable him to sell coal for 4*d* a hundredweight instead of the *7d* a hundredweight that it cost when transported by road. It would also, of course, enormously increase the demand for his coal among the businesses and residents of this rapidly growing town and thereby handsomely repay his investment in the canal. His petition was enthusiastically supported by the merchants of Manchester and Salford. The Duke's decision to proceed with the canal owed much to the insight of his local agent, John Gilbert. Gilbert had received some training in engineering as an apprentice in the works of the great Matthew Boulton[8] and had then been appointed by the Duke to look after his interests at Worsley whose mines had long suffered from flooding. The workings were drained by 'soughs', channels cut into the surrounding hillside in such a way that they sloped downwards from the flooded areas. The water then poured out through the soughs and enabled mining to continue. John Gilbert also realised that the mines would be far more profitable if their coal could be transported cheaply to Manchester. He studied maps of the area and realised that the soughs could be converted from a drainage channel to a means of transport. By making them large enough to accommodate a narrow boat they would afford a means of access to the coal workings themselves, thus reducing the need for 'drawers' (usually women or children) to drag the coal, a basket at a time, on iron-shod toboggans from the coalface to the exit. The water from the soughs could then be used to supply water to a navigable channel through which the boats could pass to Manchester.[9] Moreover, the water from the flooded mines would overcome one of the problems which was to haunt all the canal engineers: how to provide water at the 'summit' of the canal on Walkden Moor without the expense of pumping it from a lower source such as a river or lake. In effect he was turning a problem, the flooded mines, into an opportunity, a means of transport.

The craft which would enter the soughs would be narrow and crude, with their ribs and keel visible like those of an undernourished animal. They became known, for this reason, as 'starvationers' while the larger barges which were introduced at a later date to carry cargo longer distances became known as 'dukes' in honour of the Duke himself. In March 1759, despite continued opposition from the 'river navigation' interests, the act was passed and construction work could begin. The Act stipulated that the price of coal in Manchester should not exceed *4d* a hundredweight for 40 years and the tolls the Duke could levy on other people's boats would be limited to *2s 6d* (12½p) per ton. At this point the construction team was joined by James Brindley who already had some experience of mining work since he had drained a mine in Bolton with an elaborate system of waterwheels.

James Brindley, (1716–72) was typical of the early engineers who created the British canal system. Born in Derbyshire, the son of a farmer, he was apprenticed to a millwright in Macclesfield. Millwrights were the engineers of their time, with a wide range of skills in mechanical work which they imparted to their apprentices. Brindley, however, was not a very satisfactory apprentice and the cancellation of his indentures was avoided only because of his skill in repairing broken machinery. Having completed his apprenticeship the young Brindley was employed by Josiah Wedgwood to construct flint mills to produce the glazing materials required for his growing pottery business. In 1758 Brindley patented an improvement to Newcomen's design for a steam engine and the following year he joined the team constructing the Bridgewater canal. Brindley himself designed the Barton aqueduct and went on to be involved in the construction of over 300 miles of the early canal system, notably the Trent and Mersey canal. He was accompanied by three floating workshops. One was a fully equipped blacksmith's forge; one a carpenter's shop; one a stonemason's. Barely literate, Brindley would take to his bed to contemplate any serious engineering problem, doing the calculations in his head. He would then announce the results without committing the calculations to paper. It is a testimony to the confidence that he instilled in better-educated colleagues that they accepted his decisions, having no way of checking them. The novelist Arnold Bennett was a descendant of James Brindley.

James Brindley. (National Portrait Gallery)

The first 4 miles of the Bridgewater canal consisted of enlarged 'soughs' beneath Walkden Moor which emerged onto the surface near Worsley itself. This underground network eventually grew to more than 40 miles. The canal made its way to Manchester without locks but it faced one major obstacle in the form of the River Irwell whose valley had to be crossed. The Parliamentary Committee which had to approve the project required some persuading that it was possible to construct an aqueduct for barges across the valley. Brindley eventually persuaded them of the feasibility of the project by appearing before them with a large cheese and sculpting it into the required shape.[10] The aqueduct was constructed from stone and 'puddled' with clay. This process, which Sir Hugh Myddleton had used on the New River,[11] consisted of emptying quantities of clay into the bed of the canal and 'puddling' (stamping on) it so that it formed a hard, impervious lining for the bed and walls of the canal. The clay had been extracted from the Worsley mine workings where its presence had helped to cause the flooding by trapping the surface water. Limestone from the soughs was also used in the construction of the aqueduct and other spoil from the construction work was placed on the Chat Moss, to the west of Manchester, which was thereby converted into agricultural land from its earlier waterlogged condition. The new aqueduct opened in 1761 and remained in use until 1893 when it was replaced by the present Barton swing bridge. This still carries boats across the Manchester ship canal which opened in 1894. The aqueduct, the first of its kind to be built in Britain, was regarded with wonder by contemporaries and was celebrated in verse:

> Vessels o'er vessels, water under water,
> Bridgewater triumphs, art has conquered nature.[12]

The Bridgewater canal itself opened to Manchester in 1763. Rather than charge the 4*d* a hundredweight that the Act permitted, the Duke charged 3½*d* for the next 30 years, thereby halving the price of coal from its previous level.[13] Each 'starvationer' could carry 8 tons of coal, whereas a horse could only manage a maximum of 2 tons, more slowly, on a cart. As anticipated, the demand for the Duke's coal grew rapidly. The output of the Worsley mines rose correspondingly and reached 300,000 tons a year, compared with the 90,000 tons that the Sankey Brook had carried from all the mines it served. So many were employed in the mines that the Duke's agents resorted to recruiting miners from North Wales.

To Liverpool

In 1717, Liverpool, a community little more than a village, had built the first wet dock in England, a sealed enclosure in which water could be maintained at the high tide level so that loading and unloading could proceed uninterrupted. This marked the beginning of its rise as a great trading port. By 1811 it was second in population only to London itself, a development which it owed in part to the Duke's next enterprise. Even before the Worsley to Manchester canal had been completed he had decided to construct a branch of the canal to the Mersey estuary. This was a much more ambitious project. The original canal was about 11 miles long whereas the new canal, having crossed the Irwell at Barton Bridge, would run for nearly three times that distance through north Cheshire before reaching the Mersey near Runcorn. Nevertheless the enormous profits anticipated for his mines by the Bridgewater canal encouraged the Duke to press ahead with this much larger investment. In 1761, two years before the first Bridgewater canal opened, he petitioned Parliament for a new act authorising the Mersey extension. He immediately encountered opposition from the 'river navigators' who had created the Irwell route to Manchester and who saw his projected canal as a threat to their own interests. The Duke replied that hauliers charged 40*s* (£2) a ton to take goods from Manchester to Liverpool, that the Irwell navigation charged 12*s*; and that his canal would charge 6*s*. Moreover, he reminded the Parliamentary Committee which considered his act that at times of low rainfall and low tides only lightly loaded craft could navigate the Irwell and even then they were sometimes marooned in the shallows. A propaganda pamphlet produced by Brindley and circulated among Members of Parliament roundly abused 'Cheshire Gentlemen' for seeking to obstruct the Duke's plan which, it asserted, was part of a scheme which would eventually link the ports of Liverpool and Hull.[14] Brindley and the Duke asserted that one horse could draw 50 tons of freight in a barge and they called upon the eminent engineer John Smeaton, builder of the Eddystone lighthouse, to argue the case for them. The Parliamentarians were convinced and the Duke's act was passed in March 1762.

Not all of the 'Cheshire Gentlemen' were appeased. Sir Richard Brooke of Norton Priory, just east of the canal's terminus at Runcorn, did his best to impede the canal by refusing to allow it to cross his land. While the dispute was being resolved by a jury convened to decide the matter, the freight had to be carted by road around the obstacle. By 1776 the Bridgewater canal had reached Runcorn, ten locks having been constructed for the final descent to

the Mersey and in the same year the Duke opened his wharves at Liverpool to
through traffic from Manchester, with fatal consequences for the ailing river
navigation via the Irwell. The Duke went to great lengths to ensure that the
canal did not freeze over in winter – a charge that had been levelled at the
project by the river navigation interests. In 1767, the year before he sailed with
Captain Cook on *The Endeavour* to the South Seas, Sir Joseph Banks visited
Worsley and the canal network which surrounded it. He recorded the sight of
one of the Duke's ice-breakers, sturdy vessels manned by men with clubs who
smashed a path through the ice to keep the canal open. The canal did more
than carry freight. In 1766 the Duke opened a passenger service from Worsley
to Lymm, charging a penny a mile and a service was later added from
Manchester to Warrington where there was an onward connection to
Liverpool. The journey was made on a boat called *Duchess-Countess*, pulled at a
canter by two horses and equipped with a knife on its prow to cut the tow-
ropes of any slower craft which were in the way.[15] The journey took five hours
and it says much about the quality of road transport at the time that the
service attracted a sufficient complement of passengers for it to become a
regular service with its own timetable.[16] The service survived until 1872.[17]

The new canal put great strains on the Duke's finances. Like the later canal
and railway builders he often had to offer generous compensation terms to
landowners whose properties he needed to cross. The alternative was to await
the decision of juries, as in the case of Norton Priory, which could involve
substantial legal costs as well as delays. By the time the Liverpool link opened,
the Duke's canal debts, secured against his numerous estates, exceeded
£250,000. They peaked in 1787 at almost £350,000 and thereafter declined
as revenues from his canal interests accumulated. At one point the profits from
his canals enabled him to repay the debts at a rate of more than £60,000 per
annum: an unimaginably large sum for the time which reflects the profitability
of his investments. By the time of his death in 1803 they had fallen to
£162,000 and within three years they had been paid off in full.[18]

North Sea to Irish Sea

The most ambitious and costly of the Duke's projects began in 1766 when the
Liverpool link was still ten years short of completion. This was to be a canal
linking the Mersey to the Trent via the Potteries and thence to the port of Hull,
thereby providing an inland waterway across the breadth of Britain. Josiah
Wedgwood, who had founded his pottery business in Burslem in the same year,

1759, that the Duke had obtained his Act for the original Bridgewater canal, was an enthusiastic supporter of the new canal. The prospect of having his china transported gently and cheaply to the great ports instead of having it bumping slowly along rutted tracks at great expense was very attractive indeed and the register of shareholders in the Trent and Mersey canal reads like a 'Who's Who?' of industrial pioneers. Besides Wedgwood himself, who later became chairman of the canal, we find the Duke of Bridgewater, James Brindley, who was to engineer the canal, and Matthew Boulton whose partnership with James Watt would form one of the cornerstones of the Industrial Revolution.[19] Nothing could more clearly illustrate the profitability envisaged from canal investments than the decision of these experienced and dispassionate entrepreneurs to support this ambitious venture with their own hard-earned money.

Once again the promoters of the bill faced opposition from river navigators, this time from those who had made the River Weaver navigable to some craft. The opposition was joined by others with interests in coastal shipping which would be threatened by the short cut from Hull to Liverpool and by Members of Parliament who represented towns which would be bypassed by the canal. Brindley's advocacy helped to win the day. The new canal, 94 miles long, promised to connect Liverpool and Manchester not only with Hull but also with Bristol. The Staffordshire and Worcestershire canal would link with the Trent and Mersey near Stafford and thence connect it to the Severn at Stourport, a town created by the new network. Brindley's pamphlet[20] drew attention to the advantages that Holland had gained from its system of navigable waterways on drainage channels and presented a map which was headed: 'A Plan of the Navigable Canals Intended to be made for opening a Communication between the Interior parts of the Kingdom and the ports of Bristol, Liverpool and Hull'. The freight rates promised were 2½d (about 1p) per ton per mile – less than a quarter of the cost by road for Wedgwood's precious china. The act authorising the construction of the Trent and Mersey was passed in May 1766 on the same day as its partner enterprise, the Staffordshire and Worcestershire canal.

The greatest obstacle faced by the new canal was Harecastle Hill, north of Stoke-on-Trent, through which it would be necessary to cut a tunnel over 1.5 miles long. The difficulties which Brindley faced in executing this work were to leave the canal with a serious flaw. The hard rock through which he had to bore the tunnel led him to decide that he would make it wide enough only for narrow boats which meant that the wider boats in use on the Duke's

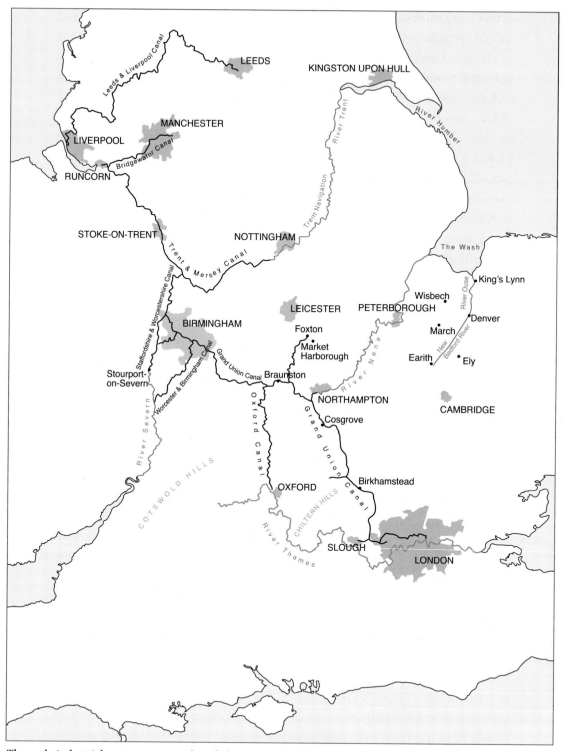

The early industrial waterway network and the New Bedford River.

canals were unable to make use of the network further south. For this reason a second Harecastle tunnel, built by Thomas Telford, opened in 1827.

The Trent and Mersey canal opened in 1777 and provided a vital waterway linking the rapidly growing industrial base of the West Midlands with the coal of Manchester and the ports of Liverpool, Hull and Bristol. It also provided a rather circuitous link with London via the Oxford canal after 1790 and when this was threatened by the proposal to build a more direct route via the Grand Junction canal the proprietors of the Trent and Mersey, including the Duke himself, showed that they could be just as ruthless in their opposition to new waterways as the 'river navigators' had been to theirs. Another pamphlet was produced, in about 1800, called 'Observations on the Proposed Grand Union [*sic*] Canal' which argued that 'the proposed Canal is not founded either in Necessity or public Utility and will not open any new Communications or Sources of Commerce'.[21]

THE GRAND JUNCTION CANAL

On 20 July 1792, a meeting was convened at the Bull Inn, Stony Stratford,[22] in Buckinghamshire, by the promoters of a new canal, to be called the 'Grand Junction Canal'. It would run from London to Braunston, in Northamptonshire. There it would link with the Oxford canal which would carry it onwards to Birmingham and hence to the northern canal network which the Duke and his associates had built. The scheme had been proposed by the Marquis of Buckingham whose home at Stowe was close to the route of the proposed canal. So many potential shareholders attended the meeting that the Bull Inn was unable to accommodate them, so the meeting was adjourned to the parish church. William Praed,[23] MP for St Ives in Cornwall, was appointed chairman of the committee to promote the Act of Parliament which would authorise the construction of the canal. The act was passed in April 1793, despite opposition from the Oxford Canal Company whose shareholders were worried about the loss of traffic to the new canal. The year 1793 marked the climax of 'canal mania'. The earlier canals had been financed by men like Bridgewater and Wedgwood who expected the new form of transport to benefit their mining and manufacturing interests. The profitability of these early waterways now attracted a new type of financier: speculators who expected to make quick and substantial profits from their investments. In that year, twenty canals were authorised and a further thirty-five in the years either side. The promoters were permitted to raise £7,880,600 in capital.[24] So much money

William Jessop (1745–1814) was the son of a shipwright. William had the good fortune to be apprenticed at the age of 14 to John Smeaton, the greatest civil engineer of his age, who had been entrusted with the rebuilding of Plymouth's Eddystone lighthouse when the original structure was destroyed in a gale in 1755. Jessop worked with Smeaton on a number of canal projects, notably the Forth–Clyde canal. He set up in business on his own account in 1772 and in the 1790s was involved in many of the inland waterway projects as the most experienced of the early canal engineers. One of these was the Ellesmere canal (now part of the Shropshire Union) which included the spectacular Pontcysyllte Aqueduct, near Llangollen, designed by the young Thomas Telford who thus gained his first experience of canal engineering under Jessop's direction. Jessop designed the Surrey Iron Railway which opened in 1803, using horses rather than steam for traction as well as designing London's West India Docks and Bristol Floating Harbour.

was made by speculating in canal shares, rather than building canals, that comparisons were made with the South Sea Bubble phenomenon and an MP suggested that children would be at an advantage if they were born with webbed feet.[25] The Grand Junction Act authorised the promoters to raise £600,000 to build the canal and specified the rates that could be charged for freight. They ranged from a farthing per ton mile for limestone to a penny for manufactured goods. One of the founding shareholders was the Duke of Bridgewater. Some care had been taken in choosing the best route. An initial survey by James Barnes had been endorsed, with some modifications, by the experienced civil engineer William Jessop. On 1 June 1793, William Praed was elected as chairman of the canal company and Jessop was appointed as its engineer. Barnes took the post of resident engineer with responsibility for day-to-day supervision of the work.

Obstacles: landowners

There were five major obstacles to the completion of the canal. The first was the existence, in the proposed path of the canal, of a number of powerful landowners who were determined to exact from the company the best possible terms in payment and compensation. The Earl of Essex was appeased with £15,000 for the right to cut through his estate at Cassiobury, near Watford, while the Earl of Clarendon settled for £5,000 in return for the right to cross his estate nearby at Grove Park. Needless to say both of these wealthy aristocrats were enthusiastic advocates of the canal. A further complication arose in the form of the Corporation of London. By a royal decree dating from 1197 the corporation controlled access to the River Thames as far upstream as Staines so Praed and his fellow directors had to agree the terms on which the canal would be allowed to connect with the river. The city fathers finally agreed to an arrangement whereby they would receive a share of the tolls levied by the canal on boat owners, amounting eventually to a minimum payment of £1,000 a year. The remaining obstacles were those of topography rather than finance.

The Chilterns

The first such obstacle comprised the Chiltern Hills which the canal needed to cross in the vicinity of Tring. To surmount this obstacle Barnes built fifty-six locks to raise the canal 380ft from its junction with the Thames at Brentford to what became known as 'Tring Summit', at which point it is above the dome of St Paul's Cathedral. There followed a descent towards Leighton Buzzard to the north of the Chilterns. At the summit itself, to avoid the need for more locks, Barnes cut ruthlessly through the hills, piling up the spoil in ridges on either side of the canal. Disposal of the spoil carried its own problems. 'Barrow runs' were built, consisting of crude wooden runways which ran up the steep sides of the ridges. The barrows were hauled up by horses on ropes and pulleys, guided by a labourer whose job was to keep the barrow on the runway. Having discharged his load the labourer would pull the empty barrow back down the steep runway – a hazardous task. The discharge of large quantities of soil on either side of the summit created an artificial environment which soon became overgrown with luxuriant shrubs, grass, trees and other vegetation. To this day this stretch of the canal, 2½ miles long, is known locally as 'Tring Jungle'.

Having overcome the obstacle of the Chilterns, Barnes was faced with the problem which assailed all canal builders: how was he to ensure a ready supply of water at the summit? Every time a boat used a lock, whether ascending or descending, water passed down from the summit in one direction or the other. To solve this problem he built four huge reservoirs covering almost 200 acres at Wilstone and Marsworth, close to the summit, in which water accumulated during the winter months. He also constructed the

Tring reservoirs, Grand Union Canal. *(Stephen Halliday)*

Wendover canal: a branch of the main canal which runs from Bulbourne junction, at the summit, to the small town of Wendover. It was hoped that this canal, 6 miles long, would feed water from chalk streams to the main canal and to its reservoirs. Unfortunately it had the opposite effect. The science of geology was in its infancy and it was not understood that water tends to sink through chalk more readily than it passes over it. Instead of supplying water to the Grand Junction, the Wendover arm, after its opening in 1796, was soon drawing water from it and distributing it over the adjacent fields. During droughts it was closed. The use of extra quantities of clay for 'puddling' the little canal failed to solve the problem of leakage and the arm was finally closed in 1904. A 'stop lock', an earthen barrier, was built close to the Wendover arm's junction with the main line at Bulbourne to prevent water leaking from the main canal. The remaining stretch of the arm from the stop lock to Wendover remains in existence, isolated from the rest of the system, a haven for wildlife.[26] The reservoirs at Wilstone and Marsworth are also the haunts of a wide variety of fishes, dragonflies and, in particular, birds. Ornithologists use specially constructed hides to observe both common and rare varieties of duck, goose, grebe, heron and gull as well as birds less often associated with stretches of water including sparrowhawk and, more recently, the red kite. Bulbourne junction was an important feature of the canal, with workshops where lock gates were made and their machinery repaired. The workshops remained in use until 2004.[27]

The tunnels

Two further obstacles were to prove the most expensive ones: the tunnels at Braunston and Blisworth. The tunnel at Braunston, close to the northern connection with the Oxford canal, was begun in June 1793 and completed in three years. Over a mile long, the tunnel presented severe problems to engineers who had little experience of building tunnels on such a scale. The construction methods were simple. First the course of the tunnel was marked on the surface above the intended route, using marker posts aligned by using a telescope. Then 'header' shafts were sunk at intervals between the surface markers to the depth at which, it was calculated, the canal would run. Labourers then descended to the bottom of the shafts and began to tunnel in each direction, aiming for the adjacent shaft and hoping to meet its tunnellers head-on. The tunnel contains two kinks which make it impossible to see through it from one end to the other, a feature accounted for by the crude alignment methods available to the tunnellers. In the circumstances their efforts were commendable.

The longer Blisworth tunnel, which at 3,056yd remains the longest on the canal, was a greater problem.[28] It runs from Stoke Bruerne, the present site of the Waterways Museum, to Blisworth, and the work was beset with problems from the start. Natural springs ran across the route of the tunnel which caused frequent flooding as well as making the terrain unstable. Work began in May 1794 and proceeded slowly and with many interruptions. As a temporary expedient a railway was laid along the line of the workings to which goods were transhipped from boats whose journeys terminated at each end of the uncompleted tunnel. The contractors resigned when they realised how much money they were losing on the work and William Jessop proposed to abandon the tunnel altogether and construct instead a long flight of locks. Barnes, the resident engineer, wanted to persist with the tunnel and proposed to take over the work himself, dispensing with the services of a contractor. Barnes won the day with the support first of John Rennie and later of Thomas Telford who inspected the completed work in March 1805 and declared it satisfactory. So it should have been. It had cost about £90,000, three times the original estimate.

The length and breadth of the nation

The opening of the tunnel on 25 March 1805 was a grand occasion. The canal had been collecting revenue from boats on the southern reaches of the

Thomas Telford (1757–1834) and John Rennie (1761–1821)
were two of the greatest engineers of their age. Telford, the son of a
shepherd, was born in Scotland and apprenticed to a stonemason. In
1792 he moved to England and worked on the construction of Somerset
House and Portsmouth dockyard. He built his first bridge over the River
Severn at Montford and went on to work with William Jessop on the
Ellesmere (later Shropshire Union) canal for which he designed the
Pontcysyllte aqueduct over the River Dee near Llangollen. He later built
the Caledonian canal, the Menai Suspension Bridge and the St
Katherine's Docks in London. He also built more than a thousand miles
of road. He played a leading part in the foundation of the Institution of
Civil Engineers and was its first president. John Rennie was also born in
Scotland and was apprenticed to a millwright before attending
Edinburgh University. He worked for five years for Boulton and Watt
and later built docks at Hull, Liverpool and Greenock as well as naval
dockyards at Chatham, Portsmouth and Plymouth. He became engineer
to the Kennet and Avon canal and was later involved in drainage works
in Ireland and the Fens, where he designed the Eau Brink Cut on the
River Ouse. He worked on the design of Scottish lighthouses with Robert
Stevenson, grandfather of the writer Robert Louis Stevenson, and built
some of the early London Docks. He is particularly remembered in
London for the bridges he designed: Southwark, Waterloo and London
Bridges though the last was completed to his design by his son, also
John Rennie, after the father died in 1821. Rennie was buried in St
Paul's Cathedral.

canal since 1795 but it was now finally open from Brentford, on the
Thames, to Braunston and thence to the northern canal system. This
obscure Northamptonshire village thus became the focal point of the canal
network. Birmingham, to the north of Braunston, would soon have more
canal mileage than any other city in Europe, as it still does. The little town of
Berkhamsted was home to 'the Port of Berkhamsted' on the Grand Junction
canal, close to the Duke's home at Ashridge but as far as it is possible to be
in England from the sea. Britain had a system of inland transport of
unprecedented speed and cheapness which would enable the factories of
Josiah Wedgwood and his fellow entrepreneurs to gain access to markets the
length and breadth of the nation.

Braunston Junction: left for Birmingham, right for London, back the way you have come for Oxford. *(Stephen Halliday)*

'Legging it'

One of the curious consequences of the long tunnels was the emergence of the 'legger'. Telford's Harecastle tunnel had a towpath but other tunnels did not, so the towing horse had to be detached from its boat and either led to the far end of the tunnel via paths or enjoy a well-earned rest as a passenger in the boat itself. On sailing barges the sails would be lowered. At this point 'leggers', who plied for trade at each end of the tunnel, would step onto the boat and 'leg it' through the tunnel. Planks, called 'wings' would be attached to the boat, one protruding from each side. On each wing would lie a legger who would leg the boat through the tunnel by pushing his feet against the wall on his side, in effect 'walking' along the side of the tunnel. In low tunnels the leggers lay on their backs and 'walked' along the tunnel roof. It took 65 minutes to 'leg' a boat through Blisworth tunnel for which the leggers each received 1*s* for a loaded boat and 9*d* for an empty one – a good rate of pay for the time which reflected the exhausting nature of the work.[29] 'Ben the legger' (William Benjamin) legged 60,000 miles in the course of his life working the Braunston tunnel on the Grand Junction Canal.[30] The leggers were noted for their strength, their rowdiness and their capacity for drink. The advent of boats powered by steam engines which did not need their services was viewed with hostility by this tough and formidable body of men.

The Great Ouse Aqueduct

The canal's final obstacle was a river, the Great Ouse, whose deep valley crosses the line of the canal at Cosgrove, on the northern outskirts of Milton Keynes. Nine locks were originally built to traverse the valley which significantly slowed the passage of the boats. Jessop and Barnes therefore agreed to build an aqueduct across the valley. A contractor was engaged to build an embankment to carry the aqueduct and at first all seemed well. However, in 1807, two years after the canal opened to through traffic, the aqueduct began to show signs of subsiding. The Grand Junction Company became involved in negotiations with the contractor and on 18 February 1808, while these were proceeding slowly and acrimoniously, the embankment collapsed. A local carpenter was called in and built a temporary replacement which opened to traffic within four months. It was replaced by an iron aqueduct, known as the 'Iron Trunk' or 'Pig Trough' which opened in 1811 and remains in use. It is a curious feature of the canal whose towpath is now mainly used by walkers and cyclists who enjoy a striking panorama of the valley of the Great Ouse far below as it makes its way towards Northampton, Ely and the Fens. The opening of the Grand Junction throughout its length connected London with the manufacturing areas of the Midlands and the North.

Napoleon

Seventeen miles north of the aqueduct lies a curious relic of the Napoleonic wars. In 1803, faced by the threat of invasion by Napoleon, the government decided to take measures to protect the kingdom. The Royal Military Canal was laid as a line of defence across Romney Marsh, near the anticipated site of any landings, and at the same time it was realised that it would be prudent to have a strategic store of supplies at a safe distance from the coast.[31] The site chosen was at Weedon in Northamptonshire, as far from the coast as possible but accessible by boat along the new canal. The government purchased 150 acres of land to accommodate a huge ordnance depot and a barracks, entrance to the site being controlled by a portcullis through which boats passed to the depot's private wharves. Two fine pavilions were also built whose superior design gave currency to a story that, in the event of invasion, they would be used to shelter the royal family. Since the invasion never took place the story was never put to the test. In the 1930s the barracks became the Army School of Equitation and the ordnance depot remained in use until 1965. Many of the structures remain, their immense size out of scale with the neighbouring

Weedon Bec, ordnance depot and refuge for royalty. *(Stephen Halliday)*

buildings. They are used as stores and workshops for the small companies which now thrive in the area.

Opposition

The canal was not always received with enthusiasm. Disputes arose between millers on its route who claimed that the new waterway was taking water that they needed to power their plants. At Apsley paper mills, close to the present site of Hemel Hempstead, the mill owners Longman and Dickinson, names which were to endure in printing and publishing, prosecuted the Grand Junction Company for drawing their mill water from the River Bulbourne which runs adjacent to the canal at this point. The Duke of Northumberland installed a water-gauge at a lock at Hunton Bridge, nearby, and agreed to supply from his land 500 locks of water to the canal below the lock if the canal supplied the equivalent to the millers above the lock. For the canal and its neighbours, water was the currency upon which their existence depended. The Grand Junction often solved the problem of recalcitrant millers by buying them out and in this way acquired a substantial amount of property in the vicinity of the canal which was to prove a valuable asset two centuries later.

Limehouse basin, the end of the Regent's Canal, the lock-keeper's house (to the left of the picture) now surrounded by luxury flats. *(Stephen Halliday)*

Other complainants were not so easily placated. In particular, pamphlets flew over disputes concerning the use of the company's wharves in the centre of London. One of these was on the Thames at Whitefriars, near the present site of Blackfriars station. Another was at Paddington in an area later known as 'Little Venice'. The directors of the company had realised that there were advantages in offering a shorter route to the fringes of the metropolis than the journey along the Thames from the canal's end at Brentford. They therefore constructed the 'Paddington Arm' which opened in 1801 and terminated in a basin 400yd long with wharves, warehouses and livestock pens. It prospered as a terminus for boats delivering produce to the rapidly expanding metropolis. By 1810 over 180,000 tons of freight a year was passing through the Paddington wharves, much of it consisting of bricks for the buildings that were springing up throughout the capital. It also became the starting point for a passenger service to Uxbridge which began in 1802 and was known as the 'Paddington Packet'. The boats were manned by crews wearing smart blue uniforms with yellow capes and yellow buttons and prospered for many years until the opening of Paddington station nearby, in 1854, offered a much faster service for passengers. In 1812 the Regent's Canal Company built a connection from the Paddington basin to Limehouse via Regent's Park and the City. It opened in 1820 and remains a feature of the London landscape, passing close to the Regent's Park zoo and terminating at Limehouse basin with its distinctive harbourmaster's pavilion, now surrounded by attractive riverside residences. In 1929 the Grand Junction merged with the Regent's Canal and the Warwick Canal companies to form the Grand Union canal network, the name by which it is still known.

The success of the Paddington basin was such that disputes arose over access to the terminus. The first dispute, however, concerned the Whitefriars wharf. It was instigated by Thomas Payne whom the company had appointed to manage its wharf and the title page of the pamphlet which argued his case indicates the strength of the feelings engendered: 'Particulars of the very hard treatment inflicted upon him by that company . . . and wantonly ruining of him, a Poor old Lame Man, upwards of four score years of age'.[32]

The pamphlet, written by a man called Augustus Cove who had his own differences with the company, alleged that Payne had been appointed as the company's wharfinger in 1797 at the age of sixty-eight and had succeeded in attracting a considerable volume of business to the wharves, including that of the rapidly expanding carrier Thomas Pickford. Payne had then been sacked for failing to give priority to Pickford's boats over others which had arrived earlier. Payne pursued his grievance for ten years, his principal adversary being Thomas Homer, clerk (in effect company secretary) to the Grand Junction Company. It is with some glee that a manuscript note in the margin of the pamphlet records that Thomas Homer had been sentenced to transportation for swindling a later employer, the Regent's Canal Company. The only other compensation that Thomas Payne appears to have received for his grievance was the 23s profit that Cove made on his pamphlet and donated to Payne 'a little before he died'.[33]

The second dispute, involving Augustus Cove himself, also involved Pickford's and was pursued in a pamphlet entitled *The Tocsin sounded, or a Libel extraordinary!* a 185-page diatribe published in 1813.[34] It described 'the enormous crimes of swindling perfidy and the blackest ingratitude etc. etc. transacted upon the person and property of Augustus Cove by, and through the express means of, the Grand Junction Canal Company'. Cove, it appeared, had leased a wharf at Paddington in 1803. The wharf had prospered and he had agreed to lease another wharf but was 'aggrieved and injured' when he learned that the second wharf had been leased to Pickford's instead, without his knowledge. Violence ensued when, according to Cove, he was beaten up by two ruffians engaged by Pickford's for the purpose. Referring to this criminal behaviour by the company's servants Cove unwisely wrote to the company threatening that 'if the deaths of any of them should ensue, it would not be denominated murder, but justifiable homicide'. Cove was further enraged when, as a consequence of this threat, he was briefly committed to Newgate gaol as an accused felon. Cove lamented in the conclusion to his intemperate pamphlet that 'any further litigation on his part would probably only add to the losses which he has already sustained' and had to be content with warning his readers 'Beware of Public Companies but particularly of the Grand Junction Canal Company'. These episodes illustrate the wealth that could be generated by the new canal system and the ruthlessness that such prosperity could engender on the part of the big concerns like Pickford's, who wanted to dominate the business, as well as the strong feelings that such behaviour could provoke.

Despite these episodes the canal flourished. By 1836 it was carrying almost a million tons of goods and its annual revenue approached £200,000. Its stock was valued at over £1¼ million and it was possibly the world's largest joint stock company at this time. In the same year, however, an ominous event occurred for the future of the canal system: London's first terminus station opened at London Bridge. Two years later Robert Stephenson's London to Birmingham railway began to compete for freight with the Grand Junction canal, following the same route through the Chilterns that the canal had taken 40 years earlier.

THE DUKE'S LAST DAYS

By this time the Duke was dead. He died on 8 March 1803, before the Grand Junction was complete though eight years after it had begun to earn revenue. Much of his time in his later years was spent at Ashridge House, the family's ancestral home, though in 1801 he also bought a house at Woolmers Park, near Hertford, from the brewer Samuel Whitbread. His interest in water was revived when he discovered a spring running through the grounds of Woolmers and conceived a scheme to pipe it to London in competition with his neighbours the New River Company.[35] His death two years later, before the plan came to fruition, must have come as a relief to the heirs of Sir Hugh Myddleton. On his death the dukedom lapsed but the earldom passed to his cousin, John William Egerton who proceeded to demolish most of Ashridge House and replace it with a castellated pseudo-medieval structure. These Egertons were no more successful in producing healthy progeny than their

Ashridge House, Berkhamsted, home to the Canal Duke. *(Stephen Halliday)*

ancestors had been. When John William Egerton died the title passed to his brother Francis and when he also died childless in 1829 the title became extinct and the estate passed to Earl Brownlow who had married into the family. It is now a management college. The canal duke was not forgotten. His simple memorial in Little Gaddesden church nearby records that 'He sent barges across fields the farmers formerly tilled' but a more conspicuous monument is a tall column which stands on the crown of the Chiltern escarpment, the Bridgewater Monument.

INGENIOUS DEVICES

The coming of the railways prompted the canal companies to adopt measures to reduce the time boats took to complete their journeys. In the twentieth century diesel engines replaced horses and enabled the crews to dispense with the services of 'leggers' though the atmosphere in long tunnels like those at Blisworth, Harecastle and Braunston was fouled by the exhaust emissions. However, the main obstacle to shorter journey times lay in the locks and it was

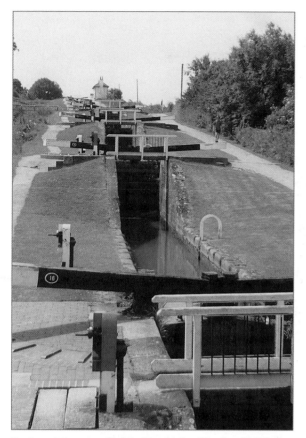

Foxton staircase: a flight of ten locks. *(Stephen Halliday)*

to this problem that canal engineers turned their attention in an attempt to meet railway competition.

A particularly long delay occurred at Foxton, on the Leicester arm of the Grand Union canal. After leaving the main canal at Norton Junction, a few miles short of Braunston, the Leicester branch makes its way through the narrow Watford Gap, which it shares with the London to Birmingham railway and the M1 motorway, and begins the climb towards Market Harborough. At Foxton, just short of the town, ten locks were required to take the canal over a steep hill. The locks were constructed as a 'staircase' in which each lock opened directly into the next with no flat, or 'pound' water between the locks. Even so it took a boat 45 minutes to rise 75ft. In 1898, therefore, the Grand Junction Company designed the 'Foxton Inclined Plane' which reduced the transit time for two boats to twelve minutes.[36] This was achieved by the use of watertight tanks known as 'caissons', mounted on wheels. One caisson was positioned by the canal at the top of an artificial slope and the other by the canal at the bottom. Four boats would enter the caissons: two in the top caisson and two in the bottom caisson. The wheeled caissons were mounted on two railways which ran side-by-side up and down the slope. When both caissons were loaded with water and boats, a braking mechanism was released. The weight and momentum of the caisson moving down the slope pulled on a set of cables which, through a pulley mechanism, drew the other caisson up the slope. Some adjustment had to be made if the boats in one caisson weighed more than the other but this could easily be done by regulating the amount of water in each caisson. Moreover, there was no loss of water, as in a lock, since water moved both up and down the slope in the caissons. In this way a load of

Foxton Inclined Plane. *(Foxton Inclined Plane Trust)*

over 200 tons could move up a one-in-four slope as an equivalent load moved down it. This ingenious mechanism worked satisfactorily for ten years but was decommissioned in 1911 because other limitations on the capacity of the canal had meant that the hoped-for increase in traffic had not materialised. The locks were brought back into use and in 1928 the machinery was scrapped. In March 2002 British Waterways announced that the inclined plane was to be restored in a programme which is expected to be completed by 2006. Details of the scheme are to be found on the Foxton Inclined Plane Trust's website: *www.foxcanal.fsnet.co.uk*

BOAT LIFTS

Charles Darwin's grandfather Erasmus (1731–1802) had designed an experimental boat lift to move boats between waterways at different levels but more than a century passed before his ideas were applied to create a connection between the Trent and Mersey canal and the River Weaver near Northwich, in Cheshire. A 50ft drop between the canal and the river was bridged in 1875 with the Anderton boat lift. Again, two watertight chambers

The Falkirk Wheel in mid-operation: terrifying to behold as it transfers narrow boats between the Edinburgh & Glasgow Union canal and the Forth & Clyde canal. *(Ruth and Jeremy Duffy)*

were built to accommodate boats, one at the top and one at the bottom, each weighing over 250 tons when loaded. In this case there was a vertical drop rather than a slope. The lift worked until 1983 though the river water caused damage to the hydraulic mechanism of the lift which thus required regular and expensive maintenance. The closure of the lift in 1983 followed the discovery of serious corrosion to the machinery but this also has been recently restored and is the only working boat lift in England. A more spectacular version is to be seen in Scotland, in the form of the 'Falkirk Wheel'. This is a rotating boat lift which transfers boats between the Edinburgh and Glasgow Union canal and the Forth–Clyde canal near Falkirk, midway between Edinburgh and Glasgow. It opened in June 2002, the only one of its kind in the world and for that reason is hard to describe. It resembles two huge scoops attached to opposite sides of a wheel. Each 'scoop' can accommodate eight boats and the descending scoop counterbalances the ascending one. The transit time is fifteen minutes for the sixteen boats. It looks terrifying and may be seen on its own website: *www.falkirk-wheel.com*

NAVVIES

The waterways created a new class of labouring man – the 'navvy'. The term originally derived from the word 'navigator', referring to those who created the inland navigation, and was later applied also to the men who created the railways and other great works of civil engineering. They were sometimes called 'bankers' because they built embankments. From the earliest days the sight of hundreds of men engaged in great enterprises made a deep impression on witnesses. An American visitor, watching men at work on the Bridgewater canal, wrote:[37] 'I surveyed the duke's men for two hours and I think the industry of bees, or labour of ants, is not to be compared with them. Each man's work seemed to depend, and be connected, with his neighbour's.' The scale of the works involved, often in remote rural locations, required new methods of assembling and managing workforces of a size which had previously been unknown outside the military, with which there were some similarities. Contractors, like recruiting sergeants, gathered their workforces from areas where there was surplus labour available and offered them, en masse, to engineers like Jessop and Brindley. Many of the men came from rural communities in Ireland and Scotland where there were few opportunities for profitable employment. Others were criminals who were refugees from justice and whose identities were unlikely to be too carefully scrutinised by contractors who were happy to hire a labourer who was likely to be loyal, if not well-behaved. In 1793, at the height of 'canal mania', it was estimated that the workforce was approaching 50,000 and the diversion of so many to canal construction was seen as a threat to the harvest. In the spring of that year a Bill was introduced to Parliament to restrict the migration of labourers from farms to canals. The debates on the Bill uncovered some curious views among MPs. An MP called Courtenay, speaking of the Irish element in the labour force, commented that: 'The people from that country, who worked in bogs, knew nothing about the corn harvest, and to send them to work at the harvest was to make them starve, or to turn highwaymen and robbers.'[38] Thus was born the foolish myth of the bog-trotting Irish navvy, though others, including the acerbic Thomas Carlyle, cast the Irish element of the labour force in a much more flattering light. In 1846 he inveighed against the behaviour of the navvies but exempted the Irish from his criticism, writing: 'I have not in my travels seen anything uglier than that disorganic mass of labourers, sunk threefold deeper in brutality by the threefold wages they are getting . . . the Irish are the best in point of behaviour. The postman tells me that several of the poor Irish do regularly apply to him for money drafts, and send their earnings home. The English, who eat twice as much beef, consume the residue in whisky and do not trouble the postman.'[39]

Carlyle's comments on the brutal behaviour of these gangs of men is echoed by others. An engineer called Peter Lecount, who worked with Robert Stephenson on the construction of the London and Birmingham Railway, recorded their impact on small peaceful communities, writing: 'These *banditti*, known in some parts as 'Navies' [*sic*] or 'Navigators' and in others by that of 'Bankers' are generally the terror of the surrounding country.'[40]

The *Carlisle Patriot*, reported the case of a navvy called Hobday who was sentenced to fifteen years' transportation for maiming another navvy. The newspaper wrote of Hobday: 'for nine years he has never slept in a bed or worn a hat; his custom was to put on his boots when new, and never remove them until they fell to pieces, and his clothes were treated in much the same way, except that his shirt was changed once a week'.[41]

The existence of different national groups, English, Scots and Irish, may have helped to promote conflicts but the presence of men like Hobday ensured that, in the absence of 'foreign' elements, there was never a shortage of pretexts for drunken violence. Drunkenness was promoted by the behaviour of some contractors who, in defiance of the Truck Acts,[42] paid their men in tokens which could only be exchanged at the contractor's own 'truck shop' or 'Tommy shop' where food and, particularly, strong drink were available at exorbitant prices, thus effectively devaluing the men's wages. This practice was itself a provocation to violence. A historian of the canals has written that: 'There was a strong tradition among the navvies of never refusing a fight if one was offered, and never staying out of someone else's fight if they happened to be around at the time.'[43]

Occasionally the navvies were encouraged to engage in acts of violence by their employers. In 1796 Lord Stanley was alleged to have used some navvies to beat up opponents at a Parliamentary election but the most celebrated incident involved Isambard Kingdom Brunel and the 'Battle of Mickleton' in Gloucestershire. On 23 July 1851, in a manoeuvre which would have done credit to the Duke of Wellington, Brunel, at the head of 2,000 of his navvies, drove from the field a similar force headed by a contractor with whose work Brunel was dissatisfied.

Some navvies, of more orderly disposition, did very well for themselves. Edward Banks, (*c.* 1769–1835) an agricultural labourer from Yorkshire, left home with 2s in his pocket and joined the workforce building the Forth–Clyde canal in Scotland. He prospered, became a contractor and ended his career in London building London, Southwark and Waterloo bridges to John Rennie's designs.[44] He was knighted in 1822.

ZENITH AND DECLINE

Some companies could afford enormous dividends. In 1810 the Aire and Calder navigation in Yorkshire received tolls to the value of £129,758 and paid out £48,000 in dividends, 37 per cent of their turnover – a dividend which would have embarrassed Croesus and which fully justified the confidence of its investors.[45] The Oxford canal paid a dividend of 25 per cent the previous year though others were less richly rewarded. The Grand Junction at this time could only pay 5 per cent – a respectable reward for investors at a time of very low interest rates but hardly the riches that 'canal mania' fifteen years earlier had seemed to promise. In 1839 the younger John Rennie calculated that Britain was served by 2,236 miles of navigable rivers and 2,477 miles of canals – a network of inland waters unmatched in any other country at that time.[46] By this time the waterways were carrying over 40 million tons of freight a year throughout Great Britain.[47] It represented the high point of their prosperity and for many years after this date factories continued to be built adjacent to canals. In 1879 Cadbury's chose Bournville for the site of their chocolate factory because of its proximity to the Worcester and Birmingham canal via which they received deliveries of chocolate, sugar and milk on their own fleet of seventeen boats.[48] An Ovaltine factory was built at Kings Langley in Hertfordshire as late as 1913 because of its proximity to the Grand Junction canal. The canals were the arteries of the industrial revolution. Even at this time they attracted some disapproving comments. William Cobbett, in his *Rural Rides*, published in 1830, remarked on the quality of the agricultural land in the vicinity of Cricklade, Wiltshire. He noted ruefully that 'while the poor creatures that raise the wheat and the barley and cheese and the mutton and the beef are living on potatoes, an accursed *canal* comes through the parish to convey away the wheat and all the good food to the tax-eaters and their attendants in the Wen'.[49] Cobbett's Wen was London, of which he thoroughly disapproved. Wordsworth, on the other hand, found solace in the sight of sailing barges on canals and recorded his feelings in a moving passage in *The Excursion*, in 1814:

> The Earth has lent
> Her waters, air her breezes, and the sail
> Of traffic glides with ceaseless intercourse,
> Glistening along the low and woody vale.

In 1838, the year that Robert Stephenson's London to Birmingham railway opened, Pickford's was operating 116 canal boats. After 1840 they transferred their freight to the railways. The rapid expansion of the railway network meant that the canal network could no longer offer the fastest means of transport for passengers or produce, though they could offer a cheaper service for low-value bulky goods like coal and building materials. In 1906 the waterways were still carrying over 40 million tons of freight a year, the same tonnage as in 1839, but the railways were carrying ten times as much, so the waterways had not benefited from the huge increase in industrial activity which occurred in Victoria's long reign. Almost half of their freight consisted of coal and most of it was carried for less than 20 miles.[50] Moreover, they had managed to maintain the tonnage they were carrying only by cutting their rates, sometimes by as much as two-thirds.[51] The same year, 1906, marked the appointment of the Royal Commission on Inland Waterways which pondered long, published eleven volumes of evidence but achieved very little beyond drawing attention to the fact that the original canal builders had been the authors of the canals' misfortunes. By constructing waterways to meet local markets, with no standard gauge for tunnels or locks, the early engineers had made it impossible for wider, more cost-efficient craft to pass through the system. The Bridgewater canal itself continued to carry a reasonable amount of freight until the 1960s when the decline of the Lancashire coalfield removed the commodity for which the canal had been built. The final straw was the intensely cold winter of 1962/3 when most of the waterway system was immobilised for months by the great freeze. Customers who had remained loyal to the waterways were obliged to transfer their goods to road and rail carriers who were less affected by the extreme weather. Once lost, most of this traffic was never regained though some survived the devastation. Roses, for example, continued to receive cargoes of limes and lime juice at their quay on the Grand Union canal at Hemel Hempstead until 1981.

'NUMBER ONES' AND THEIR BOATS

It was during this long period of decline in the late nineteenth and early twentieth centuries that there developed a community of canal folk with a distinctive way of life. Following the defection of Pickford's to the railways, referred to earlier, some of the canal companies acquired their own fleets of boats, many of which were eventually taken over by a specialist canal carrier called Fellows, Morton and Clayton. A director of the company travelled throughout the entire network to produce *Bradshaw's Canals and Navigable Rivers of England and Wales*: a 480-page guide to every waterway with details of lock capacities, tunnels, wharves and every other facility on the network.[52] Alongside such companies there developed a separate group of self-employed boating families who plied their own craft, often living on the boats as well as using them to earn their living. These were known as 'Number Ones'.

In 1861 the census of population revealed that approximately 18,000 people were living on canal boats, of whom 3,000 were women. As early as 1795 one writer recorded a female captain of a boat.[53] In 1951 the census recorded fewer than 5,000 people – still a substantial number.[54] Families with as many as five children were accommodated in a narrowboat cabin approximately 8ft long by 6ft wide by 5ft high, ingeniously equipped with bunks, cupboards, a table and a stove. One narrowboat, about 70ft long, carrying 25 tons of freight, would also tow a 'butty boat' which effectively doubled the cargo and had its own cabin with a rudder for the steersman. Some of the boats were 'fly-boats' which offered a faster service than the 'slow boats' by travelling continuously without mooring overnight. Fly-boatmen could work as many as a hundred hours a week. Craft of other designs worked some canals. In the northern canals broad-beamed barges could be accommodated in the wider locks and in the same area were found 'Tom Puddings' – as many as thirty-two broad boats, linked in a chain, pulled along by one tug at the front and usually carrying coal – perhaps as much as 450 tons in one chain.

The early Victorian factory acts did not even attempt to regulate the working hours and conditions of canal boatmen and their families but in 1877 the Canal Boats Act set up an inspectorate to check the living conditions of the boat population and encourage them to send their children to school. Their living conditions and wages compared reasonably well with those of their peers dwelling in slum tenements in the great cities and an inspector's report of 1906 gave a reassuring account of the healthy lifestyle of the children, half of whom had been born on the boats. Nevertheless the families were an object of concern to Victorian philanthropists, some of whom were concerned with the moral rather than sanitary effects of life on the canals. The London City Mission set up an outpost at Brentford on the Grand Junction canal in 1896 to administer religion, education and medical attention to the boat people and a floating chapel was set up at Oxford at about the same time.[55] Attempts were made to persuade the boating families to send their children to schools on their routes but the families were not always welcome in schools or in shops, developing a reputation akin to that of travelling families a century later. This was reflected in the impressions of the young Graham Greene who encountered them on the Grand Junction canal in his home town of Berkhamsted during his childhood. He recalled them sixty years later in his autobiography, *A Sort of Life*: 'a sense of immediate danger was conveyed by the canal – the menace of insulting words from strange, brutal canal workers with blackened faces like miners, with their gypsy wives and ragged children'.[56] Perhaps the resemblance to gypsies was more than coincidental. One tradition has it that the roses, castles, hearts, diamonds and clubs (never spades, they were unlucky) that became a feature of the attractive decorative painting on the canal boats and their implements were derived from the gypsies of the Carpathians in Romania.[57]

During the Second World War many women were recruited to operate the canal boats. Susan, wife of the actor Sir Donald Wolfit, has left a graphic account of the time she spent aboard a narrowboat, sharing its tiny cabin with two other women as they carried cargo throughout the network in the last years of the war. Training typically consisted of two round trips between Limehouse basin and the Coventry coalfields under the supervision of a boatman, after which the boatwomen were left to their own devices and paid £3 a week to deliver coal to companies like Heinz, Glaxo and Nestlé.[58] Susan Woolfitt (*sic*) gives a particularly moving account of her encounter with the formidable but kindly 'Sister Mary, the boaters' nurse' who was based at Stoke Bruerne at the southern end of the Blisworth tunnel.[59] 'Sister Mary' (Mary Ward) had trained as a nurse in Belgium under Edith Cavell[60] and such was her celebrity throughout the waterways that she was one of the first subjects chosen for Eamonn Andrews' programme *This is Your Life* in 1958.[61]

REVIVAL

Even as the Royal Commission of 1906 was failing to come to the aid of the inland waterways, a solution to their plight was beginning to emerge. In 1908 a man called George Westall published a book called *Inland Cruising on the Rivers and Canals of England and Wales* which extolled the novel idea of canals as an outlet for leisure time rather than a means of transport. Eight years later Peter Bonthron followed with the more explicitly titled *My Holidays on Inland*

Waterways.[62] The idea was slowly taken up by others, notably L.T.C. Rolt whose account of his journey on the canal network, published in 1944 under the title *Narrowboat* led directly to the foundation of the Inland Waterways Association. The Inland Waterways Association advocated 'canals for pleasure' and its president, the humorous writer A.P. Herbert, wrote that 'A particular case in this respect is the Paddington basin in London, at present a forlorn spot but one with inherent possibilities as London's Venice.'[63]

In 1941 Frank Pick, the former vice-chairman of London Transport, recommended that the inland waterways be taken into public ownership and this was achieved in 1948. After a slow start, caused by the under-investment which was to bedevil all nationalised undertakings, the waterways have re-emerged as a source of pleasure rather than profit. Two thousand miles of waterways accommodate 25,000 licensed boats, most of them used for boating holidays though some provide permanent homes for a new generation of water gypsies and 3½ million tons of freight is still carried.[64] Some canals previously abandoned have been brought back into use, notably the Forth–Clyde canal. The 2,000 miles of canal towpath have also been used to carry fibre optic

Little Venice, Paddington. (*Stephen Halliday*)

cables in the 'Easynet' network, so the waterways, the original means of communication in our first industrial age, have been used to accommodate the very latest in communications technology. The waterways are also being adapted to help overcome the increasingly pressing problems of water shortage. Surplus stocks of water in the north and west of Britain will be transferred via the waterways to shortage areas in the south and east. Half of Bristol's water is already supplied via the canal network.[65]

Much of the network's income is now derived from property as British Waterways has taken advantage of the demand for waterside properties on 'brownfield' sites close to city centres in Birmingham, Leeds, Glasgow, Gloucester, Sheffield, London and elsewhere. The formerly derelict sites at Paddington Basin now known as 'Little Venice', as A.P. Herbert had hinted, have become particularly desirable residences. Thus the inland waterways enter the twenty-first century more optimistically than they entered the twentieth. They derive their income from pleasure boating, a £300 million property portfolio and fibre optic networks. The liquid arteries of the industrial age have become a source of pleasure for holidaymakers and fashionable waterside residences for affluent city dwellers.

POSTSCRIPT: THE DEFENCE OF THE REALM

Some reference has already been made to the establishment of an ordnance depot, and royal refuge, at Weedon Bec on the Grand Junction canal, to be used in an emergency during the wars against Napoleon. A more enduring relic of that conflict is to be found in the Royal Military canal which makes its way across Romney Marsh, on the borders of Kent and Sussex. Although it is less than 80 miles from London, this strange, flat, thinly populated landscape in Kent's southern tip seems to belong to another, calmer world. It covers an area of about 100 square miles stretching from the pleasant town of Hythe in the north-east to the picturesque communities of Rye and Winchelsea in the south-west, though technically the southern area bears the name Walland Marsh. It runs out to sea at Dungeness, with its nuclear power station, while its less well-defined inland boundary roughly follows the B2067 road from Hythe to Tenterden. It contains communities with strange names like Snargate, Snave, Brenzett and North Fording Bungalow. It is home to a unique railway, the Romney, Hythe and Dymchurch Railway, whose 15in-gauge locomotives and rolling stock (roughly one-quarter standard gauge) have, since 1927, carried passengers the 14 miles along the coast from Hythe to Dungeness. This is one of a number of unique aspects of the marsh which has featured in Britain's defences against invasion, its watery landscape being adapted to overcome its vulnerability.

The last successful invasion of Britain, that of William the Conqueror in 1066, took place just a few miles to the west at Pevensey Bay, a fact which emphasises the attractiveness of this part of the coast to seaborne enemies. Romney Marsh itself is a particularly tempting landing place for an invader. It is close to the French coast and its long stretch of flat, sandy beaches would be inviting to an enemy fleet. There are no cliffs or other features behind which defenders could conceal themselves in any numbers. The unique character of the marsh explains the peculiar history of its government.

The Lords of Romney Marsh

A Royal Charter granted by Henry III in 1252 created 'The Lords, Bailiff, Jurats and Commonalty of the Level and Liberty of Romney Marsh', commonly referred to as 'The Lords of Romney Marsh'. This corporation consisted of the twenty-three Lords of the Manors of Romney Marsh and twenty-four 'Jurats', the latter being defined as 'lawful men of Romney Marsh, time out of mind hereunto chosen and sworn'. They remained responsible for the drainage of the marsh and for its sea defences until the Land Drainage Act of 1930. In 1462, in an attempt to encourage further settlement in this vulnerable and under-populated part of his kingdom, Edward IV granted a further charter which allowed the Jurats to erect gallows to do 'full execution and judgement on felons and other malefactors' while inhabitants of the marsh were exempted from national taxation and from jury service outside its boundaries. As late as 1860 one group of residents, living near Dymchurch, cited the charter in a successful appeal against the imposition of rates by Kent County Council.[66] The Justices of the Peace Act, 1949, removed the last of the corporation's formal powers and it now functions as a charity with the responsibility for managing a number of listed properties inherited from its earlier responsibilities. For this purpose the 'Lords' hold an annual meeting known as the 'Grand Lath' on the Thursday of Whitsun week.

Romney Marsh and the Cinque Ports

By the time the Lords of Romney Marsh were created in 1252 two of its towns, New Romney and Hythe, already bore some responsibility for the defence of the realm owing to their status as members of that unique body, the Cinque Ports, created by Henry II in 1155. These five (French *cinque* but pronounced 'sink') ports were expected to provide ships in time of war to defend the coasts. In return they were exempted from most taxes and, in effect, allowed to operate as 'privateers' (semi-official pirates) preying on the King's enemies. The other three ports of Dover, Hastings and Sandwich fell outside the marsh but later in Henry's reign, Rye and Winchelsea were added to their number so that the confederation's official name became (and remains) 'The Cinque Ports and Two Ancient Towns'. Their responsibilities and privileges remained in force until the Royal Navy was created by the Tudors. Most of the harbours are now silted up and some of the 'ports', notably Romney and Winchelsea, are some distance inland. The Office of Lord Warden of the Cinque Ports remains an honour conferred on public figures like Sir Winston Churchill and the late Queen Mother. In the late medieval period the marsh towns continued to show their vulnerability to attack. Despite being fortified, Rye was subjected to violent attacks twice (1377 and 1448) during the Hundred Years War and Winchelsea suffered this fate on seven occasions, its population being consequently reduced from over six thousand to a few hundred.

In 1539 Henry VIII built Sandgate castle, near Folkestone, at the eastern end of Romney Marsh as a defensive measure in his wars with the French. It was one of ten castles he built between Deal and Falmouth. The marsh does not appear to have been much affected by the invasion alarms associated with the Spanish Armada of 1588 but was the source of much anxiety in 1803. In that year Napoleon exhibited the Bayeux Tapestry in Paris to remind his citizens of England's vulnerability and began to assemble 100,000 troops and a fleet of 2,000 invasion barges at Boulogne. Contemporary cartoons and verses drew attention to the threat:

> The French are all coming, so they declare,
> Of their floats and balloons all the papers advise us,
> They're to swim through the ocean and ride through the air
> In some foggy evening to land and surprise us.[67]

A Royal Military canal

The British army had been subjected to a number of reforming measures by the Commander-in-Chief, the somewhat maligned Duke of York,[68] so it was reasonably effective but also very small. It was in no position to defend England's long south-eastern coastline, so the government turned its attention to its most vulnerable features. The flat area of Romney Marsh, between the cliffs of Folkestone and Hastings, was an obvious landing point for the French troops and it was immediately opposite their assembly points at Boulogne. The Prime Minister, William Pitt, first tried to sink the invasion barges by infiltrating them with floating mines called catamarans, just as Sir Francis Drake had used fireships against the Armada, but this failed. He therefore considered an alternative plan to flood the marsh in the event of invasion. The commander of the Kent military district was Sir John Moore, who was later to meet a heroic death at Coruña in Portugal. Moore, an experienced soldier, pointed out that the plan contained several flaws. Depending upon the state of the tide, it could take several days to flood the marsh in such a way as to impede an army, whereas only a few hours notice would be given of an invasion. A false alarm, on the other hand, could lead to the pointless sterilisation by seawater of tens of thousands of acres of good agricultural land. There had already been one such alarm in October 1803 and another was to occur in August 1804 when the French carried out an invasion rehearsal.[69] This was a fiasco. Invasion barges full of terrified soldiers collided with one another and with the harbour walls at Boulogne, enraging Napoleon who was observing the spectacle and greatly amusing the British observers who, through their telescopes, were watching the drama unfold. It is perhaps significant that it was shortly after this debacle that Napoleon marched his troops away from Boulogne in search of easier conquests in the east.

In the meantime Pitt had to take precautions and he was impressed by the ideas of Colonel John Brown, commandant of the Royal Staff Corps (later incorporated in the Royal Engineers). Brown proposed to construct a Royal Military canal from Shorncliffe, west of Folkestone to the River Rother at Rye, which would have the effect of cutting off the marsh from the rest of Kent and Sussex. The spoil excavated in building the canal would form a defensive parapet behind the waterway and behind the 35ft parapet would be a road. The whole structure would thus form a double defensive line, with waterway and parapet, which would have to be crossed by any invading force. In addition, both the waterway and the road could be used to move troops and supplies to meet any invaders. Brown, a Scotsman from Elgin, had considerable experience of surveying military defences and roadways and had worked with the distinguished engineer John Rennie[70] who was now called upon to evaluate the proposal.

Rennie's verdict was favourable, though he suggested extending the canal to Cliff End, Hastings, incorporating the Rivers Rother, Tillingham and Brede. This

John Rennie. *(National Portrait Gallery)*

plan was adopted, giving a total length of 28 miles, thereby protecting all the low-lying land between the cliffs at Hastings and Folkestone by turning Romney Marsh into an island. Twenty-five miles would have to be excavated. The Commander-in-Chief, the Duke of York, who was concerned about the burdens on his effective but small army commended the plan, writing 'These works from their construction require but a feeble garrison for the defence; nor, viewing the permanency of the work, are they to be considered expensive.'

Pitt moved swiftly to support the plan. As Lord Warden of the Cinque Ports he was familiar with the dangers that the area presented and he was also known to many local landowners whom he now summoned to a meeting at New Hall, Dymchurch, on 21 October 1804. New Hall is now the home of a museum devoted to the history of the Lords of Romney Marsh. Pitt's meeting was one year to the day before Nelson destroyed the intended French invasion fleet at the battle of Trafalgar. Pitt's arguments won the landowners' support, not least his assertion that the alternative would be to flood their lands and his assurance that the new canal, henceforward known in the area as 'Pitt's ditch', would act as a drainage channel in winter and a reservoir in summer.[71] The road would also be a useful and reliable route across the marsh, whose primitive paths were subject to flooding. In the words of the local newspaper, the *Kentish Gazette*, 'the great merit of this plan is that it combines defence with utility'. It also caught the imagination of the populace, the Sussex *Weekly Advertiser*, declaring the project 'one of the greatest military works in this or any other kingdom'.[72]

'A Field-Marshal in my profession'

Work began on 30 October, only nine days after Pitt's meeting with the landowners. Rennie was appointed engineer to the canal while Brown, the originator of the scheme, had the rather ambiguous title of 'military director', a situation which was resolved the following year when Rennie resigned his position. According to Samuel Smiles the dispute arose over Rennie's fee of 7 guineas a day. The quartermaster-general objected that this was as much as a field-marshal earned to which Rennie allegedly replied 'Well, I am a Field-Marshal in my profession.'[73] Whatever the reason, Rennie, in Brown's words 'departed in a huff'.[74] This left Brown effectively in charge though Rennie's influence had been helpful in securing the loan of a precious Boulton and Watt

New Hall, Dymchurch, meeting place for William Pitt, now a home and museum. *(Stephen Halliday)*

steam engine from the Kennet and Avon canal which pumped out floodwaters from the course of the canal as the work progressed.

The influx of a huge workforce of burly navvies had a predictably disturbing effect on this quiet locality.[75] In January 1805, The *Kentish Gazette* reported on the 'increase of population hitherto unknown in that part of the country' which led to a shortage of accommodation for families.[76] This presumably would not have worried the husband who was the subject of the following story in the same newspaper two months later and which sounds like an extract from Thomas Hardy's *Mayor of Casterbridge*:[77]

Last week, the wife of one of the men employed in cutting the canal at Shorncliffe was conducted by her husband to the market place at Hythe, with a halter round her neck, and tied to a post; from whence she was purchased for sixpence by a mulatto. She was a young woman apparently not more than twenty years of age, tall, and of a likely form and figure; her face, however, exhibited evident marks of incompatibility of temper; *vulgarly*, she had a pair of black eyes; notwithstanding this, the new partner led her away with much apparent satisfaction from his bargain.

Rennie had preferred to use experienced contractors to carry out the work but Brown recruited his own labour force from two regiments of troops who could be quartered in camps and barracks. They were more easily subjected to discipline and they were cheaper, earning 2*s* a day as against 5*s* for a labourer. By the summer of 1805, fifteen hundred men were at work and making rapid progress at the very time that Napoleon's plans were coming to fruition and about to meet their doom. In July 1805, Napoleon told his admiral Villeneuve to break the blockade on the French fleet which Nelson was besieging at Cadiz. Villeneuve had seen Nelson at work at the battle of the Nile and was in no hurry to face him but the emperor instructed his hesitant admiral 'Make us the masters of the channel for three days and with God's help I will put an end to the career and existence of England.'

Work on the canal proceeded rapidly. Its channel, 60ft wide and 7ft deep, was 'puddled' with clay as earlier canals had been.[78] As each section came into use, eight barges were used to transport shingle from Hythe beach to make the towpath on the seaward side and the military road behind the parapet on the landward side. The canal was not straight. Every 500yd a 'kink' was built into the design with gun emplacements so that cannon could fire upon any intruders in the next 500yd stretch. Wooden bridges were built at intervals to enable cattle to cross in times of peace though these could quickly be destroyed in the event of an invasion. Each bridge had its own 'station-house' manned by soldiers or excisemen whose job was to intercept smugglers. By August 1806, less than two years after work had started, the section between Shorncliffe and the River Rother was brought into use. Ten months earlier Nelson's victory at Trafalgar had ended the threat of invasion and, with it, the need for the canal but this is more obvious now than it was at the time. Besides, the project had now acquired its own momentum and pressed on relentlessly, the full length being completed as far as Cliff End in 1809. It had cost £234,000. By this time Napoleon was fully occupied elsewhere and other military priorities were regarded as more pressing so the canal had to wait until 1812 before it was equipped with some captured cannons.

'Very improvident for the country'

As soon as the canal was completed the commissioners opened it to commercial traffic. Barges paid from 1*d* to 3*d* per ton mile, depending upon the cargo, the tolls being collected by NCOs of the Royal Staff Corps whose soldiers had built it and who were accommodated in a huge barracks built at Shorncliffe, near Hythe. Grazing land along the canal was also let, as were the fishing rights once the canal had been stocked with fish. In August 1810 a passenger service was inaugurated along the canal between Hythe and Rye which continued intermittently until 1851 when it was finally killed off by competition from railways. Private pleasure boats were also permitted include a canoe belonging to an Ensign Douglas of the 71st Light Infantry which was licensed in October 1841.[79]

The canal enjoyed a brief period of prosperity in the 1840s, transporting materials for the construction of the railway between Ashford and Hastings but the completion of the railway marked the end of the canal's status as a largely self-supporting entity. The Duke of Wellington, congenitally suspicious of the French, was one of its supporters but by the 1850s its annual revenue of about £1,200 was regularly exceeded by the cost of running it which, even with army pensioners collecting the tolls, amounted to £1,600. The management of the canal was in the hands of the commissioners to the Board of Ordnance who were concerned about the drain it imposed on their finances. An investigation into the canal's prospects by Captain George Wrottesley of the Royal Engineers led him to conclude that:[80] 'viewing the project dispassionately, at this distance of time, it must be allowed to have been a very

Royal Military Canal, Hythe. *(Stephen Halliday)*

improvident one for the country'. He recommended that the canal be sold if a buyer could be found but the only tentative approach, from the projected Hastings, Rye and Tenterden Railway, eventually came to nothing.

From the 1860s, following Wrottesley's recommendations, the War Office began to lease stretches of the canal to interested parties along its length. The eastern stretch, between Shorncliffe and the River Rother, was leased to the Lords of Romney Marsh for 999 years at an annual rent of 1s[81] though the Borough of Hythe purchased that part which passed through the little town and turned it into ornamental waters. It became the centre of a 'Venetian Festival' held in Hythe. The local MP, Sir Philip Sassoon,[82] bought another stretch of the canal. Much of the Royal Military canal now belongs to the National Trust and is managed by the Environment Agency to act as a drainage channel. It survives as a pleasing if unexpected feature of the landscape and ensures that Romney Marsh remains technically an island. The canal has become a visitor attraction, with a rich collection of water birds, dragonflies and frogs as well as pleasure boats, with no trace of its original warlike purpose. Like the rest of the waterway network the canal has become a source of pleasure rather than a thing of war or commerce.

MAJOR BRITISH CANALS

By some calculations there are well over 400 canal systems in Great Britain if one includes river navigations, navigable drainage ditches and branches of the main trunk canals. The curious reader can visit British Waterways website and count them! The following are the principal canal systems and river navigations, listed in chronological order. In some cases, such as the Leeds–Liverpool canal, the route followed is obvious. In other cases details have been given. Where the canals were built by well-known engineers their names are shown.

Fossdyke: *c.* AD 120; a Roman canal, 11 miles long, linking the Trent with the River Witham at Lincoln.

Exeter ship canal: 1566; 5 miles; the engineer was John Trew, a neglected figure who deserves to be remembered for his pioneering use of locks on this canal.

Aire and Calder navigation: 1702; 34 miles from Goole to Leeds; branch to Wakefield.

Sankey Brook navigation: 1757; 8 miles from St Helens to the Mersey near Warrington.

Bridgewater canal; 1763: John Gilbert and James Brindley; Worsley to Manchester; 28 miles with branches; the ancestor of the inland waterway network.

Birmingham canal navigation: Birmingham is the hub of the canal system, with more miles of canal than any other city; the first was the Birmingham to Wednesbury canal, built in 1769; the network eventually comprised over 200 locks and over 500 private canal basins.

Calder and Hebble navigation: 1770; John Smeaton and James Brindley; 21 miles from the Aire and Calder navigation at Wakefield to Sowerby Bridge, near Halifax.

Staffordshire and Worcester canal: 1772; James Brindley; 46 miles, linking the Severn at Stourport with the Trent and Mersey canal near Stafford.

Trent and Mersey canal: 1777; James Brindley; 93 miles from Runcorn, on the Mersey, to the Trent near Burton. Linked to the River Weaver since 1875 by the spectacular 'Anderton Boat Lift' at Northwich, restored to use in 2002 after a 20-year closure.

Coventry canal: 1790; James Brindley; 38 miles from Coventry to a junction with the Trent and Mersey canal near Lichfield.

Oxford canal: 1790; James Brindley; 78 miles to link the Coventry canal with the Thames at Oxford. This completed Brindley's 'Grand Cross' by linking the Thames, Severn, Trent and Mersey.

Forth-Clyde canal: 1790; linking the North Sea with the Atlantic; 35 miles; John Smeaton and Robert Whitworth; took 22 years to build because construction was suspended during the American War of Independence; closed among much controversy in 1962; reopened in 2001.

Basingstoke canal: 1794; William Jessop; 31 miles from the River Wey at Byfleet to North Warnborough, near Basingstoke, Hants.

Llangollen canal, formerly the Ellesmere canal: 1805; William Jessop and Thomas Telford; 46 miles, forms part of the Shropshire Union canal linking the Rivers Severn, Dee and Mersey. It includes Telford's spectacular Pontcysyllte aqueduct.

Kennet and Avon canal: 1810; John Rennie; 86 miles from the Thames at Reading to the Avon near Bristol.

Worcester and Birmingham canal: 1815; 30 miles, serving many industrial premises including the Cadbury complex at Bournville.

Leeds–Liverpool canal: 1816; 127 miles with some particularly impressive flights of locks to cross the Pennines.

Caledonian canal: 1822; Thomas Telford and William Jessop; 60 miles of canal linking Inverness with Fort William via Loch Ness to spare vessels the long and hazardous passage around Cape Wrath.

Edinburgh and Glasgow Union canal: 1822; 30 miles from Edinburgh to Falkirk where it links with the Forth–Clyde canal. Linked to the Forth–Clyde canal by the amazing 'Falkirk Wheel' since June 2002.

Manchester Ship canal: 1894; designed by E. Leader Williams to enable ocean-going vessels to reach the port of Manchester.

Grand Union canal: formed in 1929 by an amalgamation of a network of canals including the Warwick and Birmingham (1799); the Warwick and Napton (1800); the Grand Junction (1805); and the Regent's canal (1820); with branches it has a length of 135 miles.

4

WATER AS POWER

Waterwheels, Steam and Electricity

The lifting power of a wheel is much stronger and more certain than that
of a hundred men.

Pirotechnica, *Vannoccio Biringuccio,*
writing of waterwheels, 1540

. . . a new invention, for raising of water, by the important use of fire.

Extract from the first patent for a steam engine,
awarded to Thomas Savery in 1698

The Rocket is so much superior to all the old locomotive engines in use
as to entitle Mr Stephenson to the most marked and liberal consideration
for the skill and ingenuity displayed in its construction.

Mechanics Magazine, *reporting*
on the Rainhill trials, 1829

Water is the oldest form of power known to mankind with the exceptions of
sun and fire. Indeed, water power is itself a form of solar power. The
evaporation caused by the rays of the sun created the streams which powered
waterwheels and which now produce hydroelectric power. Between these two
sources of water power came the steam engine, described in its early days as
'An Engine to raise Water by Fire'. Water may yet prove to be the newest form
of power as engineers continue their quest to find economic ways of harnessing
the power of tides.

EARLY WATERWHEELS

No one can be sure when waterwheels were first used to power machinery, though there is some evidence that they were used in India in the fourth century BC.[1] The Greek engineer Philo of Byzantium (*c.* 260–*c.* 180 BC) is credited with many inventions, including a number of water-powered artefacts, at Alexandria in *c.* 200 BC and one of these may have been a waterwheel, though there is little evidence of its practical application. A drawing of a waterwheel is to be seen in one of the Roman catacombs in the third century AD and in England traces of a Roman waterwheel have been found at the small Roman fort at Haltwhistle Burn in Northumberland, west of Hexham and south of Hadrian's Wall. They were used extensively in Rome in the sixth century AD to grind flour and at Barbegal, near Arles, a 'flight' of about sixteen waterwheels, the outfall of one leading on to the next in a descending line, was used to provide power to a large flour mill. In 762 a waterwheel is mentioned as being in use in Kent and it seems probable that St Albans Abbey used some form of water power soon after its foundation in 793.

By 1086 that invaluable compendium of life in early medieval England, *Domesday Book*, recorded 5,624 watermills in use including a tidal mill at Dover which was recorded as causing 'disaster to vessels by the great disturbance of the sea'. Two of the Domesday mills paid their rent in iron from which we may infer that, at this early stage, water was already being used to process metal. In the following century the Cistercian order of monks was responsible for the further spread of the device. The Cistercians' search for tracts of virgin land took them to remote areas where fast-flowing streams were a ready source of power which they harnessed for milling, tanning and for fulling cloth. The addition of cams and cranks to waterwheels enabled them to be harnessed so that they could hammer, pull, polish and even blow as well as grind, so by the sixteenth century they were being used in a variety of industrial processes including forging, sawing, stamping, rolling and for powering bellows. In the late sixteenth century the historian William Camden, in his *Britannia*, wrote that in the iron industry in Sussex he had observed 'ponds and pools for the driving of Mills which, beating with hammers upon iron, fill the neighbourhood round about night and day with continual noise'.[2] Paper-making was another activity which came to depend upon water power and the demand for paper after the invention of printing ensured that there were 350 water-powered paper mills by 1763.[3] Most of these wheels were probably about 10–15ft in diameter, 2–4ft wide and drawing 5–10 horsepower but some were much larger and more elaborate. The largest single wheel was probably that installed by Peter Morice in the first arch of London Bridge in 1582 which pumped up to 2,500 tons of water to a height of 120ft each day to supply the City of London with drinking water. It remained in place until the old London Bridge was demolished in 1822 and replaced by Rennie's new design.[4] The most elaborate use of waterwheels was in an engine in Cornwall which consisted of ten waterwheels, one above the other, the outfall from one feeding the one below it, the whole 'tower' being used to power pumping machinery.

COMPETING DESIGNS

In medieval England most mills were 'undershot' or 'overshot' mills, two of five varieties which eventually came into use. The undershot mill was the simplest type of mill in which a fast-flowing stream passed through the vertical wheel as its blades reached the bottom, carrying the blades with its flow and causing it to rotate. The third variety derived from the undershot wheel in the form of the 'horizontal' wheel whose paddles protruded sideways into the stream and were similarly driven by the flow. Neither of these designs was very powerful and the horizontal wheel, which was cheap to build, was never common in England. In the overshot wheel, water entered the bucket-shaped blades of the wheel from the top, causing the wheel to rotate by the force of gravity. In the eighteenth century the relative power imparted by different types of mill became an issue because some rivers were becoming so heavily populated by watermills that there was no room for any more on the rivers around communities like Birmingham, Manchester and Nottingham and there were clashes between mill owners and boatmen. As observed in chapter 3 a mill weir erected across the River Exe as early as the twelfth century had impeded navigation to the point where Exeter was cut off from the sea.[5] One authority has estimated that, by the eighteenth century, England could have contained as many as 20,000 watermills, with 60 on a particularly crowded 3-mile stretch of the River Mersey.[6]

Encouraged by the growing shortage of water power, a number of eminent engineering pioneers now applied themselves to studying the relative efficiency of different types of mill. At this time many engineers learned their trade as millwrights since the skills that the work required were readily translated to civil and mechanical engineering projects. The Scottish engineer William Fairbairn wrote in his *Treatise on Mills and Millwork* (1871) that: 'The millwright was in former days to a great extent the sole

Sir William Fairbairn (1789–1874) William Fairbairn was born in Kelso, in the Scottish borders, the son of a farmer. After a rudimentary education he left school at the age of 14 and worked at Percy Main colliery in North Shields as an apprentice engine-wright and subjected himself to a rigorous scheme of study in his free time. He was placed in charge of the steam engine which worked the colliery's pumps and became acquainted with George Stephenson, who worked in the area, and later with his son Robert. In 1810 he travelled to London and, after many vicissitudes caused by the 'closed shop' operated by societies of millwrights, he eventually settled in Manchester where he established a successful business making, mending and improving machinery for the cotton manufacturing industry. In 1824 he installed at Zurich two watermills of advanced design which worked effectively even when there was little water to drive them. He was a pioneer in the use of lightweight components made of iron to replace heavier timber and iron structures, thereby improving the efficiency of machinery. He invented a riveting machine which revolutionised the manufacturing of boilers. Fairbairn's knowledge of iron enabled him to construct the world's first iron-hulled ship, the *Lord Dundas*, at his Manchester works in 1831 and four years later he established a shipyard at Millwall where Brunel's *Great Eastern* was later built. He also applied his knowledge of iron in working with Robert Stephenson on the design of the tubular iron Conway and Britannia bridges in North Wales. He later claimed to have built or designed 1,000 bridges. He was knighted in 1869 for his pioneering services to the engineering profession.

representative of mechanical art, and was looked upon as the authority in all applications of wind and water as a motive power for the purposes of manufacture. He was the engineer of the district in which he lived, a kind of jack of all trades.'

The great engineer John Smeaton (1724–92) who is regarded by many as the founder of the civil engineering profession, prepared for the Royal Society an 'Experimental Enquiry concerning the Natural Powers of Wind and Water to turn Mills and other Machines'.[7] He concluded that the overshot wheel was twice as efficient as the undershot but also advocated a fourth design, the 'breast wheel', in which water entered the wheel half-way up (at 3 o'clock or

9 o'clock) since this imparted the maximum velocity upon impact. The engineer John Rennie (1761–1821)[8] installed a variant of the breast wheel in the celebrated Soho works of Boulton and Watt during the brief period that he worked there in 1784. Further improvements to the waterwheel at this time included the introduction of lighter wheels made of iron whose mass absorbed less of the energy the wheels generated. After 1770 iron wheels became common, as did the very light 'suspension wheel'. This was like a bicycle wheel, the outer rim being kept in place by tension between a number of lightweight radiating 'spokes'. Instead of imparting power through a heavy axle, it was transmitted by cogs on the wheel rim, thus helping to maximise the power-to-weight ratio of the mechanism.

Waterwheel technology was by now approaching its zenith but two further inventions led to the development of the 'water turbine', the fifth variant on the original concept and not strictly a waterwheel. Both of the innovations were the work of Frenchmen; the first was the military engineer Jean Borda (1733–99) who demonstrated that curved blades would improve the output of a waterwheel. He was swiftly followed by his compatriot Benoit Fourneyron (1802–67), the true inventor both of the turbine itself and of its name. The word 'turbine' is derived from a Latin word meaning 'spinning'. Fourneyron was from Gémonval in eastern France, close to the Swiss border where, in the 1820s, he was employed in the local coalmines as an engineer. He conducted a series of experiments to identify better ways of dealing with the ever-pressing problem of pumping floodwater from the mines. Horizontal waterwheels were a much more common power source in France than in England. Borda discovered that, by incorporating Borda's curved blades in a horizontal wheel, and by distributing water onto all the blades at once from above, he could make the wheel rotate much more quickly, with less input of power, than was possible with any conventional design. They were smaller, faster and much cheaper to build than vertical wheels. From this time the water turbine gradually replaced the conventional waterwheel as a source of hydraulic power.

RICHARD ARKWRIGHT'S WATER FRAME, 1771

The growth of the cotton industry during the late eighteenth century gave an impulse to the further development of water power and eventually caused its decline in favour of the more flexible and manageable steam power. A series of inventions by people like the Lancashire inventor John Kay (the Flying

Shuttle, 1733) and his fellow Lancastrian the weaver James Hargreaves (the Spinning Jenny, 1764) had mechanised the process by which cotton from India and Egypt was turned into thread and cloth. The new machines required substantial reservoirs of power. In 1769 the Preston wig-maker Richard Arkwright (1732–92) employed a clockmaker from Warrington, also called John Kay (no relation), to design machinery which was more productive than earlier ones but required a substantial power source. He opened an enterprise using some of the new machinery near Nottingham, powered by horses, but two years later, in 1771, Arkwright and his partners moved to Cromford, near Matlock in Derbyshire, where a tributary of the River Derwent could provide the water power that his 'water frame' required. It was because of the early use of watermills in this way that cotton factories came to be called 'mills'.[9] The Cromford site was the world's first true factory complex, five storeys high, housing and employing hundreds of people, and operating 23 hours a day. Arkwright favoured the employment of weavers with large families so that the mothers and children (from the age of ten) could operate the cotton-spinning machinery in 12-hour shifts while the fathers weaved cotton cloth in their neighbouring homes. In the next 20 years Arkwright built mills throughout Derbyshire and Lancashire and when he died in 1792, having been knighted by George III, he left the enormous sum, for the time, of half a million pounds. Arkwright was the first to use the next development of water power in the textile industry in the form of a Boulton and Watt steam engine, though he used it initially only to pump water for his water frames, the full application of steam power to the machinery coming in 1783.

Within a few years of Arkwright's first factory at Cromford, water frames had been adopted by many other textile manufacturers. The growth of the new industry may be measured by the fact that between 1763 (8 years before Arkwright's first water frame) and 1860, cotton imports to Britain grew from less than 3 million pounds' weight to 1,084 million.[10] Other water-powered industries were springing up to meet the needs of the new industry. As observed in Chapter 6, one of these was seen in the bobbin mills of the Lake District whose fast-flowing streams provided a ready source of water power for light industry. The intrusion of such industries was most unwelcome to William Wordsworth.[11] Some traces of the industry survived until the 1970s when the decline of the Lancashire textile industry and the development of plastic bobbins brought about its demise. By this time the industry had moved from water to steam power.

THE GREAT LAXEY WHEEL

Despite the gradual replacement of water by steam power from the late eighteenth century, the most magnificent waterwheel of all was yet to be built. This was the 'Lady Isabella' wheel of the Great Laxey mining company on the Isle of Man. Made of cast iron, 22m in diameter, the height of an eight-storey house, it was opened in September 1854 to pump water from a lead mine 412m below sea level to a disposal point 40m above sea level.[12] This late use of a waterwheel was attributable to the shortage of coal on the island as an alternative power source. The Laxey wheel's opening, on 30 September 1854, when a bottle of champagne was broken on the mechanism and it was named 'Lady Isabella' after the wife of the island's governor, was a great occasion.

The Great Laxey Wheel, Isle of Man. *(Manx National Heritage)*

A banquet was held for the bishop, the governor and the legislature, with milk supplied in place of ale for the 'totalists' (teetotallers) in the company and, in the words of the local newspaper 'the shouts from the strong lungs of the workpeople vied with the booming of the cannon in proclaiming the satisfactory accomplishment of a great undertaking'.[13] The great wheel pumped water from the mine from 1854 until 1929 when the mine closed, and is now one of the island's major tourist attractions.

'AN ENGINE TO RAISE WATER BY FIRE'

The first person to register a patent for a steam engine was a military engineer from Devon, Thomas Savery (*c.* 1650–1716) though there had been earlier experiments in Italy and France.[14] There had also been conjectures by Edward Somerset, Marquis of Worcester (1601–67), a former soldier in the army of Charles I. In 1655, shortly after Savery's birth, the Marquis published a book called *A Century of Inventions*. Many of the inventions he described were highly fanciful but number 68 was a plausible account of a machine for 'driving up water by fire' which some commentators have cited as evidence that he conceived the steam engine. There is no evidence that the Marquis ever made one. The problem that confronted Thomas Savery was the familiar one of pumping water from waterlogged mines to the surface. Savery's engine consisted of a sealed vessel into which steam was introduced under pressure, forcing the water up a pipe and out of the mine. Cold water was then sprinkled on the vessel to condense the steam. This created a vacuum which sucked more water from the mine through a valve. Savery submitted a working model of his 'Fire Engine' to the Royal Society and demonstrated it to King William III at Hampton Court in 1698, following which his patent was granted for 'a new invention by him invented, for raising of water, and occasioning motion to all sorts of mill works, by the important use of fire, which will be of great use for draining mines, serving towns with water, and for the working of all sorts of mills, when they have not the benefit of water nor constant winds'. He called his engine 'The Miner's Friend; or an Engine to raise Water by Fire', yet it is clear from the wording of the patent that Savery foresaw many uses for his engine in addition to pumping and that his engine was seen as especially suitable for use in conjunction with watermills. In a pamphlet he wrote in 1702 to promote the sales of his engine, he particularly recommended it as a means of recirculating water to reservoirs for overshot mills. Savery's engine,

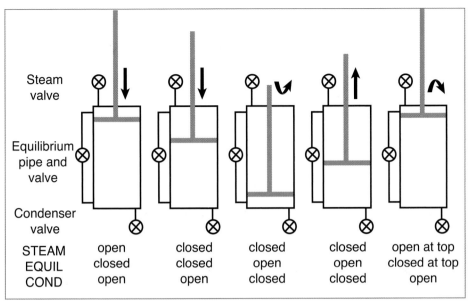

The workings of an early steam engine.

though ingenious, had difficulty raising water much more than 60ft without using pressures which risked causing his vessels to explode, and enormous quantities of fuel were required to generate the necessary amount of steam. Deep mines required an ascending series of Savery's engines at intervals of about 60ft, each pumping water to the level above: good for the sales of engines but uneconomic for mine-owners. The engines were used, however, to pump water into tanks in private houses.

THOMAS NEWCOMEN AND THE 'ATMOSPHERIC ENGINE'

Savery managed to have his patent extended from the usual fourteen to thirty-five years so he effectively monopolised the business until 1733. This was a great impediment to Thomas Newcomen (1663–1729), a blacksmith from Dartmouth, who invented the 'atmospheric' steam engine. This was a great improvement on Savery's design but because of Savery's patent Newcomen was obliged to go into partnership with the older man and derived little financial reward from his invention. It is possible that Newcomen was used by Savery to make some of the components for his 'Fire Engine' and that this may have aroused Newcomen's interest in designing an improved version. It is also possible that Newcomen's work was stimulated by his work as a smith in West Country mines which exposed him to Savery's engines. What is certain is that,

The Newcomen engine, invented in 1712.

in 1708, Newcomen registered a patent, in conjunction with Savery, for a revolutionary design.

Newcomen's engine, for the first time, made use of a piston operating within a vertical cylinder which was open at the top. The piston was slightly narrower than the cylinder and Newcomen created an airtight seal by ringing the outside of the piston with wet rope. Steam was introduced into the bottom of the cylinder, causing the piston to rise. When the piston reached the top of the cylinder the steam inlet valve was closed and cold water was sprayed onto the exterior of the cylinder. The resulting condensation of the steam created a vacuum in the cylinder, whereupon the piston fell under atmospheric pressure, beginning the process again. The top of the piston was attached to a pivoted beam which moved up and down with the piston and operated the pump. The use of the piston and beam meant that motion was applied both on the up and down strokes. Moreover, the power of the engine depended not upon the pressure of the steam, as in Savery's case, but on the size of the piston and cylinder on which atmospheric pressure worked. Newcomen engines were characterised by large, low-pressure cylinders and by slow-moving pistons and were relatively safe mechanisms. In 1712 Newcomen and his partner, a man called John Calley, installed their first 'atmospheric engine' in a colliery near Dudley in Staffordshire. The cylinder was 8ft long, 21in in diameter and worked at about 6 strokes per minute, raising water from a depth of 156ft, a depth which would have required three Savery engines. The engines cost about £1,000 each, a huge sum for the time, and the fact that Newcomen had installed over a hundred machines by the time of his death is evidence both of their effectiveness and of the importance of the problem they were designed to solve. The engines were also extremely durable, some of Newcomen's own installations remaining in use into the twentieth century.

JAMES WATT

Newcomen's engines were very effective but they were also very inefficient in their use of fuel. The process of cooling the cylinder with cold water meant that enormous amounts of energy had to be used reheating it each time. This did not matter too much in the early applications in coalmines where fuel was readily available but it discouraged the adoption of the design by factories or other facilities situated far from the coalfields. The next major step in the development of steam power was the work of James Watt (1736–1819) who is often wrongly credited with the invention of the steam engine. He certainly did not invent it but the improvements he made to its design ensured that it found a much wider range of application than Newcomen's would ever have done. The tale that he was inspired to devise a steam engine by watching the lid of a kettle rise as it boiled was long regarded as a myth but a letter written by Watt and auctioned in London in March 2003, specifically mentions the incident.

James Watt was the son of a merchant of Greenock, Scotland, who at the age of 19 went to Glasgow to learn the trade of a mathematical instrument-maker. In 1757, after a short time in London, he set up in business as an instrument-maker in Glasgow and quickly gained a good reputation. In 1763, aged 27, he was asked to repair a Newcomen engine and while doing so he realised the enormous cost in fuel of the alternate heating and cooling process

James Watt. *(National Portrait Gallery)*

which the older design required. Watt's solution was to release the steam from the piston cylinder to a separate condenser. In this way the cylinder could be kept at a constant temperature with a dramatic saving in fuel. He also realised that, by injecting steam at each end of the enclosed cylinder, above and below the piston, he could impart more power to the mechanism than could Newcomen's atmospheric pressure. He went into partnership with a Scottish ironmaster called John Roebuck with a view to producing his new design but in 1773 Roebuck went bankrupt.

Having lost his original partner Watt now formed one of the most celebrated partnerships in industrial history with the businessman Matthew Boulton (1728–1809) at the Soho works in Birmingham. Boulton, the son of a silver stamper, founded the Soho works with money from his wife's dowry. It specialised in machine tools, notably for minting coins. He supplied machinery for the Royal Mint which remained in use until 1882. The Soho works prospered and grew to a size where water power was no longer adequate for its needs. Boulton tried, with little success, to adapt Newcomen's steam engine as a source of power for his plant. In 1767 he met Watt and learned of his experiments with steam engines. Boulton bought out Roebuck's share of the failed enterprise and took Watt into partnership himself. Watt's mechanical skill, together with Boulton's capital and determination, led to the development of Watt's condensing steam engine, three times as efficient as Newcomen's and better adapted to driving machinery. Watt was granted a patent for his 'Condensing Engine' in 1769 and later registered many other patents. The addition of a crank to the piston enabled Watt's engines to impart a rotary motion which made the device suitable for use in cotton and other factories. It was James Watt who was commemorated in Westminster Abbey for his inventiveness, but without Matthew Boulton's support, James Watt would be a far less celebrated name in industrial history.

The two men were as ruthless as Savery had been in exploiting the patents that Watt was granted and they made it difficult for others to make further improvements in the application of steam power. Watt charged his customers for the use of his engines according to the amount of money they saved by using one of his engines rather than a team of horses – hence the concept of 'horsepower'. The users of his machines paid him one-third of the money they saved each year. This monopolistic practice did not discourage people from using his engines. By 1800 there were over 500 Boulton and Watt engines in mines and factories. Watt died a very wealthy man.

RICHARD TREVITHICK AND THE LOCOMOTIVE

By the early nineteenth century, then, steam engines were well established as an alternative source of energy to waterwheels but only in stationary applications. No one had yet devised a steam engine which could move. A prominent manufacturer of steam engines, Matthew Murray (1765–1826), observed that a steam engine was about as portable as a church and doubted whether it would be possible to build an engine which would have the necessary balance of power and weight that would enable it to move along rails. His company declined the invitation to build 'locomotives' for the Stockton and Darlington Railway, though after his death his successors did build them for the Great Western.

Not everyone agreed with this pessimistic assessment of the suitability of using steam as a means of propulsion. The most important doubter, and true father of the locomotive, was Richard Trevithick (1771–1833). Trevithick, known as 'the Cornish Giant' because of his height (6ft 2in) and prodigious strength, revealed an aptitude for engineering while working at tin mines near Camborne in his native county. Cornwall, because of its concentration of deep tin mines, had more steam engines than any other place on earth. The principle of moving coal in horse-drawn wagons along wooden planks or rails had long been in use since the flat, regular surface of the wood enabled heavier loads to be hauled than was possible on rough road surfaces. As many as 20,000 horses were being used in this way in the eighteenth century. The problem with using steam engines in place of horses lay with their weight. The unwieldy cast-iron mechanisms of early engines were heavy enough but to this had to be added the weight of the water and the coal to turn it into steam. In a stationary engine at a mine or mill this was of no importance but in an engine which was required to move and to draw loads, it was critical.

Trevithick's innovation in the 'Cornish engine' was to put the tube with the fire *inside* the boiler where it was surrounded by the water it had to heat. In this way all the heat generated by the fire was transferred to the water, none being lost to the surrounding atmosphere as with earlier designs. A smaller fire could thus generate a higher steam pressure through a smaller boiler. An adaptation of this system was to be critical to the later success of Robert Stephenson's *Rocket* at the Rainhill trials of 1829. An early experiment with a miniature locomotive was successful and on Christmas Eve 1801, a larger version transported Trevithick himself and a small group of friends up a hill near Camborne. Boulton and Watt lobbied the government to forbid his experiments on the grounds that the high pressures generated by his engines made them dangerous. There was some truth in their arguments, though they were certainly motivated by the threat that Trevithick's designs posed to their monopoly rather than by any concern for public safety. Nevertheless Trevithick continued with his experiments and in 1804 he produced the first steam engine to run successfully on rails. It was built for the Penydarren ironworks in Merthyr Tydfil, South Wales and hauled 10 tons of iron and 70 people 9 miles at a speed of almost 5mph. A huge piston-driven flywheel transferred power to the drive wheels by a system of cogs.

This locomotive, and its successors, had demonstrated the potential of steam as a form of motive power but they all ran into the same problem: the 7-ton engine caused the cast-iron rails to break after a few journeys. Trevithick's most spectacular demonstration took place in the summer of 1808 when he erected a small circular track close to the present site of Euston station and offered onlookers a ride on the locomotive *Catch Me Who Can* at 12mph for the substantial price of 1*s*. There were plenty of takers but once again the rails broke and the trial ended. Further experiments with the application of steam succeeded only in reducing him to penury, from one episode of which he was rescued by Robert Stephenson. Stephenson paid Trevithick's fare back to Britain after an unsuccessful foray by the older man in South America but Stephenson (and his father George) became admirers of Trevithick's pioneering work and argued, without success, that he should be awarded a government pension. Trevithick died in poverty at an inn in Dartford, Kent in 1833.

However, Trevithick's experiments had not escaped the attention of those who sought to apply steam power in another area where weight was less critical and water readily available: in transport by water. After some early experiments in America by John Fitch, the engineer William Symington (1763–1831) designed the first working steamboat, the *Charlotte Dundas* which worked the Forth–Clyde canal from 1802. However, the death of his patron the Duke of Bridgewater, who had recognised the possibilities for such a craft on his canal network, deprived Symington of the financial support he needed and, like Trevithick, he died in poverty. In 1843 I.K. Brunel designed the *Great*

Britain, a steamship which was revolutionary in several ways. It was the first large iron-hulled steamship driven by propellors (rather than paddles) which enabled it to offer a regular service across the choppy waters of the Atlantic. James Watt had proposed the use of the propellor, which he called the 'spiral oar', in the 1780s but it was Brunel's ruthless determination which installed it in the most powerful ship of its day, able to carry unprecedented numbers of passengers and quantities of cargo. The *SS Great Britain* transported troops to the Crimea and emigrants to Australia, as well as the first English cricket team to tour that country. She was later used to take Welsh coal round Cape Horn to San Francisco and it was on one of these voyages, in 1886, that she was marooned in the Falkland islands. From there she was rescued in 1970 and brought home to Bristol where she remains as the most outstanding example of the early application of steam to marine transport.

STEAM RAILWAYS

By the time of Trevithick's death the concept of the public railway system was well established, despite the failure of his attempts to make steam railways something more than an adjunct to mining enterprises. This process is normally associated with George and Robert Stephenson and *The Rocket* but other developments were necessary before their famous triumph at the Rainhill trials of 1829. One of the most important contributions was made by Goldsworthy Gurney (1793–1875) whose experiments with steam cars are described in Chapter 7.[15] At a young age he met his fellow Cornishman, Trevithick, and it was this contact which probably aroused his interest in steam locomotives and led to Gurney's invention of the steam jet whose concentrated emission of steam increased power output. Its use in *The Rocket* was decisive in enabling the Stephensons' engine to sustain high speeds. The process by which the Stephensons learned of the steam jet and adapted it to *The Rocket* is not entirely clear but it is likely that the point of contact was the world's first public railway, the Stockton and Darlington railway, which opened in 1825.

Goldsworthy Gurney had been in correspondence about his steam jet with Timothy Hackworth (1786–1850) a neglected railway pioneer who was born in Wylam, near Newcastle, also the birthplace of George Stephenson himself. While working at Wylam colliery at his trade of blacksmith, Hackworth helped to design the colliery locomotive *Puffing Billy*.[16] George Stephenson (1781–1848) was following a similar career at the nearby collieries of Dewley and Killingworth. Almost entirely self-educated, Stephenson progressed rapidly from keeping cows off the colliery railways to repairing its engines. By 1814 he was designing colliery locomotives and in 1819 he built an 8-mile railway from Hetton to the River Wear at Sunderland, worked partly by his locomotives and partly by stationary engines which hauled the colliery wagons on cables. His work attracted the attention of a man called Edward Pease who in 1821 had obtained an Act of Parliament authorising him to construct a horse-drawn railway to connect the collieries around Darlington with the River Tees at Stockton. Having seen Stephenson's locomotives at work at Killingworth colliery, Pease had the Act of Parliament amended to enable his railway to dispense with horsepower and, instead, 'to make and erect locomotive or moveable engines'.

In 1824 Pease joined with George Stephenson and his son Robert (1803–59) to form a company in Forth Street, Newcastle, to make locomotives

for the new railway. George recruited Timothy Hackworth as locomotive superintendent and together the two men designed and produced the new railway's first engine, *Locomotion*, in 1825. George also identified a supplier of wrought-iron rails much stronger than the cast-iron rails whose habit of breaking had bedevilled Trevithick's early locomotives. On 27 September 1825, *Locomotion*, with George Stephenson at the controls, drew thirty-six wagons of coal, flour, workmen and visitors the 9 miles from Darlington to Stockton in less than two hours. The train included a purpose-built passenger coach called *The Experiment*. Since it had no suspension the ride must have been

George Stephenson. (*National Portrait Gallery*)

very uncomfortable but the train, the track and the passengers survived the journey which thus inaugurated the world's first public passenger service, though in the months that followed, steam engines were used only for freight and passenger carriages were drawn by horses at a more stately pace. Forty thousand people turned out to watch what the local newspaper called 'The Steam Horse' as it moved at the amazing speed of up to 15mph.[17] The railway reduced the cost of moving coal by one-third and George Stephenson's renown as a railway engineer was assured.

The Rocket

Stephenson was now appointed as engineer to the proposed, and much larger, Liverpool and Manchester Railway, leaving Timothy Hackworth in charge of locomotives for the Stockton and Darlington Railway. In this capacity Hackworth adopted Goldsworthy Gurney's steam jet for an improved locomotive design, the *Royal George* which entered service in 1827. It was probably by this means that George Stephenson learned of the steam jet which he was shortly to adapt for *The Rocket*. The new line was not without its opponents. Local canal owners bitterly opposed the new line. By 1825, £70 shares in the Bridgewater canal were valued at £1,250 and the owners saw the proposed line, correctly, as a severe threat to their huge dividends. The *Quarterly Review* suggested that, on grounds of public safety, the trains should be limited to a speed of 9mph. Having overcome such opposition, Stephenson struggled with the problems of building the 31-mile railway across the unstable peat bog of Chat Moss[18] and building a nine-arch viaduct across the Sankey valley. In the meantime the directors of the Liverpool and Manchester Railway were deliberating on the type of motive power to be used for the new line. Stationary engines, which would haul the trains on cables, were tried and tested but locomotives, attached to the trains themselves, were now seen to be working on the Stockton and Darlington Railway.

The directors therefore announced that they would hold trials of competing designs at Rainhill, south of St Helens, in October 1829. Each locomotive would have to haul a load three times its own weight at a speed of at least 10mph over a distance equivalent to a return trip between Liverpool and Manchester. No locomotive was to weigh more than 6 tons in order to avoid damage to the track. A prize of £500 was offered to the winner. Ten locomotives were originally entered but only three were in a condition to take part in the trials when they started. Three judges were

Robert Stephenson. *(National Portrait Gallery)*

appointed (two of them engineers) to report to the company's directors on the performance of the competitors.

The three surviving contenders for the prize, as reported in *Mechanics Magazine*[19] were *Novelty* of Messrs Braithwaite and Erickson of London; Timothy Hackworth's *Sans Pareil*, from Darlington; and *The Rocket*, described as being to the design of George Stephenson's 26-year-old son Robert, from Newcastle. *Rocket* and *Sans Pareil* weighed more than 4 tons; *Novelty*, at less than 3 tons, was substantially lighter. In addition to the steam jet, *Rocket* had another design feature which was crucial to its success. Like Trevithick's design, the heating system was inside the boiler but instead of using one large tube, as Trevithick had done, Stephenson used many small ones, thus increasing the heated surface in contact with the water, generating greater heat with less fuel. The 'Grand Mechanical Competition Rail-Road Race' as it was called by *Mechanics Magazine* began on 6 October and continued to almost the end of the month. It is hard to overstate the drama of the occasion. Grandstands were erected to accommodate the thousands of spectators who came to witness the event. *Mechanics Magazine* devoted four issues to a day-to-day account of the progress of the trials, giving details of locomotive design, weight hauled, fuel consumption and speeds reached. *The Times* and other local and national newspapers also followed the event with close interest. *Novelty* and *Sans Pareil* suffered mechanical problems and failed to complete the trial so the directors were left with no choice but to award the £500 prize (and the contract for locomotives) to *Rocket* and the Stephensons. The verdict of *Mechanics Magazine* was unambiguous. It declared that *Rocket* was 'so much superior to all the old locomotive engines in use, as to entitle Mr Stephenson to the most marked and liberal consideration for the skill and ingenuity displayed in its construction'[20] and it compared his achievement with that of John Harrison, inventor of the marine chronometer. It reported that *Rocket* had approached speeds of 30mph and observed that a journey time of an hour from Liverpool to Manchester could now be contemplated rather than half a day.

The Liverpool and Manchester Railway was opened on 15 September 1830 and is chiefly remembered for the accident which occurred when William Huskisson, MP for Liverpool and President of the Board of Trade, was run over and killed by *Rocket* shortly after the opening ceremony. Despite this tragedy the railway was a most successful enterprise carrying almost half a million passengers in its first full year and making substantial profits for its shareholders. *Rocket* worked on the railway until the late 1830s when it was sold to a railway in Carlisle. It is now in the Science Museum. The age of the steam railway had begun and was followed by a boom in railway construction which underpinned the economy of the mid-nineteenth century in Britain and rapidly spread to other nations. In 1845 *The Times* estimated that over a thousand railway promotion schemes were in the course of preparation, though the financial crisis of 1847, when the Bank of England raised interest rates, stilled the enthusiasm of investors and caused the boom to collapse.

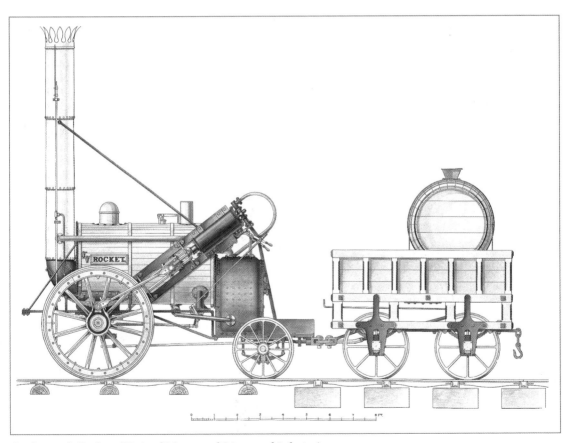

Stephenson's Rocket. (*National Museum of Science and Industry*)

Nevertheless, by 1852 about 7,000 miles of track had been built and Britain's mainline railway system was virtually complete. The steam railway reduced the cost of transport for goods and people and created new industries like seaside holidays for working people as well as new communities like suburbs for commuting workers. Coalmines, steelworks and factories could now reach national markets more quickly than they could even by using the canal network which now began its long decline. The success of the Great Exhibition of 1851 was substantially attributable to the steam railways. They brought 6,039,195 visitors to the spectacle in Hyde Park, almost as many as visited the Millennium Dome 150 years later from a population which had increased threefold in the intervening time. In the years that followed, British railway expertise was exported to the world, Stephenson himself designing Germany's first locomotive *Der Adler* (*The Eagle*). British engineers also ensured that the standard gauge of 4ft 8½in was adopted throughout most of the world, despite its curious origin: a gauge used in a Northumberland colliery for its horse-drawn wagons; a colliery in which George Stephenson worked.

London time

In 1841 the Great Western Railway opened, reducing the journey time from London to Bristol from two days to five hours and the timetable of Brunel's famous railway contained an innovation which was itself a testimony to the power of steam. The Great Western had decided that all its timetables would use 'London time' based on the time at Greenwich, rather than the local variations which reflected the fact that the sun reaches Bristol approximately ten minutes later than it reaches London. When economic activity was based upon small local communities with little, slow travel between them, this didn't matter. But as these local economies were brought together by the power of steam, the opportunity for confusion caused by differences in time between cities became a problem which was quickly recognised by the railway companies, especially those whose lines ran east to west. If local time was used, then a journey from Bristol to London appeared to take longer than one in the opposite direction. In 1845 the Liverpool and Manchester Railway petitioned Parliament to impose London time throughout the country. The petition failed but from this date more railway companies began to adopt London time as the Great Western had done. Greenwich time was checked every day and transmitted to signal boxes and stations, with whom local watch and clockmakers were allowed to check the accuracy of their instruments. It was not until 1880, however, that the power of steam over the clock was recognised with the passage of the 'Statutes (Definition of Time)' Act which introduced London (Greenwich) time throughout the kingdom.

Steam beneath the streets

Steam locomotives were not confined to the surface. In January 1863, the world's first underground railway opened between Paddington and Farringdon in the City of London. It was designed to collect the hundreds of thousands of commuters who were being brought each day to the railway termini on the fringes of London – Paddington, Euston, St Pancras and King's Cross – and take them to their offices in the City without the need to pass through the capital's crowded streets. The new railway lay just below the surface of the Marylebone Road–Euston Road–Pentonville Road–City Road–Farringdon Road route and Daniel Gooch, who had designed Great Western engines for Brunel, designed a special 'condensing' locomotive to emit less steam than conventional engines. Steam was led through a pipe back to the water tank but the success of the design was compromised by two factors. First, the condensing pipe did not prevent the emission of smoke in the underground tunnels. Second, the Great Western insisted on running its own trains straight through from its main line at Paddington to Farringdon using conventional engines (requiring the addition of a third rail to accommodate the GWR's 7ft-gauge rolling stock). Blow holes were built into the roads above the railway tunnels through which smoke and steam could escape but as traffic increased the atmosphere in the tunnels became appalling. A letter to *The Times* described a journey in 1879: 'The condition of the atmosphere was so poisonous that I was almost suffocated. On reaching the open air I requested to be taken to a chemist close at hand. Without a moment's hesitation he said "Oh, I see, Metropolitan Railway" and at once poured out a wine glass full of what he designated *Metropolitan Mixture*. I was induced to ask him whether he often had such cases to which he rejoined "Why, bless you sir, we often have twenty cases a day".'[21]

In 1898 a Board of Trade Committee was appointed to enquire into the problem of the ventilation of the tunnels, through which over 500 steam trains a day by then were passing. The Metropolitan Railway's General Manager, John Bell, assured the committee that the fuming chasms of his railway were particularly beneficial to people with asthma, bronchitis and other respiratory problems. Bell attributed his own recovery from tonsillitis to the 'acid gas' of

Gooch condensing engine, designed for London's first underground railway. Note the condensing tube. *(London's Transport Museum)*

the tunnels and produced a driver, Mr Langford, to support his assurances with testimony to the effect that thirty-four years in an atmosphere of smoke and steam had done him no harm. However, Langford's evidence was somewhat compromised when he added that only 'very seldom' was the atmosphere so thick as to prevent him from seeing the railway signals![22] The problem was not solved until early in the next century when electricity replaced steam as the motive power on the Metropolitan, District and Circle lines.

STEAM ON THE ROADS

Steam traction is inseparably associated with railways but Goldsworthy Gurney was not the last person to experiment with it as a means of road transport. The problem faced by its advocates was that which had defeated Trevithick: weight. The combination of metal, fuel and water produced vehicles that were so heavy that an excessive proportion of the energy generated by the engine was devoted to coping with the sheer mass of the apparatus itself, before any freight or passengers were added. Some success was achieved in the late nineteenth century with steam-driven 'agricultural traction engines' which did not have to carry great burdens and which were the ancestor of the mechanical plough. 'Showmen's engines' were also developed to drive roundabouts and other entertainments at fairs but these, when used, were stationary and were only required to move their own weight when passing from one venue to another. Some success was achieved in the late nineteenth century in designing steam-driven cars, usually powered by kerosene. One of these, an American-designed 'Stanley steam car', reached a speed of 120mph in 1906 and several of the thirty-three vehicles which participated in the first London to Brighton Run on 14 November 1896 were steam-powered.

Lighter internal combustion engines eventually replaced steam engines in farms and fairs, though many have survived, often rescued from dereliction, to be exhibited at events throughout the country. One of the most notable is Camborne's 'Trevithick day', an event held each April to celebrate the town's most famous son. The one application to road vehicles which survived and flourished into the late twentieth century was the steamroller, used for road surfacing, in which the weight of the vehicle was an asset. During the Suez crisis of 1956 the shortage of oil prompted the government to look into the possibility of bringing steam-operated lorries out of retirement. It was estimated that about 900 working vehicles could be located.[23]

Steam road vehicles are now, with few exceptions, the preserve of groups of dedicated enthusiasts who gather at rallies during the summer months to exhibit the artefacts that they have been repairing and polishing during the winter.

Foden 5-ton steam-powered road vehicle, built in 1917. (*Stephen Halliday*)

Steam railway locomotives are likewise to be found on carefully restored railways which have been rescued from the late Dr Beeching. There is a romance about a steam locomotive, whether it be a humble tank engine, the *Flying Scotsman* or the celebrated *Rocket* which no diesel or electric version has come close to matching. Paradoxically these amazing mechanisms with their gleaming brass fittings and shining paint are in better condition in museums or on steam railways than they were when they were in regular service up until the 1960s.

HYDROELECTRIC POWER

In many applications, on railways and elsewhere, steam has given way to another form of water-generated power: electricity. It could be argued that this represents a return to the waterwheel since hydroelectric plants operate by passing water through a water turbine which drives a generator. It is estimated that hydroelectric power accounts for about 15 per cent of worldwide electricity supply though it is more abundant in mountainous regions with fast-flowing rivers than in a small country like Britain. Thus in Canada it accounts for about 60 per cent of electricity generated, in the United States for about 10 per cent and in Britain for little more than 1 per cent.[24]

As with waterwheels there are different types of hydroelectric plant. The first are 'low head' plants, also called 'run of the river' plants in which the flow of a river is used to drive a turbine. Many early plants were of this kind, usually with a generating capacity of 25 megawatts[25] or less. They are dependent upon the seasonal flow of a river, with little or no capacity to store water and are therefore vulnerable to intermittent reductions or interruptions of supply. Most hydroelectric power is generated by 'high head' plants, in which huge dams store water in reservoirs from which water is channelled to turbines, usually at speed from a height. They were long regarded as environmentally desirable because they do not generate the gases associated with fossil fuels, though more recent studies suggest that they are damaging in other ways. These issues are discussed in the epilogue. The third form of hydroelectric power is the 'pumped storage' plant which exploits the fact that demands for electricity vary enormously throughout a 24-hour period. Such a plant is found at Dinorwig in North Wales which since 1984 has been home to Europe's largest pumped storage generating station. At night, when demand for electricity is low, surplus electricity is used to pump water from a low-level reservoir, Llyn Peris, to a higher reservoir, Marchlyn Mawr. During the day, when demand for electricity peaks, the water is released from the higher reservoir through turbines which power six generators to produce 288 megawatts of electricity. Pumped storage systems of this kind now generate about two-thirds as much electricity as conventional hydroelectric plants. This ingenious use of electricity is not new. In 1863 the architect Richard Norman Shaw (1831–1912) designed a house at Cragside, near Rothbury, Northumberland, for William (later Lord) Armstrong (1810–1900) who was responsible for a number of inventions in the application of hydraulics to industry and had made a fortune from armaments production. The house was the first in the world to have permanent electric lighting, the electricity being generated by the flow of water from one artificial lake to another. Such was the wonder the house engendered among contemporaries that it was described as 'the palace of a modern magician'.[26]

THE POWER OF THE TIDES

Britain may lack fast-flowing mountain streams but it is surrounded by tidal waters and since medieval times the power of tides has been harnessed as a source of power. Reference has already been made to the tidal mill at Dover recorded in Domesday Book.[27] For half a century serious attempts have been made by engineers to turn this potential source of energy into electricity. Its advocates remind us that, like conventional hydroelectric plants, tidal power does not produce greenhouse gases as fossil fuels do and that, once the enormous capital cost of the necessary infrastructure has been absorbed, there is little cost associated with running such a power source. However, the limitations of tidal power are reflected in the fact that only two commercial-scale plants have been built, one in Nova Scotia, Canada and one across the River Rance near St Malo, in Brittany. The latter has operated satisfactorily since 1966 generating 240 megawatts of electricity but it is significant that the larger plant which was planned to follow it, across the whole of the St Malo bay, has never been built. An inescapable problem associated with tidal plants is that they only operate effectively when the tide is ebbing or flowing reasonably fast and these conditions only apply for about twelve hours a day. This would not matter if the tidal flow coincided with peak demand for electricity but since the tides are conditioned by the moon, which takes no account of human needs for electricity, this happy situation remains elusive. For this reason, among others, plans to build tidal power barrages across the Severn estuary, the Wash and the Solway Firth have remained firmly on paper, though smaller-scale plants are contemplated. One has been commissioned on the coast of Islay, an island off the west coast of Scotland. Designed by researchers from Queen's University, Belfast, it harnesses the power of waves to compress air in a chamber in such a way that the escaping air drives a turbine, producing 50 kilowatts of electricity for the island.

HYDROELECTRIC POWER: THE PROBLEMS

Hydroelectric power, whether from rivers or tides, was once thought of as the cleanest form of energy, particularly in comparison with fossil fuels, but doubts are now emerging. The construction of the huge reservoirs associated with 'high head' power plants has often been accompanied by severe damage to the environment. Some of the more recent and controversial examples are discussed in the epilogue but even in Canada, whose vast land area and long history of hydroelectric power generation should make it well disposed to the process, doubts are emerging. In Quebec 10,000sq.km of land have been submerged and in many cases this has been at the expense of the settlements of native peoples. There is some evidence that the decay of vegetation thereby submerged emits greenhouse gases which are as harmful as those from fossil fuel plants. Dams can prevent fish like salmon from swimming upstream to spawn and can also trap sediment. Instead of being carried downstream to refresh the soil of a floodplain, sediment collects in the bottom of a reservoir, thus reducing its storage capacity. For this reason the World Bank has become more reluctant to fund huge 'high head' projects in third-world countries and there may be a revival of smaller-scale 'low head' or 'run of the river' systems in such communities.

THE FUTURE OF WATER POWER

There is every reason to suppose that water will continue to be a major source of power, and controversy, in the twenty-first century. Steam has become less important as a source of power for transport in western nations, though in countries like India and China, where coal is abundant, railways still employ thousands of steam locomotives. Steam remains a significant force in manufacturing, the purpose to which James Watt originally applied it. As steam power declines in relative terms, the demand for electricity advances and with it the demand for 'clean' methods of generating it. It is too early to predict with confidence whether tides, dams or 'run of the river' technology will assume the most prominent place in producing clean energy but whichever it is, water will certainly be involved.

5

WATER AS DEADLY DANGER

Sir Joseph Bazalgette and the Great Stink

By the mere action of the lungs of the inhabitants of Liverpool, a stratum of air sufficient to cover the entire surface of the town, to a depth of three feet, is daily rendered unfit for the purposes of respiration.

Dr W.H. Duncan, Liverpool's Medical Officer, explaining the causes of cholera to a Royal Commission in 1844

Although great differences of opinion existed, and continue to exist, as to the causes of the disease, yet an inspection of the houses in which deaths occurred was sufficient to show that, however occult might be the connection between death and defective drainage, the places formerly most favourable to the spread of disease became quite free from it, when afterwards properly drained.

Sir Joseph Bazalgette, builder of London's sewers, explaining how he was banishing cholera from London, 1864

CHARLES DICKENS – AN ALARMING VISIT

In April 1850, Charles Dickens visited the works of the Grand Junction Water Company at Kew. The company had been set up as an offshoot of the Grand Junction Canal Company earlier in the century[1] but had since become independent of its parent. Dickens gave an account of his visit in *Household Words* of which he was then the editor.[2] He had asked the company engineer 'How many companies take their supplies from the Thames, near to, and after it has received the contents of, the common sewers?' The engineer assured him that only one water company, the Lambeth, took water from the Thames below Chelsea which at that time was on the western extremity of the built-up area. Dickens observed that, since the Thames was a tidal river as far upstream as the weir at Teddington (Tide-end-town), any sewage entering the river in the metropolis would be borne by the incoming tide to the water intakes of all the water companies which took supplies from the river. The engineer assured Dickens that problems of water pollution were more likely to be caused by dirt entering cisterns in houses than by pollution in the river. His complacency echoed that of a spokesman for the company twenty-two years earlier who had informed

A DROP OF LONDON WATER.

'A Drop of London Water'; at this time much of London's drinking water was drawn from the polluted river. (Punch, *1850*)

the Royal Commission on Water Supply of the Metropolis that: 'The impregnating ingredients of the Thames are as perfectly harmless as any spring water of the purest kind in common life: indeed there is probably not a spring, with the exception of Malvern, and one or two more, which are so pure as Thames water.'[3]

There were those who had their doubts, besides Charles Dickens. In the same month that Dickens published his alarming account, an engineer called William O'Brien published an article in the *Edinburgh Review* entitled 'The Supply of Water to the Metropolis' in which he wrote: 'There are 141 public sewers between London and Battersea Bridges; Richmond, Isleworth, Brentford, Mortlake, Chiswick and Hammersmith furnish 68 more – and the whole of their contents are received into the Thames, and returned by the reflux of the tide – we perceive a state of things which renders exaggeration truly superfluous.'[4]

He was right. Londoners were drinking one another's sewage and, as a result, by the time the articles appeared, over 20,000 Londoners had perished in the cholera epidemics of 1832 and 1849. Almost 11,000 more were to die in another epidemic in 1854 and over 5,000 in cholera's final attack, on a small area of Whitechapel, in 1866. To these figures must be added deaths from the other great water-borne scourge, typhoid. Since typhoid deaths came in a steadier stream rather than sudden epidemics, and since it was often confused with typhus, deaths from typhoid are more difficult to identify with certainty but they may well have exceeded deaths from cholera. In the years that followed, controversy raged over the causes of cholera and the remedies to be applied. The most alarming feature of cholera and typhoid, as far as the authorities were concerned, was that they affected all classes equally. Premature deaths from disease and malnutrition were associated with poverty, filth and, occasionally, with degenerate behaviour such as drunkenness. Cholera and typhoid did not defer to rank or class. The most eminent victim of typhoid was probably Albert, the Prince Consort, who died in 1861.[5] Polluted water, the real cause of these diseases, killed indiscriminately. Paradoxically the contemporary belief that they were transmitted through the air (the 'miasmatic' theory) made the atmosphere itself the principal suspect and when the crisis arrived, in the form of 'The Great Stink' of 1858, fear finally prompted frightened Parliamentarians to take the necessary action they had long delayed.

THE 'NECESSARY CHAMBER'

The cause of London's cholera epidemics could be traced to the very first Mayor of London, Henry Fitzalwyn. In 1189, in an early attempt at building regulations, Fitzalwyn had decreed that the 'necessary chamber' (the cesspool) should be at least 2ft 6in from the neighbouring building if it was made of stone and at least 3ft 6in if it was made of other materials. The centuries that followed provided abundant evidence of the need for this and similar measures. In 1290 some Carmelite Friars petitioned Parliament 'to abate a nuisance, viz. a great stench, which they cannot endure and which prevents them from performing their religious duties'.[6] By 1300 the disposal of sewage in the Sweetwater Bourne in Sweetwater Lane had earned the latter thoroughfare the unofficial name 'Shiteburne Lane'.[7]

This was not supposed to happen. The preferred method of sewage disposal was to store it in Fitzalwyn's 'necessary chambers' from which it was removed, usually at night, by men known as 'rakers', 'gong-fermors' or 'nightsoilmen'. The work was well paid. In 1281 thirteen men took five nights to clear the cesspools of Newgate jail, each man being paid sixpence a night, three times the normal wage. The sewage was taken on carts to farmers who were happy to buy it as manure for their fields. It did not have to be taken far. 'Moor Fields', just beyond Moorgate, were just that: fields rather subject to flooding in wet weather whose cultivators were glad to purchase the smelly cargo of entrepreneurs like Joseph Waller of Islington, whose business card in the Museum of London advertises his services as 'chimney sweeper and nightman', and who kept 'carts and horses for emptying bog houses, drains and cesspools'. From time to time lord mayors and, occasionally, kings complained about the pollution of streets and streams by refuse. In 1357 King Edward III addressed the mayor and sheriffs of the City in stern terms about the 'fumes and other abominable stenches' arising from 'filth accumulated upon the bank of the river'. He decreed that 'no man shall take any manner of rubbish, earth, gravel or dung out of his stables or elsewhere to throw and put the same into Rivers of Thames or Fleet'.[8]

The aim of such decrees was to ensure that London's network of rivers, flowing down into the Thames, was used for the purpose nature intended: to convey rainwater into the Thames and thence to the sea. Moreover, until the early nineteenth century it appears that both the Thames and its tributaries were kept reasonably free of pollution. In 1756 an Irish doctor called Charles Lucas had written that London's water is 'undoubtedly one of the principal causes why our capital is the most healthful city in the world' and in 1818 a publisher called Samuel Leigh had claimed that London's 'healthfulness is equal to that of any other metropolis in existence' and suggested that its 'plentiful supply of water which is furnished by different water companies, must also have an effect on the cleanliness, and consequently on the health, of the inhabitants of London'.[9] As late as 1844 a professor of chemistry called Booth wrote to the magazine *The Builder* reassuring readers that 'the free currents of air which are necessarily in constant circulation from its [*sic*] proximity to the majestic Thames have been considered (and not improperly) as a great cause of the salubrity of the metropolis'.[10] This was the expression of a theory which was made more explicit by Professor Booth in a following sentence: 'From inhaling the odour of beef the butcher's wife obtains her obesity.' This theory, known as the 'miasmatic' explanation of disease causation, held that epidemics were caused by foul air, not by polluted water. It was to confuse the deliberations of sanitary reformers for the next fifty years.

DISASTER: THE WATER-CLOSET

By the time that Professor Booth was writing his pompous letter to *The Builder*, the capital's sewage disposal system was in crisis and the water supply increasingly polluted. In 1816 fourteen salmon weighing 179 pounds were caught in the river. Four years later no catches were recorded and this remained the pattern for the next half-century. Three reasons account for the fact that, in the space of a few years, a clean river had become an open sewer. The first concerned the growth of London. In 1801, at the time of the first census, London's population was recorded as 959,000. By 1821 it had increased by more than 40 per cent to 1,378,000 and by 1861 it had more than doubled again to 2,807,000 – by far the largest city in the world. As the population expanded so did the built-up area, so that the fields which previously lay just beyond Moorgate were now beyond Highbury. As the fields retreated, the nightsoil carts faced longer journeys with their rank contents, making the business less economical. The construction of the canals brought some relief. As late as 1904 the records of the Grand Junction Canal Company show that 45,669 tons of manure were being conveyed by barges from Paddington basin to the fields of Hertfordshire, though by that date most of the cargo would have been horse manure gathered from London's streets. The second blow to the recycling businesses of the nightsoilmen came in the form of guano: solidified bird droppings excavated from guano mountains in South America and imported from the late 1840s onwards. This was more easily handled and less malodorous.

However, the real culprit was the water-closet. This had been invented in the sixteenth century by a courtier called Sir John Harington but he only made two

Thomas Cubitt (1788–1855) Thomas Cubitt's contribution to the building of London compares with that of Sir Christopher Wren. He was trained as a ship's carpenter and saved enough money during a voyage to India to set up as a builder upon his return. He was the first major builder to employ a permanent (as distinct from jobbing) workforce on large contracts and he became involved in speculative building as a means of providing them with regular employment. In this way he built much of Bloomsbury, Highbury, Belgravia, Pimlico and Clapham, providing dwellings for the aristocracy as well as the middle classes. At the request of Queen Victoria he reconstructed Osborne House on the Isle of Wight as a home for the royal family and built the east front of Buckingham Palace (facing the Mall). He also removed the Marble Arch from its incongruous position in front of Buckingham Palace to its present site. At Prince Albert's request he negotiated the purchase of the land on which the South Kensington Museums were built with the profits of the Great Exhibition of 1851. He left over £1 million pounds in his will which, at 386 pages, was the longest on record.

of the devices: one for himself and one for his godmother, Queen Elizabeth I. The idea was neglected until the late eighteenth century when a number of improvements were made to Harington's design, the most notable by a Yorkshire carpenter called Joseph Bramah. Bramah was a serial inventor who in his lifetime registered eighteen patents. In 1778 he was installing a WC in a private house when he realised that he could improve the mechanism to make it both more efficient and easier to produce in large numbers. By 1797 he had made over 6,000 closets and the company he founded continued to produce them until 1890. In 1861 Thomas Crapper, a businessman, founded a competitive business in Chelsea which marketed its wares under the memorable slogan 'a certain flush with every pull'. Crapper's business continued to trade from 120 King's Road until 1966.

By the early nineteenth century a water-closet was a desirable status symbol for householders with social ambitions. They were installed in the new dwellings that were being built in places like Bloomsbury, Belgravia, Highbury and Clapham by builders like Thomas Cubitt (1788–1855) from the 1820s onwards.

In 1844 Cubitt told the Royal Commission on the State of Large Towns and Populous Districts that in the previous twenty years the number of closets installed in London had increased tenfold.[11] A further stimulus to the popularity of the increasingly fashionable device arose from the Great Exhibition of 1851. An enterprising manufacturer called George Jennings installed his WCs in the Crystal Palace where he charged visitors a penny a time for using them. Some 827,000 took advantage of the novel facility and, in the process, ushered a new phrase into the language: 'spending a penny'. Jennings and his fellow entrepreneurs also placed unbearable strains on the system of sewage disposal inherited from Henry Fitzalwyn. Every time a WC was flushed, the mechanism despatched to the cesspool a very small quantity of potential manure accompanied by a much larger volume of water – ten or twenty times as much water as manure. The cesspools filled ten times as quickly with liquid which was difficult for nightsoilmen to extract and transport and which farmers did not want to buy. The liquid content of the cesspools overflowed or leaked into surrounding watercourses and thence to the Thames, carrying with it a multitude of germs into the city's water supply.

By this time the authorities had come to appreciate that the attachment of a modern invention, the WC, to what was still fundamentally a medieval system of waste disposal, the cesspool, had its disadvantages so in 1844 the Metropolitan Buildings Act required new buildings in London to be connected to the street sewers – a practice which had been forbidden in earlier centuries. Thomas Cubitt described the consequences which followed: 'Fifty years ago nearly all London had every house cleansed into a large cesspool. Now scarcely any person thinks of making a cesspool, but it is carried off at once into the river . . . the Thames is now made a great cesspool instead of each person having one of his own.'[12]

THE EMPIRE'S SECOND CITY

By the time that Thomas Cubitt gave this evidence London had already suffered the first of its four great cholera epidemics. The water-borne cholera bacillus, carried from victims via the sewers into the Thames and hence the capital's drinking water, claimed 6,536 victims in 1831–2.[13] However, it was the second city of the empire, Liverpool, which was the first to take active measures to protect its population from sewage and to take in hand the supply of clean drinking water through a publicly managed body.[14] By 1811 Liverpool was second only to London among British cities in the number of its inhabitants, a position which it held until it was overtaken by Glasgow in the 1860s. This human tide was not accompanied by any corresponding

George Cruikshank cartoon lampooning the Southwark Water Co., *c.* 1830. *(Thames Water)*

investment in public hygiene. Liverpool's proximity to the sea should have made it fairly easy to dispose of its waste, as observed by the distinguished engineer John Rennie in 1816. His report 'The Sewers and Soughs of Liverpool'[15] recorded that 'no town in the British dominions is better situated than the town of Liverpool for a complete system of sewers but there are few sewers in the town, and these not only deficient in capacity, but ill-calculated to perform the purposes for which they are designed'. For many years the population had been swollen by the arrival of impoverished Irish families, a situation exacerbated after 1845 by the Irish famine. This prompted the Liverpool Town Council to promote its own Sanitary Act which laid down some minimum standards for the construction of dwellings, prohibited the building of houses without drains and, thirty years after London, allowed house drains to be connected to the street sewers. The act also created, for the first time in a British city, the post of Medical Officer of Health.

That first Medical Officer was Dr William Henry Duncan (1805–63). Scottish by parentage, Duncan had qualified in Edinburgh and worked at the

Liverpool Infirmary where he campaigned relentlessly for better dwellings for the poor. Diseases like cholera, typhoid and dysentery were rife in Liverpool but many years were to pass before there was a clear understanding that they were carried in polluted water. The orthodox explanation for epidemics was accepted: that they were caused by a 'miasm' of foul air which carried the diseases into the body via the nose and lungs. At a time when the atmosphere of cities like London and Liverpool was heavy with the smell of human sewage this was a reasonable view to take. A Liverpool builder called Samuel Holme, a fellow campaigner of Duncan's, told a Royal Commission[16] in 1844 that there were dwelling-places that he could not bear to enter because of the foul smells. Duncan was more emphatic, telling the same body that 'By the mere action of the lungs of the inhabitants of Liverpool, a stratum of air sufficient to cover the entire surface of the town, to a depth of three feet, is daily rendered unfit for the purposes of respiration,' a radical expression of the miasmatic theory.

Duncan devoted the next sixteen years to campaigning tirelessly for the inspection, cleansing and whitewashing of insanitary dwellings and for the construction of an effective system of sewers and water supply. In the ten years after Duncan's appointment, Liverpool built 146 miles of sewers, compared with 30 miles built in the previous twenty years. The sewage was carried to the River Mersey which was not the source of Liverpool's drinking water. The town council bought out two private companies which had been delivering an inadequate supply of fresh water to the town and augmented them with additional supplies from Rivington, north of Wigan. For the first time the growing community had a reliable supply for drinking, cooking and washing, Thomas Hawksley being the engineer who managed the project.[17]

Duncan died in 1863 'worn down by the uneven contest'[18] of struggling with Liverpool's health problems. He was 57 years old. His obituary in the *Liverpool Daily Post* concluded that the health of Liverpool had so improved as a result of his exertions that 'there is therefore no longer any occasion for a medical officer at a salary of £700 a year'.[19] Wiser counsels prevailed.[20] The year after Liverpool appointed Dr Duncan, London appointed its own medical officer, (later Sir) John Simon. London's problems with contaminated water had become much worse than Liverpool's and would demand a more radical solution.

MICHAEL FARADAY

As observed above, the condition of the Thames was the subject of smug self-satisfaction into the 1840s, by which time the capital's sewage had been pouring into the river for thirty years. The problem reached one of its many climaxes in July 1855, when *The Times* published a letter which gave the following account of a journey along the Thames:

Sir,

I traversed this day, by steam boat, the space between London and Hungerford Bridges, between half past one and two o'clock . . . the appearance and smell of the water forced themselves at once upon my attention. The whole of the river was an opaque, pale brown fluid. . . . I tore up some white card into pieces and then dropped some of these pieces into the water at every pier the boat came to; before they had sunk an inch below the surface they were indistinguishable. . . . Near the bridges the feculence rolled up in clouds so dense that they were visible at the surface.

The smell was very bad, and common to the whole of the water . . . the whole river was for the time a real sewer. . . . The condition in which I saw the Thames may, perhaps, be considered as exceptional. . . . I fear it is rapidly becoming the general condition. If we neglect this subject, we cannot expect to do so with impunity, nor ought we to be surprised if, ere many years are over, a hot season gives us sad proof of the folly of our carelessness.

I am, sir, your obedient servant
M. Faraday, Royal Institution, July 7th 1855

Michael Faraday was at that time the most famous scientist in Britain and probably in the world, so his views commanded more attention than do most letters to *The Times*. He was also correct in his warning about 'a hot season'. Three years later, in the hot, dry summer of 1858, the condition of the Thames caused 'The Great Stink' which finally persuaded a wavering government to take action.

'VAGUE, SPECULATIVE, DISQUISITIOUS, UNINTELLIGIBLE SCHEMES'

The problem had not been altogether ignored before 1858. Between 1848 and 1855 six sewers commissions had struggled with the problem of creating a unified system of sewerage for London. Much of their time was spent quarrelling. Personal animosities were so fierce that one commission was disbanded and a new one constituted with the government's representative,

Lord Morpeth, stipulating that 'neither of the prominent parties in the late disputes and differences should reappear in the latest Commission'. To such animosities were added disputes between local authorities about how much each should contribute to the costs of any scheme. Finally, the commissions' unfortunate engineer, Frank Forster, was besieged by advocates of different theories concerning the solution to the capital's problems, many of which were clearly the work of crackpots. He gave the task of evaluating 137 schemes to two of his assistant engineers, Edward Cresy and Joseph Bazalgette. Of these, 116 were given serious consideration while the remaining 21 were described as 'vague, speculative, disquisitious or collateral . . . few of which can be said to possess any practical value'. One of these, submitted

Joseph Bazalgette, *c.* 1865. *(Thames Water)*

under the pseudonym 'Onalar' was described as 'long, unconnected and unintelligible'.[21] Several of the plans, including one from the newsagent W.H. Smith (later to be a Member of Parliament and First Lord of the Admiralty) involved conveying sewage by rail. A later proposal recommended that London's sewage be pumped to Hampstead Heath to the north and Shooters Hill to the south, and allowed to flow away in all directions in order to improve the fertility of the soil. One cannot help reflecting that, had this scheme been accepted, Hampstead would not have become one of London's most fashionable residential districts.

In 1852 the engineer to the commissions, Frank Forster, died, the victim of 'harassing fatigues and anxieties of official duties', according to his obituary.[22] His replacement was one of his assistants, Joseph Bazalgette, who now set about the task of devising a viable plan from the good and bad ideas that he had inherited. Bazalgette, like many other great Victorians, was of French descent.[23] His grandfather, Jean Louis Bazalgette, had arrived in England in the 1770s, having made a considerable fortune in Jamaica. In London he set up in business as a tailor, demonstrating both a considerable ability to make money and an equal capacity for making imprudent loans. He loaned over £20,000 to the Prince of Wales and the Prince's equally improvident brothers, one of whom, the Duke of Kent, was to be the father of the future Queen Victoria. He also loaned money to the Prince's close friend, the playwright, Sheridan, whose capacity for spending other people's money rivalled that of his master. It took an Act of Parliament for Jean Louis to recover most, though not all, of his money.[24] By his first marriage, Jean Louis had three children. One of them was a son, Joseph William, born in 1783. He entered the Royal Navy and was promoted to sub-lieutenant on 15 October 1805, six days before the battle of Trafalgar. He had one son, also Joseph William, the engineer, who was born in Enfield in 1819 and became an articled pupil of the eminent engineer Sir John MacNeill who had himself been an assistant to the great Thomas Telford.[25]

In 1842, aged 23, Joseph set up his own civil engineering practice, specialising in railway work at the height of the railway boom. He was based in Great George Street, off Parliament Square, the 'Harley Street' of the engineering profession where the Institution of Civil Engineers still has its headquarters. As a result of overwork, Joseph became ill but quickly recovered to gain the post first of assistant engineer and then engineer to the sewers commission. He also gained a considerable reputation for competence. When the sewers commission was replaced by a more powerful body, the Metropolitan Board of Works, in 1855, Bazalgette applied to the new body for the post of chief engineer and gave as his referees the great railway engineer Robert Stephenson and the even more celebrated Isambard Kingdom Brunel. Such a combination was hard to beat. He was given the job.

A GOVERNMENT FOR LONDON

The Metropolitan Board of Works was London's first metropolitan government. Prior to that date most of London's local government outside the Square Mile of the City of London itself lay in the hands of vestries, loosely based on parishes, each jealously guarding its own interests regardless of the effects on its neighbours and anxious, above all, to keep down the rates. Overlaying these was a confusing variety of paving and lighting boards and local sewers commissions. The City, of course, under its Lord Mayor, had since medieval times operated quite independently of the rest of the Metropolis. An idea of the confusion which resulted may be gained by examining the experience of the rector of Christchurch, Regent's Park, who had enquired of the government what could be done to improve sanitation in his parish. He was told: 'In the parish of St Pancras, where you reside, there are no fewer than sixteen separate paving boards, acting under twenty-nine Acts of Parliament, all of which would require to be consulted before an opinion could be pronounced as to what might be practicable to do for the effectual cleansing of your parish as a whole.'[26]

The Metropolitan Board of Works had been set up by an Act of Parliament of 1855 to bring some order to this chaotic situation. The board had more authority than the sewers commissions which preceded it but to allay the fears of local vestries that they were being displaced, the board's forty-six members were elected by those vestries rather than directly by the ratepayers. The board remained in office until 1889 when it was replaced by the directly elected London County Council. It was enjoined by the Act to 'make such sewers and works as they may think necessary for preventing all and any part of the sewage of the Metropolis from flowing into the River Thames in or near the Metropolis'. It also had the responsibility for creating new streets, parks and other public spaces. Its powers exceeded anything previously seen in London. It had the right to inspect the construction projects of vestries and to require alterations to them to conform to the board's own plans. It also had the right to levy rates in each vestry area. These powers even extended to the Square Mile itself despite the protests of the city fathers.

BAZALGETTE'S PLAN

Bazalgette was appointed as Chief Engineer to the board on 25 January 1856, within four weeks of its taking office. He had the advantage of familiarity with the schemes which had been considered by the ill-fated commissions and by May he was able to present a comprehensive plan. He did so with a self-effacing modesty that was to become a hallmark: 'Almost every suggestion which can be made upon the subject has been so often repeated in some shape or other that it would be difficult to detect which were the first authors of the various schemes propounded. Having had the advantage of access to all, I cannot pretend to much originality; my endeavour has been practically to apply suggestions, originating in a large measure with others, to the peculiar wants and features of different districts, with which my position has made me familiar.'[27]

A much more flattering verdict was delivered by Sir George Humphreys who, as Chief Engineer to the London County Council, was responsible for maintaining and extending Bazalgette's system seventy years after it was built. Men in such a position do not always offer compliments to their predecessors,

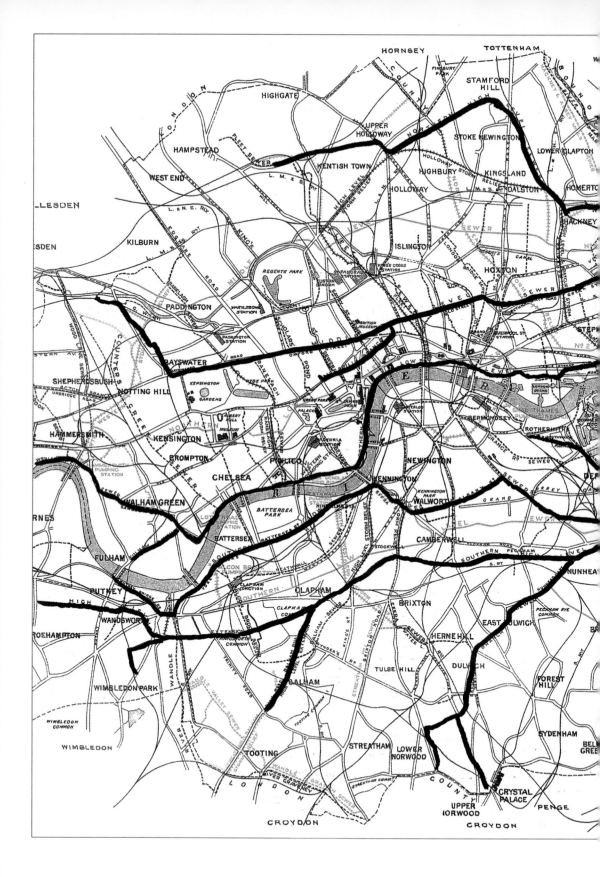

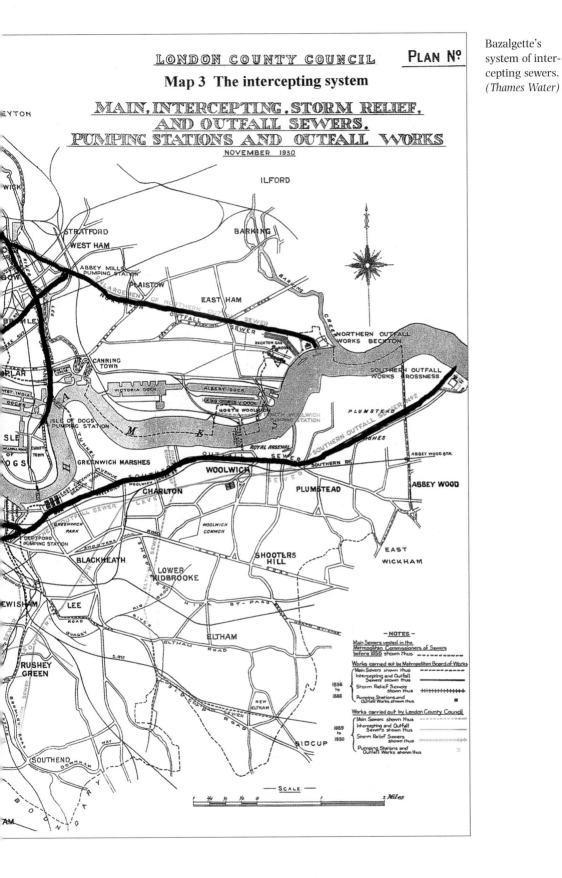

Bazalgette's system of intercepting sewers. *(Thames Water)*

preferring sometimes to complain about a lack of foresight which has made the present incumbent's work so much harder! Commenting on Bazalgette's self-deprecatory statement, Humphreys wrote in 1930: 'This fair and frank statement, disclaiming credit which he considered was not due to him, must not be allowed to deprive Sir Joseph Bazalgette of the great credit to which he is entitled as the engineer who not only evolved a practical scheme out of these various proposals but also carried it out in so efficient a manner that to-day, with trifling exceptions, the whole work is still carrying out the function for which it was created.'[28] It should be added that Sir George's view is still shared by the engineers of Thames Water who operate Bazalgette's system in the twenty-first century.[29]

Bazalgette himself described the arduous and frustrating nature of the task in an interview with *Cassell's Saturday Journal* in 1890, less than a year before his death. He described the problems of routeing a sewer, which must have a gradual and continuous fall, across a network of railways, roads and canals: 'It was certainly a very troublesome job. We would sometimes spend weeks in drawing out plans and then suddenly come across some railway or canal that upset everything, and so we had to begin all over again. It was tremendously hard work. I was living over at Morden then and often used to drive down there from my office at twelve or one o'clock in the morning.'[30]

Bazalgette's plan called for the construction of huge intercepting sewers which would run parallel to the Thames on each side of the river. They may be seen in the diagram on page 140–1. They would intercept sewage and much of the capital's rainwater and conduct both to sewage works at Barking on the north side and Crossness, near Abbey Wood, on the south side. There the sewage would be released into the river at high tide so that the first movement of the sewage would be out to sea. The combined length of the intercepting sewers would be 82 miles. At their western end, where the sewers began, they would be about 4ft in diameter but as they made their way through the capital they would grow in size as they collected more and more waste. In the east end of London their diameter would reach 12ft – larger than the tunnels that would later be built for London's underground railway. In addition, Bazalgette's plan called for the construction of an additional 1,100 miles of street sewers so that all buildings and streets could be connected to his system, thereby preventing any waste from finding its way into London's underground rivers and wells.

As it passes through London, the Thames falls at a rate of 3in per mile whereas Bazalgette estimated that sewage needed a fall of at least 2ft per mile to ensure that it flowed steadily towards the sewage works without causing

Abbey Mills Pumping Station. (Illustrated London News, *1868*)

troublesome blockages. The topography of London meant that this discrepancy between the fall in the river and the fall of the sewers would mean that, as it neared its destination in the east, the sewage would be beneath the level of the river. His solution to this problem was to build huge pumping stations which would lift the sewage into outfall sewers which would take their murky contents on the final stage of their journey. The largest of these would be at Abbey Mills, near West Ham, on the north side and Crossness, near Abbey Wood, to the south. Bazalgette was confident that his proposal would solve once and for all the problem of pollution in the Thames.

Big Ben intervenes

Not everyone shared his confidence. The Act of Parliament which had set up Bazalgette's employers, the Metropolitan Board of Works, required that his plan be approved by a government minister, the First Commissioner of Works. This

The Prince of Wales opening the Metropolitan main drainage works at Crossness: interior of the engine-house. (Illustrated London News, *1865*)

office was held in Palmerston's government by Sir Benjamin Hall who had recently presided over the final stages of the reconstruction of the Houses of Parliament after the destructive fire of 1834. He may have been celebrating the fact that the great bell in Parliament's fine new clock, 'Big Ben', had been named after him though an alternative explanation for this name suggests that it was derived from that of Ben Caunt, an 18-stone boxer of formidable reputation whose retirement from the ring coincided with the installation of the bell. Either way, Sir Benjamin Hall took his responsibilities very seriously when he received Bazalgette's proposals in June 1856. A delay of over two years now ensued while Hall dithered.

Since Sir Benjamin Hall has subsequently been much criticised for the delay, a few words should be offered in his defence. Bazalgette was proposing to construct a system which was unprecedented in its size and scope. He would be using untested techniques and materials. He would need to dig up or tunnel beneath the streets of the world's largest city, thereby causing immense problems for London's traffic. Indeed the expression 'traffic jam' possibly originates with him. Moreover, if the system did not work as Bazalgette insisted it would, then sewage would continue to pollute the river and Hall would be remembered as the man who approved a flawed system. He therefore appointed two independent referees to evaluate Bazalgette's plans. One of the referees was James Simpson, engineer to the Chelsea and Lambeth water companies whose work has been already described.[31] In particular, Sir Benjamin Hall wanted to be reassured that Bazalgette's sewage works were sufficiently far downstream. He was worried lest a really high tide should bring the sewage back into the centre of London.

There now followed a debate between Bazalgette, the referees and Hall which, in the words of a later account took 'a somewhat acrimonious and personal tone'.[32] The referees calculated that Bazalgette needed to extend his system for another 15 miles downstream in order to ensure that no incoming tide ever bore sewage into the centre of the capital. This, they estimated, would cost £5,437,265 compared with Bazalgette's estimate of £2,413,376 for his plan.[33] Bazalgette considered the referees' plan to be an unnecessary extravagance and asked whether the extra cost would be borne by the capital's ratepayers or whether the government would make a contribution. The government demurred. Parliament debated.

The Great Stink

In February 1858 Palmerston's government fell and Sir Benjamin Hall was succeeded by Lord John Manners in the Conservative administration led by the Earl of Derby in the Lords and by Benjamin Disraeli in the Commons. A more significant event, however, was the hot, dry summer which followed and which had been fearfully foreseen by Michael Faraday three years earlier. *The Times* described the consequences in a leading article on 18 June: 'What a pity that the thermometer fell ten degrees yesterday. Parliament was all but compelled to legislate upon the great London nuisance by the force of sheer stench. The intense heat had driven our legislators from those portions of their buildings which overlook the river. A few members, bent upon investigating the matter to its very depth, ventured into the library, but were instantaneously driven to retreat, each man with a handkerchief to his nose. We are heartily glad of it.'

The temperature may have fallen but the point had been made. One of those seen fleeing from the library, handkerchief to nose, was Benjamin Disraeli, Leader of the House of Commons and Chancellor of the Exchequer. 'The Great

Sewer interior. *(Thames Water)*

Stink', as the press dubbed it, concentrated the minds of the government in a way that the disputes of engineers had failed signally to do. On 15 July, Disraeli introduced a bill to the House of Commons which removed the government's veto and gave Bazalgette and the Board of Works all the authority they needed to proceed with the work of constructing the main drainage system. The bill became an act in just eighteen days. The speed with which the bill was passed owed much to fear. At that time the court of Queen's Bench was situated within Westminster Hall, a few yards from the Commons chamber. The business of the court had been interrupted when the foul odours from the Thames which entered the court were described by a surgeon as 'dangerous to the lives of the jurymen, counsel and witnesses. It would produce malaria and perhaps typhus fever.'[34] Later knowledge showed that the surgeon was wrong in his diagnosis but Bazalgette was not complaining.

'The most extensive and wonderful work of modern times'

In the time they could spare from quarrelling with Sir Benjamin Hall and his allies, Bazalgette and his staff had not been idle. He had continued to work on detailed engineering drawings and contract specifications so that, within a few

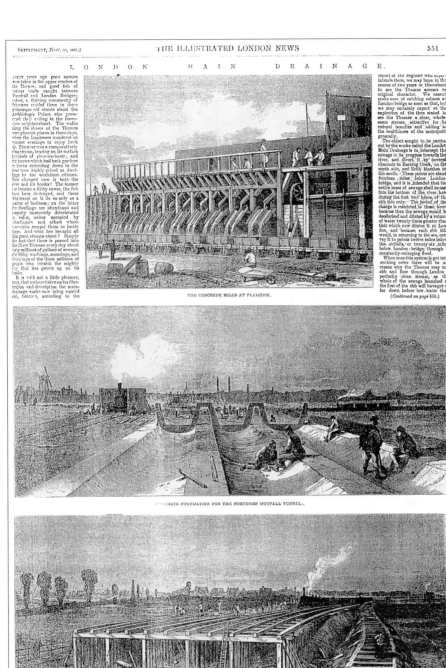

Building the sewer outfall at Barking: this page from the *Illustrated London News*, November 1861, conveys the scale of the operation with a temporary concrete mill and railway to make and convey the materials.

weeks of Disraeli's act reaching the statute book, work had begun. It would take sixteen years to complete and would be the largest civil engineering project of the age, perhaps of any age, carried out under the direction of one engineer. Bazalgette's huge intercepting sewers had to traverse the existing dense network of roads, railways and canals. Usually this was done by tunnelling beneath them as in the case of the New River and the Grand Junction canal but there were occasions when tunnelling would have taken a sewer too low to maintain a steady fall. In such cases roads or railways had to be raised or lowered to enable the sewers to pass. When the northern high-level sewer, beginning in Hampstead, had to cross the Metropolitan Railway without stopping the traffic, Bazalgette designed an aqueduct to be built 5ft above the intended level. It was then lowered into position a few inches above the engine chimneys.

Two problems are worth examining in more detail. All the northern sewers came together in a junction at Abbey Mills pumping station, near West Ham, where the sewage is lifted into 'outfall' sewers for the last few miles of its journey to the sewage treatment works at Barking. This outfall sewer, the largest of them all, had to cross low, marshy ground which was already intersected by roads and railways. A temporary cement works was built at Barking to produce the huge quantities of this material that was required to complete the works. A temporary railway also was built to convey the cement and other materials to Abbey Mills. The Barking and North Woolwich railway lines were lowered to enable the sewer to pass over it and five roads were raised by between 6 and 16ft so that the sewer could pass beneath them. As work on the sewer proceeded, the marshy ground was stabilised and the temporary railway retreated towards Barking. When the sewer was completed, the railway and cement works were dismantled and removed. The top of the outfall sewer is now a pleasant path, cycle track and nature trail through this otherwise rather unattractive part of east London. Very few walkers and cyclists know what is flowing beneath them.

The Victoria Embankment

Bazalgette's second major problem lay in finding a route for the northern low-level sewer which served the most densely populated area. The simplest solution would have been to lay the sewer beneath the Strand and Fleet Street. At the time those streets provided the only direct route from Westminster to the City and were probably the most congested streets in the world. The effect upon

London's traffic of digging them up can scarcely be imagined. Bazalgette therefore decided to create his own land. At that time 'The Strand' was just that – the strand of the river: hence the name. The houses on the south side of the Strand backed directly on to the Thames and owners of such properties could step straight from their gardens into their boats via such steps as those of York Gate, now situated in Victoria Embankment Gardens, a considerable distance from the river. The Thames was thus much wider at that point than it is now.

Bazalgette therefore decided to reclaim thirty-five acres of land to build the Victoria Embankment. This huge structure, stretching for over a mile from Westminster Bridge to Blackfriars Bridge, was designed to meet six pressing needs. First, it was to provide a route for the low-level sewer, the last line of defence against the pollution of the Thames. Second, it provided a service tunnel through which were channelled gas, water and later electricity services. Third, it provided a much-needed road from Westminster to Blackfriars as an alternative to the congested Strand. To round off this part of his work Bazalgette built Queen Victoria Street from Blackfriars to the Bank of England so that travellers could travel from Westminster to the heart of the City on roads entirely built by Bazalgette. The fourth benefit of the Embankment was a

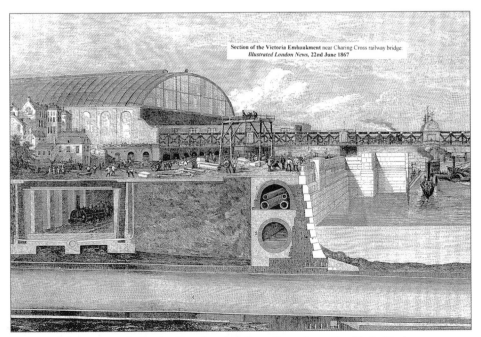

Section of the Victoria Embankment, showing the railway (now the Circle Line), sewers, service tunnel for gas, water and eventually electricity, and a projected pneumatic railway across the Thames which was never built. (Illustrated London News)

route for the District Underground Railway, now part of the District and Circle Line, which was itself seeking a means of connecting Westminster and the City. The fifth amenity was Victoria Embankment Gardens, a much-needed green space in this part of London. Finally, by narrowing the river at this point Bazalgette made it run deeper and faster, helping to keep it clean. Never, perhaps, has one engineering project conferred so many benefits upon a great city. Bazalgette later repeated the exercise with the Chelsea Embankment from Battersea Bridge to Chelsea Bridge.

Planning the Victoria Embankment was difficult enough but building it created unprecedented challenges. For most of its length it was built within coffer dams. Piles were sunk in the riverbed and the gaps between them were filled in with clay and spoil. The water was then pumped out leaving a dry area within which the embankment, and its tunnels, could be built by thousands of labourers armed with picks and shovels. For the stretch between Westminster and Waterloo Bridges the riverbed was too unstable to permit piling so Bazalgette specified the use of caissons. These metal chambers, like boilers without bottoms, were lowered into the riverbed at low tide. Gaps between the caissons were plugged with wooden pegs to make a watertight barrier behind which work could proceed.

Victoria Embankment under construction. (Illustrated London News)

One of the consequences of the vast scale of Bazalgette's projects was a shortage of bricks. He used 318 million bricks[35] in the intercepting sewers alone. In his own words to the Metropolitan Board 'the supply became quite unequal to the demand created by the extensive character of your works, and thus the price of bricks was enhanced from forty to fifty per cent'.[36] Faced with this problem, Bazalgette therefore decided to use a material which was distrusted by his fellow engineers: Portland cement. This combination of lime and clay had been invented in 1824 by a Yorkshire bricklayer called Joseph Aspdin. When properly made, with materials of the right quality processed in the correct way, it was known to be exceptionally strong when immersed in water. However, it had acquired such a reputation for poor quality that engineers like Brunel would not use it. Bazalgette took the bold decision to use the new material but to install his own quality control inspectors to test to destruction every batch. In the words of one of his contract documents: 'All cement that shall not bear, without breaking, a weight of five hundred pounds, at the least, when subjected to this test, shall be peremptorily rejected and forthwith removed from the works.'[37] Bazalgette used almost a million cubic yards of Portland cement in his works. In the process the manufacturers created their own quality control procedures within their own works on the Medway, in Kent, to avoid the embarrassment and cost of having their materials rejected by Bazalgette. Long immersion in water (or sewage) was shown to strengthen the cement, which soon became the industry's standard material.

Public interest

Bazalgette and the Board of Works showed considerable skill in managing their relations with politicians, the public and the press during the sixteen years that the main drainage took to complete. The interest shown by all in Bazalgette's work as it progressed reflects the importance attached to the task of ridding the Thames of sewage. One Sunday newspaper, the *Observer*, had been critical of Bazalgette's plans but in April 1861 it was writing 'It is two years since the most extensive and wonderful work of modern times was commenced.'[38] The *City Press* which had long reflected the resentment of the City of London that the Metropolitan Board exercised authority within its sacred walls, was also won over, writing later the same year: 'Looking at the results attained so far, we must do the Board the justice of uttering our opinion that it has accomplished wonders and if we were to contemplate the transference of its powers to the hands of government we should at the same time entertain grave

Somerset House after the opening of the Victoria Embankment. (Illustrated London News, *1870*)

doubts if the future progress of these immense undertakings would be prosecuted with one-tenth the speed or with anything like the same efficiency.'[39] Even the *Marylebone Mercury*, which had been a long-standing critic of the Board and all its activities and had penned an article in March 1861 headed 'The Uselessness of the Board of Works' was won round. In October of the same year, after a tour of the works by the paper's editor, the paper declared that 'To Mr Bazalgette no tribute of praise can be undeserved.'[40]

Further heights of acclaim were scaled when the Victoria Embankment, containing the great low-level sewer, was opened in July 1870. The importance of the occasion was reflected in the guest list. The opening ceremony was performed by the Prince of Wales who was accompanied by five other members of the royal family, twenty-four ambassadors, virtually every member of both Houses of Parliament and ten thousand ticket holders who watched the event from specially erected stands. The bands of the Grenadier and Coldstream Guards provided a musical accompaniment to the cheering of the excited crowds and *The Times* devoted its main news story to the event, commenting that it 'marked the completion of a work of which it would be difficult to speak in terms of too much praise and admiration. . . . For the principal engineer, of course, it will be a monument of enduring fame, second to none of the great achievements that have marked the Victorian age.'[41] Four years later, following the opening of the Chelsea Embankment, Bazalgette was knighted.

The Victoria Embankment was an impressive structure but it was the invisible and forgotten sewer which really mattered. Four great cholera epidemics had carried off 40,000 Londoners between 1832 and 1866.[42] To these must be added the steady flow of unnumbered victims of typhoid, dysentery and other diseases spread by polluted water. Bazalgette's greatest achievement was to banish these water-borne epidemics from London and elsewhere.

CHOLERA

From the late 1820s the spread of cholera from India across Asia and continental Europe had been the cause of much anxious speculation and comment. It is a particularly unpleasant disease, being characterised by acute diarrhoea and dehydration, usually followed by death within a few hours. The anxiety which followed its arrival in Britain in 1831 (where it first came ashore at Sunderland) was unprecedented since the plagues of the seventeenth century. In 1832 alone, thirty riots were caused by fear of this scourge.[43] In November 1831, early in the first of four epidemics which hit Great Britain, the respected medical journal *The Lancet* reported that a community of Jews in Wiesnitz, Austria, had escaped its effects by rubbing their bodies with a mixture of camphor powder, wine, vinegar, garlic and ground beetles.[44] Between 1845 and 1856 over seven hundred works were published in London alone on the subject of cholera. At the height of the second epidemic in September 1849, *The Times* published a series of articles which explored some of the theories that had been advanced to explain the rapid spread of the disease. These included the 'Telluric' theory which 'supposes the poison of cholera to be an emanation from the earth'; the 'Electric' theory which attributed the disease to atmospheric electricity; and the 'Ozonic' theory which laid the blame on a shortage of ozone. More space was devoted to the 'Zymotic' theory advocated by Justus von Liebig, Professor of organic chemistry at the University of Giessen (and inventor of the Oxo cube). Liebig believed that the putrefaction of bodies afflicted with cholera would produce ammonia which could be 'the means through which the contagious matter received a gaseous form' thereby creating a 'miasma' in the atmosphere which would spread the infection. The word '*miasma*' is derived from a Greek word meaning 'pollution'.

The perils of plums

None of the theories discussed by *The Times* involved polluted water, the real cause of the epidemics. At the time the science of microscopy had not advanced to the point where microbes in water could be identified with certainty. Cholera bacilli in water were then invisible both to the naked eye and to the scientist with his microscope. On the other hand the foul smell of London's air, infected with the odours of its sewage-laden river, was all too evident. In these circumstances it was perfectly reasonable to suppose that the disease was carried in air rather than water. Indeed, as observed earlier, we have the Parliamentarians' fear of airborne disease during 'The Great Stink' to thank for the fact that the deadlock over the construction of Bazalgette's system was broken in the summer of 1858. Liverpool's redoubtable public health campaigner, Dr W.H. Duncan, had expressed his firm belief in the dangers of an infected atmosphere, or 'miasma', in 1844.[45] Another doctor who practised in Liverpool advanced a stranger theory: plums. Dr John Sutherland (1808–91) opened a medical practice in Liverpool in the 1840s. He told the Board of Health that the death from cholera of three German seamen from the Prussian barque *Pallas* was due to the fact that they had overindulged on the cargo of plums they had been transporting from Hamburg to Hull: 'during an epidemic constitution such indulgence is well known to be fraught with extreme danger'.[46]

Duncan and his fellow 'miasmatists' were in respectable company. The great public health campaigner Edwin Chadwick (1810–90) informed a Commons Committee in 1846 that 'all smell is, if it be intense, immediate acute disease'.[47] In 1890, the year of his death, he advocated the construction of an edifice like the Eiffel Tower from which, by some unspecified means, air would be drawn down from a great height with a view to 'distributing it, warmed and fresh, in our buildings'.[48] One of Chadwick's allies was Florence Nightingale (1820–1910) who in her seminal work *Notes on Nursing*, inveighed against the practice of laying drains beneath houses on the grounds that odours would escape from them, penetrate the dwellings and cause measles, smallpox and scarlet fever.[49] That formidable lady went to her grave in 1910 convinced that air was the principal culprit in the spread of epidemic disease.

DEATH'S DISPENSARY.
OPEN TO THE POOR, GRATIS, BY PERMISSION OF THE PARISH.

Death's Dispensary: Open to the Poor, Gratis, by Permission of the Parish. (Fun, *1860*)

John Snow and the Broad Street pump

Others were providing a more thoughtful analysis of the causes of cholera. Dr John Snow (1813–58). a pioneer in the use of anaesthetics during surgery and childbirth, began to practise medicine from premises in Soho in 1843. In 1849 he published a paper 'On the Mode of Communication of Cholera' in which he argued that water polluted by sewage might be the means by which the disease was transmitted. He further argued that the practice of flushing cesspools and sewers into the river made the epidemic worse[50] and developed his thesis in a series of well-argued articles in the *Medical Times and Gazette*. He drew particular attention to the fatal effects of the water-closet:[51] 'If the general use of water-closets is to increase, it will be desirable to have two supplies of water in large towns, one for the water-closets and another, of soft spring or well water from a distance, to be used by meter like the gas.'

During the 1854 epidemic, which killed almost 11,000 citizens, Snow observed a high incidence of cholera among people who drew water from a well in Broad Street (now Broadwick Street, off Carnaby Street), near his Soho surgery. He also noted that workers at the nearby brewery, which had its own water supply, were not affected by the epidemic, despite breathing the same air. Further investigation revealed that a sewer (later found to be leaking) passed close to the well. Snow persuaded the parish authorities to remove the pump handle on the suspect well. This may have made Dr Snow temporarily unpopular but it certainly saved lives. Even so, very few were prepared to believe that the epidemic was caused by infected water despite the evidence of Snow's observations and the inexorable logic of his arguments: 'Rivers always

---

Dr John Snow (1813–58) John Snow was born in York and apprenticed to a surgeon in Newcastle. He became both a vegetarian and a total abstainer from alcohol while a student – an unusual development even in those more abstemious days. He was one of the first to use ether and chloroform as anaesthetics, administering chloroform to Queen Victoria for the birth of Prince Leopold in 1853. He is best remembered for his seminal papers on cholera, though their significance was appreciated by very few during his lifetime. The site of the pump on which he based his observations, now in Broadwick Street, is adjacent to a pub which bears his name. The site of the pump itself is marked by a granite kerbstone and a replica of the pump has been positioned nearby.

receive the refuse of those living on the banks, and they nearly always supply, at the same time, drinking water of the community so situated . . . the water serves as a medium to propagate the disease among those living at each spot and thus prevents it from dying out through not reaching fresh victims..'[52]

Most of his colleagues remained sceptical so in 1857, a year before his early death, John Snow published a comparison of death rates in Lambeth, whose water was supplied by James Simpson's Lambeth Company and the adjacent parish of Southwark, which was supplied by the Southwark and Vauxhall Company. In the 1849 epidemic Lambeth had suffered a slightly higher death rate. In the 1853–4 epidemic Lambeth's mortality rate was *one-sixth* that of Southwark. In the intervening four years Simpson had moved the Lambeth Company's intake to Seething Wells, above Teddington lock, where it was untainted by metropolitan sewage.[53] Snow offered this as further evidence that cholera was water-borne. The marked difference in the mortality rate of the two parishes, breathing the same air, cast further doubt on the 'miasmatic' explanation. Snow recommended the use of filters by water companies, as Simpson was already doing, and the boiling of drinking water during epidemics.[54]

The Whitechapel epidemic

John Snow died in 1858, the year of 'The Great Stink', still surrounded by scepticism. The role of polluted water in causing cholera was at last publicly acknowledged in 1866 when William Farr, statistician to the Registrar General, carried out an investigation into the virulent epidemic which struck Whitechapel in that year. Whitechapel was not yet connected to Bazalgette's system of intercepting sewers. The East London Water Company denied that sewage could enter its reservoirs, yet at the height of the epidemic two customers of the company announced that they had found eels in their water pipes from the River Lea (also spelt Lee). This small tributary of the Thames was still receiving sewage from water-closets, including that of a labourer called Hedges who had died of cholera on 27 June. Farr demonstrated that the epidemic was caused by the company's carelessness in allowing its reservoirs to be polluted by water from the lower reaches of the Lea. Farr wrote to Bazalgette about the pollution of the water supply. Bazalgette responded quickly, telling Farr: 'It is unfortunately just the locality where our main drainage works are not complete. The low level sewer is constructed through the locality, but the pumping station at Abbey

The John Snow public house, Soho, adjacent to the Broad Street pump. Snow was a strict teetotaller. *(Stephen Halliday)*

Mills will not be completed until next summer. . . . I shall recommend the Board to erect a temporary pumping station at Abbey Mills to lift the sewage of this district into the Northern outfall sewer. This can be accomplished in about three weeks.'[55] The temporary pumping station was built and the epidemic ended, though not before 5,596 people had died of the disease in this small area of London. Farr's verdict on the Whitechapel epidemic was damning. In his report he included a reference to the ruthlessness and skill with which the water companies had defended their interests, writing:[56]

As the air of London is not supplied like water to its inhabitants by companies the air has had the worst of it both before Parliamentary Committees and Royal Commissions. For air no scientific witnesses have been retained, no learned counsel has pleaded; so the atmosphere has been freely charged with the propagation and the illicit diffusion of plagues of all kinds; while Father Thames and the water gods of London, have been loudly proclaimed immaculate and innocent. . . . An indifferent person would have breathed the air without apprehension; but only a very robust scientific witness would have dared to drink a glass of the waters of the Lea at Old Ford after filtration.

John Snow was thus posthumously vindicated, though sceptics like Edwin Chadwick and Florence Nightingale remained unconvinced, even after the German scientist Robert Koch had identified the cholera bacillus in India in 1883 and established that it was carried in infected water.

Robert Koch (1843–1910) Robert Koch, an early practitioner of the science of bacteriology, identified the organisms that cause anthrax (1876) and tuberculosis (1882). He visited India and Africa to identify the sources of epidemics. In 1883 he identified the cholera bacillus in India and confirmed John Snow's hypothesis that it was carried in polluted water. Koch's reputation suffered a setback in 1890 when he announced that he had discovered a cure for the scourge of tuberculosis. One-and-a-half thousand doctors enthusiastically gathered in Berlin only to learn that Koch had been mistaken. Nevertheless his pioneering work in the field of bacteriology was widely applauded in both medical and wider scientific circles and in 1905 he was awarded the Nobel Prize for medicine.

By 1868, two years after the Whitechapel epidemic, Bazalgette had almost completed his system of main drainage. Another seven years would pass before the western extremities of the metropolis, around Fulham, were fully connected to the intercepting sewers, but this was a thinly populated area which was less susceptible to epidemics than densely populated areas like Whitechapel. In 1865 the Crossness pumping station, completing the southern drainage, was opened by the Prince of Wales. The four great pumping engines which lifted the sewage into reservoirs from which it could be released to the river were the largest ever built and were named after members of the royal family: Victoria, Prince Consort, Albert Edward and Alexandra. They were in fact so large that when modern replacements were built in the 1950s no means could be found of removing them so they remained in place and are now being restored.[57] Abbey Mills, serving the northern system, was opened in 1868.

The epidemic that did not happen

In 1892 there was a severe cholera epidemic on the continent, especially in Hamburg which traded extensively with London. This caused the greatest anxiety since epidemics had invariably arrived in Britain from foreign seaports. The government commissioned a report on the subject from a Parliamentary Committee and set up a committee to advise on how to deal with the expected mortality. Kaiser Wilhelm II conferred on Robert Koch such draconian powers to deal with the Hamburg outbreak that the Burgomeister complained. The *Illustrated London News* devoted three successive issues to the virulent Hamburg epidemic.[58] In the last of these it printed a dramatic picture entitled 'Death in the Cup' based upon an account by its artist, J. Schonberg who had 'witnessed in a shop where he called to make some purchase, a little girl drinking freely of water, the purity of which may be doubted. A few hours later he was told that this child was dead.' There was no British epidemic. One hundred and thirty-five people died from 'a disease reputed to be of the nature of cholera'. They were spread across sixty-four towns. Seventeen people in the capital died, nearly all of whom had contracted the disease abroad and brought it to London. But they did not pass it on to others. Bazalgette had died the previous year but his system of intercepting sewers ensured that London's drinking water was protected from London's sewage.

Bazalgette made the connection between cholera and efficient sewers before William Farr. In 1865 he described his system of main drainage to the Institution of Civil Engineers, commenting: 'although great differences of opinion existed, and continue to exist, as to the causes of the disease [cholera], yet an inspection of the houses in which deaths occurred was sufficient to show that, however occult the connection between death and defective drainage, the places formerly most favourable to the spread of disease became quite free from it when afterwards properly drained'.[59] London's water was safe.

Bazalgette designed sewage systems for many other communities including Cambridge, Norwich and Budapest, which he visited in 1869 in response to a request by the Burgomeister. He submitted a plan for the City and in his covering letter commented 'No-one can calculate how great the saving of life may be in case the City should be visited by Cholera.'[60] He also designed a system for Port Louis, Mauritius, sending his engineer son Edward to survey the town on his behalf before designing a system of pipes to be made in England and shipped out to Port Louis for assembly there.

By 1896 cholera was so rare in Britain that it was classified in official publications as one of a number of 'exotic diseases'.[61] It continued to plague continental cities with inadequate sewerage systems and remains a threat in less developed countries, particularly Asia and Africa. In the 1990s there have been epidemics in South America, India and Bangladesh and over 106,000 cases were reported to the World Health Organisation in the first nine months of 2002, the great majority being in Africa. It remains a familiar horror in refugee camps and similar communities which lack proper sanitation.

Sir Joseph Bazalgette was not the only Victorian engineer who was building sewers in towns and cities but the scale of his great works mark him as the man who set the standards for the others and developed many of the materials and techniques that they used. The significance of his achievements was well summarised in the closing paragraph of his obituary in *The Times* which appeared on 16 March 1891, the day after his death:

> When the New Zealander comes to London, a thousand years hence, to sketch the ruins of St Paul's, the magnificent solidity and the faultless symmetry of the great granite blocks which form the wall of the Thames Embankment will still remain to testify that, in the reign of Victoria, 'jerry-building' was not quite universal. Of the great sewer that runs beneath Londoners know, as a rule, nothing, though the Registrar-General could tell them that its existence has added some twenty years to their chance of life.[62]

POSTSCRIPT

Bazalgette retired from his post as Chief Engineer to the Metropolitan Board of Works when the board itself was replaced by the London County Council in

Crossness from the air, still protecting Londoners from diseases. *(Thames Water)*

1889. In the last three years of his service he modified the system of sewage discharge to reflect the changes which had occurred in the thirty years since he first designed it. The areas around the sewage works at Barking and Abbey Wood were themselves becoming populated and the residents did not appreciate a 'Great Stink' of their own in the adjacent river. Bazalgette therefore constructed settling tanks at Crossness and Barking where lime and sulphate of iron were added to assist the settling process and reduce the smell. The liquid, thus deodorised, was released to the river and the solids were loaded into sludge boats (one of which was named *Sir Joseph Bazalgette*) which dumped their cargo in the North Sea. This arrangement continued for over a century after Bazalgette's death, until December 1998. Since that date the solids have been incinerated at Crossness and Barking, the energy generated by the process being fed into the national grid as 'green' electricity. The nightsoilmen would surely approve. They recycled London's waste as manure in an agricultural economy. Their successors recycle it as electricity in a world of high technology.

6
WATER, LANDSCAPE AND LITERATURE

Wordsworth and the Lake School

Oh, many a time have I, a five years' child,
In a small mill-race, severed from his stream,
Made one long bathing of a summer's day;
Basked in the sun, and plunged and basked again.

The Prelude, Book 1,
Wordsworth

There was a Boy: ye knew him well ye cliffs
And islands of Winander! Many a time
At evening, when the earliest stars began
To move along the edges of the hills,
Rising or setting, would he stand alone
Beneath the trees or by the glittering lake.

The Prelude, Book 5,
Wordsworth

'Now, my dears,' said old Mrs Rabbit one morning, 'you may go into the fields or down the lane, but don't go into Mr McGregor's garden: your Father had an accident there; he was put in a pie by Mrs McGregor.

The Tale of Peter Rabbit,
Beatrix Potter

William Wordsworth. *(National Portrait Gallery)*

THE LAKE POETS

The 'Lake Poets' are perhaps the best known 'school' in English literature but it has not always been a complimentary term. The founders of the *Edinburgh Review*, Sydney Smith and Francis Jeffrey, denounced them as 'a sect of poets' and that illustrious journal remained hostile to them while praising other Romantic writers such as Keats. Lord Byron once described Wordsworth's poetry as 'namby pamby trash' and wrote a satirical poem called *English Bards and Scotch Reviewers* which lampooned the 'Lake School' of William Wordsworth, Samuel Taylor Coleridge and Robert Southey. He made them an object of a witty attack in his dedication to *Don Juan*.

> You gentlemen, by dint of long seclusion
> From better company have kept your own
> At Keswick, and through still continued fusion
> Of one another's minds at last have grown
> To deem, as a most logical conclusion,
> That poesy has wreaths for you alone.
> There is a narrowness in such a notion,
> Which makes me wish you'd change your lakes for ocean.

A later writer, Norman Nicholson (1914–87), who lived at Millom, on the fringe of the lakes, questioned their links with the district, writing 'They were not indigenous. They were never acclimatised. . . . They remained always separate, alien, self-conscious.'[1]

Despite these strictures the term came to be attached to some of the most prominent figures in English literature. Indeed they have become so celebrated that they have attracted their own parodists, notably Sue Limb's Radio Four series and book *The Wordsmiths at Gorsemere*, a tale of mayhem among literary folk. They include Dorothy and William Wordsmith, who takes long walks with lumps of sustaining pork in his pocket; the lecherous Lord Byro who chases Dorothy sixty-seven times around the house; and the unpredictable Samuel Taylor Cholericke whose time is occupied in preparing and consuming exotic herbal concoctions which render him insensible.[2] It must be acknowledged that only one of the 'Lake School', William Wordsworth, was born in the Lake District itself though his presence alone would be enough to identify the Lakes as a major literary centre which inspired some of the finest poetry and prose in English. The other members of the group, Coleridge, De Quincey and Southey were attracted to the area either by the presence of Wordsworth or for reasons of domestic convenience.

Thomas de Quincey. *(National Portrait Gallery)*

Thomas De Quincey (1785–1859) Thomas De Quincey was attracted to the Lake District by the presence there of Wordsworth, of whom he became an ardent admirer rather than a friend. He was the son of a wealthy Manchester merchant and ran away from Manchester Grammar School before going to Oxford, where he became addicted to opium: a product then freely available from chemists in the form of laudanum, a painkiller. He was introduced to Wordsworth by Coleridge and was invited to Grasmere but was so overawed by the great poet that two years passed before he could summon up the courage to accept the invitation, having written to Wordsworth 'I thus lowly and suppliantly prostrate myself'. When Wordsworth's daughter Catherine died, De Quincey spent two months prostrate on her grave. His increasing dependence upon drugs and his tactlessness made him a difficult guest. He lived in Dove Cottage in Grasmere when the Wordsworths departed in 1809 and scandalised the latter by marrying the daughter of a local farmer after she bore him an illegitimate child, Dorothy's verdict on the union being 'Mr De Quincey is married and I fear I may add he is ruined.' He inherited £2,100, gave £300 to Coleridge, whom he also admired, and squandered most of the rest on opium. He then turned to journalism and offended Southey by suggesting that Coleridge had only married his neglected wife because Southey persuaded him to do so. Southey urged the son of the union, Hartley Coleridge, to give De Quincey a thrashing. With Wordsworth's help De Quincey became editor of the *Westmorland Gazette* and regaled its readers with the philosophy of Immanuel Kant and accounts of Winchester assizes. This venture having predictably failed, he became a regular contributor to the *Edinburgh Review*, moving house frequently and occasionally seeking sanctuary in Holyrood House to escape his creditors. His *Recollections of the Lakes and the Lake Poets* helped to foster the idea of a 'Lake School' and is an interesting, if controversial, first-hand account of that remarkable group and their often troubled relationships. Its 'warts and all' portraits of the personalities and their quarrels exacerbated their antagonisms, especially towards De Quincey himself. De Quincey finally achieved fame, or notoriety, with his autobiographical *Confessions of an English Opium Eater*.

The Romantic Movement

Between them, the Lake Poets (who often conducted venomous quarrels among themselves) constituted a most prominent feature of the Romantic Movement in English literature which asserted itself in the early years of the nineteenth century. It emerged as a reaction to the more ordered values of the classical age which preceded it and whose writers, like Pope and Swift, admired their predecessors of Rome's Augustan period. The publication of *Lyrical Ballads* by Wordsworth and Coleridge in 1798 is an opening landmark in the Romantic revival. This seminal work, in which appeared Coleridge's *Rime of the Ancient Mariner* and Wordsworth's *Tintern Abbey* came to include poems which concerned themselves with simple events and people like Wordsworth's *Cumberland Beggar* and the shepherd *Michael*. These subjects attracted the scorn of the urbane heirs of the Enlightenment in Sydney Smith's *Edinburgh Review*. Wordsworth, in particular, was unapologetic in his advocacy of the primacy of the imagination, the individual and the natural world over those of reason, polite society and the Enlightenment. One writer has described the Romantics as 'prophetic voices crying in the wilderness, dislocated from the social hierarchy'.[3] What better wilderness to choose than the Lake District, the place of Wordsworth's birth?

Moreover, in the years that followed Wordsworth's death in 1850, the Lake District continued to attract a disproportionate number of other prominent writers, some of them being of the first rank in their numerous genres. John Ruskin, Beatrix Potter, Arthur Ransome, Hugh Walpole and many others adopted the Lake District as their home. In more recent years Melvyn Bragg, Hunter Davies and Margaret Forster have been added to their number. Many have used its landscape as a setting for their books. Others adopted its values as their own, to be defended against property developers, railways, industry or even visitors. Wordsworth himself, in his later years, actively opposed the building of railways in the Lake District and the establishment of small industries which offered better employment to the neighbouring shepherds and rural poor about whom he had written. What is it about this watery landscape that has exerted such an influence on the imagination of so many creative minds?

THE FORMATION OF THE LAKE DISTRICT

It is unlikely that they were attracted by the climate. The Lake District has more rain than any other part of the British Isles and the village of Seathwaite,

Castlerigg stone circle, with the gentle outline of the Skiddaw range in the background. *(Stephen Halliday)*

in Borrowdale, enjoys the distinction of being the wettest inhabited place in Great Britain with 125in of rain a year.[4] Both the weather and the abundance of lakes are explained by the geology of the area. In less than 900 square miles there are three distinct geological systems, a unique condition caused by the complex and violent processes by which they were formed.

The three systems run roughly east-north-east to west-south-west. North of a line from Ennerdale Water to Penrith, via Derwentwater, are the Skiddaw Slates, whose landscape is characterised by smooth, rounded hills. It includes Skiddaw itself (3,054ft) and Skiddaw Forest as well as Bassenthwaite Lake which is the only one to carry the word 'lake' in its title. For the others the Old English words 'water' or 'mere' serve the purpose. South of the Skiddaw Slates is the Borrowdale volcanic range which is bounded on the south by a line which begins at Black Combe, near the coast in the south-west. The line then runs north of lakes Coniston and Windermere, to Shap, on the fringe of the Cumbrian mountains in the north-east. In this band of hard, craggy, volcanic rocks are the highest peaks including England's highest mountain Scafell Pike (3,210ft) and Helvellyn (3,116ft). Finally, south of this central area are the Silurian Slates, sometimes referred to as the 'Windermere Group', which stretch through undulating wooded slopes to the coast in the south and towards Kendal in the east. Intruding upon this over-simplified division of the landscape are many other formations such as the Coniston Limestone which forms a barrier between the Borrowdale volcanics in the centre and the southern slopes.

The complexity of the area's geology is such that it attracted the attention of early geologists. The first was a local man, Jonathan Otley (1766–1856), a Kendal watchmaker, who made the first geological map of the area in his *Guide to the Lakes*, published in 1829. The most distinguished Lakeland geologist was Adam Sedgwick (1785–1873) who was Professor of Geology at Cambridge for an unsurpassed fifty-five years (1818–73). He was born in Dentdale, Cumbria where he carried out the early fieldwork which began to establish his reputation as a pioneering field geologist as well as an inspirational teacher.

Some 500 million years ago, during the Ordovician geological era, the area now occupied by the Lake District lay under water. During this period there was a continual deposition of marine sediment which included both rock fragments and organic substances such as fossilised remains and vegetable matter. About 450 million years ago this peaceful, watery scene was interrupted by violent volcanic activity. This phase, which lasted about 50 million years, threw up the Borrowdale volcanic range in the centre which then remained largely submerged as it cooled down once the volcanic activity ceased. The volcanic ash deposited in the water by the eruptions became the attractive green slate found in the area of Honister and Coniston. The waters then rose again, depositing more sediment on the volcanic rocks.

Between 400 and 250 million years ago a complex series of movements in the earth's crust caused the area to be lifted above the sea in a ridge roughly corresponding to the present east-north-east/west-south-west alignment. The same processes caused the intrusion of granite, such as is found at Shap, and the limestone features which are found in some places. At this time the area was joined to the European land mass and enjoyed a tropical climate, the mountains being as high as the Alps. A further uplift occurred about 100 million years ago and, in a final flourish in recent geological time there was a process of 'doming up' whereby the central area of the Lake District rose into a huge dome, traces of which may still be seen from photographs taken from high altitudes.[5] Earth movements had now finished their work in the area but geology still had much to do. Apart from the normal processes of erosion by wind and rain, the district now underwent a period of glaciation. About a million years ago the whole area was covered in ice. As the ice melted,[6] glaciers began to slide down from the top of the dome, gouging deep valleys in the slopes as they made their descent. This explains the radial pattern of the lakes themselves. Look at a map of the district and imagine yourself standing at a point midway between the highest peaks, Scafell and Helvellyn. You would be standing west of the A591 between Windermere and Keswick, in the vicinity of High White Stones (2,500ft). All the major lakes radiate from this 'dome summit'. They begin with Bassenthwaite and Derwent Water to the north and then, moving clockwise, come Thirlmere, Ullswater, Haweswater, Windermere, Coniston, Wastwater, Ennerdale Water and Buttermere. At intervals between the lakes are river valleys, many of these also created by glaciers. You would also observe smaller lakes like Grasmere and Rydal Water or 'tarns', small bodies of water marooned by the glaciers high in the mountains, such as Easedale Tarn near Grasmere or Sprinkling Tarn south of Seathwaite. Wordsworth himself commented on this feature in his own 'Guide to the Lakes', first published in 1810. He wrote that if one could 'stand on a cloud mid-way between Great Gable and Scafell we shall then see stretched at our feet a number of valleys, not fewer than eight, like spokes from the nave of a wheel'. The mountains themselves, springing up suddenly a few miles from the western coastline, are an obstacle to the rain-bearing clouds approaching from the sea. As they encounter this unexpected land mass they rise, cool down and shed their rain on the inhabitants of Seathwaite and other mountain villages. The lakes, thus replenished, provide drinking water not only for the local population but also for cities such as Manchester.[7] The glaciation which formed the lakes also explains another curious feature of the geology: the fact that large quantities of limestone, granite and other rocks are often found deposited in the midst of other rock formations. They were carried to their unfamiliar surroundings by glaciers, sometimes moving hundreds of miles in the process. This phenomenon explains why a geological map of the area can look like a jigsaw puzzle which has been assembled with many pieces in the wrong places.

EARLY VISITORS

The charms of the Lake District and its capacity to inspire the imagination were overlooked by early literary visitors. In the eighteenth century, during the ascendancy of the Augustan poets with their admiration for classical models and the values of the Enlightenment, literary visitors saw only the barren landscape of a wilderness without the beauty. Dr Samuel Johnson declared himself 'astonished and repelled by this wide extent of hopeless sterility' while

Daniel Defoe in his *Tour through the Whole Island of Great Britain* could comment on 'Westmoreland, a country eminent only for being the wildest, most barren and frightful of any that I have passed over in England or even in Wales'. The poet Thomas Gray died in 1771 soon after what Wordsworth described as 'his forlorn and melancholy pilgrimage to the Vale of Keswick' and the remoteness of the area was such that it was the only part of England not visited by William Cobbett on his *Rural Rides*. Charles Dickens, a townsman to the core, complained bitterly about 'the unutterable folly of climbing, undriven, up any steep place in the world' after climbing to the modest summit of Carrock Fell in the northern lakes and yearned for 'nice short walks in level public gardens'. Others, though, found the remote and unyielding landscape attractive. The area is rich in medieval monastic foundations such as Cartmel Priory, Furness Abbey and St Bees whose occupants were no doubt impressed by the numerous stories of early saints who came to the area. St Bees Benedictine Priory was supposedly built on the site of St Brega's (or St Bega's) hermitage, the land for which had been given to the Irish saint in about 900 by a landowner who promised her all the land on which snow fell on midsummer day: an unwise promise to make in an area with such a fickle climate.

WORDSWORTH AND THE LAKE DISTRICT

William Wordsworth was born in Cockermouth, Cumbria, in 1770, the son of a lawyer who was steward to Sir James Lowther (later Lord Lonsdale), a wealthy and irascible member of the local gentry. Wordsworth was the only 'Lake Poet' to be born in Lakeland but his presence there was responsible for drawing Samuel Taylor Coleridge and De Quincey to the area while Robert Southey settled in the area because of family connections with Coleridge.

Wordsworth's mother died when he was 8 years old and his father when he was 13, leaving William, his sister Dorothy and his two brothers in straitened circumstances since Sir James Lowther refused to pay to the orphaned children the money he owed to their late father. This matter was not resolved until Lowther died in 1802 and his successor made a just settlement with the family. In the meantime the children were split up and lived with relatives, except for William who was boarded out at Colthouse, near Hawkshead, where he attended the grammar school. Hawkshead, its nearby lake at Esthwaite and his kind landlady, Ann Tyson, made a deep impression upon the young William. In his autobiographical work, *The Prelude*, he later described the influence exerted upon him at this time by his surroundings. He first reprimands himself for concern with worldly 'meagre novelties' but then explains his recovery from such trivialities:[9]

> Bent overmuch on superficial things,
> Pampering myself with meagre novelties . . .
>> but I had known
> Too forcibly, too early in my life,

Robert Southey (1774–1843) Robert Southey was born in Bristol in 1774, the son of a prosperous draper, and was expelled from Westminster School when his precocious taste for literature found expression in a magazine, *The Flagellant*, which he founded. He went to Oxford and met the slightly older Coleridge (who was at Cambridge) with whom he founded the *Pantisocracy*, a Utopian (and unrealised) community of families who were to live in harmony on the banks of a river in New England. He travelled to Spain and Portugal and, on his return in 1800, settled in the Lake District where he lived for the rest of his life. Coleridge had also moved to the Lakes, drawn by the presence of Wordsworth. By this time Southey and Coleridge were related, Southey having married Edith Fricker in 1795 and Coleridge having married her sister Sara. The two families set up home together at Greta Hall, near Keswick. The awkward Coleridge soon left and Southey, having turned down a job with *The Times* and an invitation to become an MP, settled down to domestic life, with an enormous library, caring for Coleridge's wife and children as well as his own. He and Wordsworth were never close. He once described Wordsworth's view of poetry as 'pile-worts and daffdowndilles through the same telescope' and said that 'to introduce Wordsworth into one's library is like letting a bear into a tulip garden' a remark reported by De Quincey.[8] He earned his living mostly by journalism and by historical works such as his *Life of Nelson* and his *History of Brazil*, a country in which he is consequently better remembered than he is in England. In 1813 he became poet laureate, a post he came to dislike. He was succeeded in the post by Wordsworth and Southey's poetry is now largely forgotten. His most memorable literary work, the story of *Goldilocks and the Three Bears*, is rarely associated with him.

Visitings of imaginative power
For this to last; I shook the habit off
Entirely and for ever, and again
In Nature's presence stood, as now I stand,
A sensitive being, a creative soul.

In this way he records the process by which the natural world, that cornerstone of the Romantic Poets' imagination, took root in his soul and in his poetry which is full of references to the Lake District landscape, its lakes and rivers. In this respect he contrasted his own passions with those of his fellow poet Southey. In some explanatory notes he dictated in 1843 on his poem *The Excursion*, he wrote:

My lamented friend Southey (for this is written a month after his decease) used to say that had he been born a papist, the course of life which would in all probability have been his was the one for which he was most fitted – that of a Benedictine monk in a convent furnished with an inexhaustible library. Books, as appears from many passages in his writings, were in fact his passion and wandering, I can with truth affirm, was mine. . . . Had I been born in a class which would have deprived me of what is called a

The Grammar School, Hawkshead, attended by Wordsworth. *(Stephen Halliday)*

Liberal education it is not unlikely that, being strong in body, I should have taken to a way of life such as that in which my Pedlar [a character in *The Excursion*] passed the greater part of his days.

After leaving Hawkshead School, Wordsworth briefly attended St John's College, Cambridge, before going on a walking tour in France in 1790–1. During his visit to France he was stirred by the early events of the French Revolution, though he later became disillusioned by its excesses. He also fathered a daughter before returning to England and settling for five years in Somerset where he met and befriended Coleridge. In 1795 he had received a legacy of £900 upon the death of a schoolfriend, Raisley Calvert. This money and the final settlement of Sir James Lowther's debt to the family enabled Wordsworth to devote his time to poetry without the need to take up a regular career. In 1799 he moved to Dove Cottage, Grasmere where he lived with his sister Dorothy and subsequently, also, with his wife Mary Hutchinson. They remained in the Lake District for the rest of his life, moving successively to Allan Bank and the Rectory, Grasmere and finally to

Dove Cottage, Grasmere. *(Stephen Halliday)*

Rydal Mount. His comfortable lifestyle owed little to his income from poetry. In 1813 the influence of the Lowther family secured for him the post of distributor of stamps for Westmorland and later Cumberland as well, posts which paid him the substantial sum of £900 a year and enabled him to indulge his love of walking around his native Lakeland. He regularly walked thirty or more miles a day in his capacity as distributor of stamps, composing poetry as he went. Further legacies from admirers followed and in 1842, at the age of 72, he received a civil list pension of £300 per annum, becoming Poet Laureate the following year on the death of Southey. His earnings from his poems were modest in comparison with these other sources and enabled him to maintain his independence from editors and aristocratic patrons who might have required him to leave his Lakeland wilderness for more metropolitan areas.

LAKELAND LANDSCAPE AND POETRY

De Quincey estimated that Wordsworth walked 180,000 miles, adding that Wordsworth's legs 'were pointedly condemned by all the female connoisseurs that I ever heard lecture upon that topic'.[10] On such walks Wordsworth drew inspiration for some of his most celebrated verse. Dorothy recorded in her *Journal* one of their walks along the banks of Ullswater in April 1802:

> When we were in the woods beyond Growbarrow park we saw a few daffodils close to the waterside. We fancied that the lake had floated the seeds ashore and that the little colony had so sprung up. But as we went along there were more and more and, at last under the boughs of the trees, we saw that there was a long belt of them along the shore, about the breadth of a country turnpike road. I never saw daffodils so beautiful. They grew upon the mossy stones about and above them. Some rested their heads upon the stones as a pillow for weariness and the rest tossed and reeled and danced and seemed as if they verily laughed with the wind that blew upon them over the lake; they looked so gay, ever glancing, ever changing.[11]

The famous poem was published in 1804, within two years of this encounter, with its references to tossing and dancing daffodils.[12]

There are many other references in Wordsworth's poetry to the impression made on his youthful mind by the natural landscape of the Lake District, as in the first book of *The Prelude*, entitled 'Childhood and School-time' where he recalls the River Derwent which ran behind his birthplace in Cockermouth:

> the fairest of all rivers, loved
> To blend his murmurs with my nurse's song,
> And from his alder shades and rocky falls,
> And from his fords and shallows, sent a voice,
> That flowed along my dreams.[13]

Later in the same book he reflects upon the joys of a young child playing in a millpond:

> Oh, many a time have I, a five years' child,
> In a small mill-race, severed from his stream,
> Made one long bathing of a summer's day;
> Basked in the sun, and plunged and basked again.[14]

Childhood companionship is then evoked in his description of a day spent with friends skating on a frozen lake:

> All shod with steel,
> We hissed along the polished ice in games
> Confederate, imitative of the chase.

In the same work he addresses the lake of Windermere itself (using the archaic name 'Winander') in an almost mystical evocation of an idyllic childhood:

> There was a Boy: ye knew him well ye cliffs
> And islands of Winander! Many a time
> At evening, when the earliest stars began
> To move along the edges of the hills,
> Rising or setting, would he stand alone
> Beneath the trees or by the glittering lake.[15]

Lakes, rivers and rain-bearing clouds are frequently used by Wordsworth both in his poetry and in some of his most evocative prose. In his *Guide to the Lakes*, first published in 1810 and subsequently much revised, he describes 'clouds, cleaving to their stations, or lifting up suddenly their glittering heads from

behind rocky barriers, or hurrying out of sight with speed of the sharpest edge
. . . a resident in a country like this which we are treating of will agree with
me, that the presence of a lake is indispensable to exhibit in perfection the
beauty of one of these days'.[16] A gathering storm is observed from the summit
of Scafell Pike as 'tiny vapour swelled into masses of cloud which came boiling
over the mountains'.[17]

Rivers, in which the Lake District abounds, had a special fascination for
Wordsworth. As a schoolboy he had noticed how the boisterous mountain
stream that ran through Colthouse grew silent as it passed through the
channel in Ann Tyson's garden:

> And that unruly child of mountain birth,
> The froward Brook, which soon as he was box'd
> Within our garden, found himself at once,
> As if by trick insidious and unkind,
> Stripp'd of his voice.[18]

The series of thirty-four sonnets that he
addressed to the River Duddon occupied a
special place in his affections as he
explained in 1849, the year before his
death, in an otherwise understated account
of his success as a poet. He wrote 'My
sonnets to the river Duddon have been
wonderfully popular. Properly speaking,
nothing that I ever wrote has been popular
but they have been more warmly received.'
The progress of the Duddon from mountain
stream to the sea is a metaphor for human
life itself beginning, in an early sonnet, as
'Child of the clouds: remote from every
taint of sordid industry', passing through a
later sonnet where, in the river itself,

Lakeland stream: 'Child of the clouds, free of every
taint of sordid industry'. *(Stephen Halliday)*

> Declining manhood learns to note the sly
> And sure encroachments of infirmity,
> Thinking how fast time runs, life's end how near!

Finally, in one of the last sonnets, he foresees the reunion of the river with the sea and hence its extinction:

> in radiant progress towards the Deep
> Where mightiest rivers into powerless sleep
> Sink and forget their nature.[19]

At critical moments in his life Wordsworth called upon streams, fountains and rivers to express his feelings. In 1802, as he contemplated the decline of the ideals of the French Revolution which had so inspired him, and England's reaction to it, he used a metaphor of stagnant water to express his despair in one of his most quoted sonnets:

> Milton, thou shouldst be living at this hour.
> England hath need of thee! She is a fen
> Of stagnant waters.

At a critical point in his troubled relationship with Coleridge, Wordsworth wrote *A Complaint* which compared his relationship with his errant fellow poet with a bountiful fountain.

> Your love hath been, not long ago,
> A fountain at my fond heart's door,
> Whose only business was to flow –
> And flow it did; not taking heed
> Of its own bounty or my need.

In 1826, when Wordsworth was faced with the possibility of eviction from his last home, at Rydal Mount, it was to the tiny spring that lay at the corner of his garden that he addressed some farewell lines:

> O pellucid spring
> Insensible the foretaste of this parting
> Hath ruled my steps and sealed me to thy side.

Samuel Taylor Coleridge (1772–1834) Coleridge ran away from home at the age of 7, later attended Christ's Hospital school and proceeded to Cambridge where he acquired an alcohol and opium habit which bedevilled the rest of his life. He joined the Light Dragoons to escape his troubles and was released from the regiment at the request of his family on grounds of insanity. By this time he had met Robert Southey and in 1795 married Sara Fricker, the sister of Southey's wife. Coleridge had met Wordsworth in Somerset in 1797 when the latter briefly settled there on his return from France and the two worked together on the production of *Lyrical Ballads*. Coleridge followed Wordsworth to the Lake District and became disastrously infatuated with Sara Hutchinson, the sister of Wordsworth's wife. In 1804 he abandoned his family to the care of the long-suffering Southey and went to Malta in a vain attempt to rid himself of his dependence upon opium. From time to time he returned to the Lake District, though never to his family, and lived with the Wordsworths who found him an increasingly trying guest, William describing him as 'an absolute nuisance'. Walking and climbing activities in the lakes were interspersed with opium binges and he moved to London to stay in the house of an apothecary in the hope that this would help him to overcome his addiction. His troubled life ended in 1834 and he is buried in Highgate cemetery. *Lyrical Ballads*, which was published in 1798 in association with Wordsworth is regarded as one of the landmarks of the Romantic movement in English poetry so on those grounds alone Coleridge, along with Wordsworth, may be regarded as having been one of its prime movers. Some of his most notable poetry, including the second part of *Christabel* and his *Dejection* ode was written in the Lake District where his son Hartley Coleridge (1796–1849) was brought up. Hartley was himself a poet of some quality but inherited his father's dependence upon stimulants, in Hartley's case alcohol. This caused his expulsion from a Fellowship of Oriel College, Oxford in 1814 and also his death when he fell, drunk, into a wet ditch near his home at Rydal where one of his visitors had been Branwell Bronte, the black sheep of that otherwise distinguished literary family. Hartley died of the bronchitis which followed his night in the ditch and is buried at Grasmere among the Wordsworth graves. (*National Portrait Gallery*)

Rydal Mount, Wordsworth's final home. *(Stephen Halliday)*

The threat to his tenancy passed and Wordsworth lived at Rydal Mount until his death.

Protecting the Lakes

As Wordsworth's residences increased in size and dignity the youthful admirer of the French Revolution turned into a conservative upholder of traditional values and the Church of England. In particular, his devotion to his native Lake District did not extend to any strong inclination to encourage others to visit it. While one may applaud his desire to protect from damage the landscapes that had inspired his poetry it must be said that the language he used was insensitive, even by the standards of the time. He was particularly hostile to 'uneducated persons', urban plutocrats and railways.

In his *Guide to the Lakes* he claimed that, if the 'labouring classes' were given access to the Lakes it would be 'pretty much the child's cutting up his drum to learn where the sound came from'. He added that 'the imperfectly educated classes are not likely to draw much good from rare visits to the lakes . . . we should have wrestling matches, horse and boat races without number; and pot-houses and beer shops would keep pace with these excitements'. The references to 'wrestling matches' was unintentionally prophetic. Such bouts are a feature of the Grasmere games which are now regarded as one of the region's great traditions and it must be acknowledged that 'beer shops' or their modern counterparts are a stronger feature of the local economy than is poetry. His doomed attempt to forestall these developments called upon these invaders to be 'guided by the clergy of the Church of England' and 'after having attended divine worship . . . make little excursions with their wives and children among neighbouring fields', the neighbourhood being that of Bradford, Leeds or Manchester rather than Grasmere.[20] These strictures were prompted by the proposal to build a railway to Windermere for which occasion he wrote to the editor of the *Morning Post* in 1844 and composed a poem which began with the lines:

> Is there no nook of English ground secure
> From rash assault?

He particularly deplored the practice adopted by 'benevolent manufacturers' from Yorkshire and Lancashire of organising day excursions to the lakes for their workforce: 'surely that good is not to be obtained by transferring at once uneducated persons in large numbers to particular spots'. It was

> the Thirst of Gold
> That rules o'er Britain like a baneful star[21]

that was to blame for these assaults on his beloved lakes. Besides railways which brought excursionists, he opposed builders of houses for more permanent residents, especially when they embanked an island on Windermere in such a way as to destroy its natural shoreline: 'unpractical minds receive their impressions only from objects that are divided from each other by strong lines of demarcation'.[22] Other comments have echoes in the twenty-first century. He disapproved of the practice of planting trees which were inappropriate to the landscape which would 'grow up into nothing but deformity' and deplored the closure of small farms, observing that 'in a few years the country on the margin of the Lakes will fall almost entirely into the possession of gentry, either strangers or natives'.[23] The loss of such farms and the traditional way of life they represented was accompanied by the decline of home-based manufactures such as weaving which had traditionally supplemented farming incomes. In the same passage he added:

> By the invention and universal application of machinery, this second resource has been cut off, the gains being so far reduced, as not to be sought after but by a few aged persons disabled from other employment.

The loss of small farms was mirrored by the intrusion of industrial processes upon the rural economy. During Wordsworth's lifetime a substantial industry was created in the Lake District, creating wooden bobbins for the wool and cotton mills in the adjoining counties of Lancashire and Yorkshire. The lakes had the fast-moving streams that were required to power waterwheels and the right kind of coppice wood from which to make the bobbins. The industry survived in the face of increasing difficulties into the 1970s and one still operates as a museum at Stott Park, between Windermere and Coniston, under the management of English Heritage.[24] In Wordsworth's time there were more than sixty such mills employing thousands of workers, some of them orphaned children. Wordsworth observed of these processes that:

> Our life is turned
> Out of her course, wherever man is made
> An offering, or a sacrifice, a tool
> Or implement, a passive thing employed
> As a brute man[25]

and he regretted the decline of home-based industries in the face of factories:

> The Mother left alone, no helping hand
> To rock the cradle of her peevish babe;
> No daughters round her, busy at the wheel,
> Or in despatch of each day's little growth
> Of household occupation.[26]

Towards the end of his life he became an inveterate trespasser upon the lands of invasive landowners in a way that foreshadowed later, organised trespasses like that on Kinder Scout a century later.[27] Wordsworth's resistance to the invasion of his lakes by trippers and industry did not enjoy unqualified support in his own lifetime, even among the local literary community. Harriet Martineau (1802–76) was the daughter of a textile manufacturer from Norwich who had resisted her father's attempts to marry her off and had first come to notice as the author of an article 'On Female Education'. She made a small fortune by writing easily understood books on politics and economics. In 1845 she moved to Ambleside and wrote for the *Daily News*, campaigning for the rights of women, labourers and the poor. She smoked a pipe, brandished an ear-trumpet, walked the fells and wrote, in 1855, a *Complete Guide to the English Lakes*. Unlike Wordsworth she welcomed the coming of the railway to Windermere because she believed that it would benefit the rural poor. Her view of Nature was less romantic than that of Wordsworth. She thought it provided 'rock for foundations, the purest air and the amplest supply of running water; yet people live in stench, huddled together in cabins and almost without water'.[28]

Wordsworth's views in 1844, when he was Poet Laureate, no doubt carried some weight with the *Morning Post* but they did not count for much with the railway companies who were no doubt consoled by the knowledge that he had earlier written a sonnet in praise of 'Steamboats, Viaducts and Railways' when they did not appear to threaten his immediate surroundings:

> In spite of all that beauty may disown
> In your harsh features, Nature doth embrace
> Her lawful offspring in Man's art; and Time,
> Pleased with his triumphs o'er his brother Space,
> Accepts from your bold hand the proffered crown.

The railway was built and in the 1960s the Friends of the Lake District, Wordsworth's heirs as preservers of the natural landscape, successfully fought an attempt to close it, claiming that it had become an indispensable amenity.[29]

Towards the end of his life, in a commentary dictated in 1843 on *The Excursion*, Wordsworth expressed a wish to be buried in the churchyard at Grasmere in accordance with the ancient usages of the district:

> my own body may be carried to Grasmere church after the manner in which, till lately, that of every one was borne to that place of sepulture, namely, on the shoulders of neighbours, no house being passed without some word of a funeral psalm being sung.

His wishes were followed when he died in 1850 and he lies in Grasmere churchyard surrounded by the graves of his sister Dorothy, his wife Mary and his children.

PRESERVATION OF THE LANDSCAPE

After Wordsworth's death others assumed his mantle as protectors of the landscape which had inspired his poetry. One of the most prominent was the influential writer and art critic John Ruskin (1819–1900). Born in 1819, the son of a wine merchant, he later recorded that 'the first thing I remember as an event in life was being taken by my nurse to the brow of Friar's Crag on Derwentwater', an event that he described as 'the creation of the world for me'. In 1871 he went to live at Brantwood, on Coniston Water in the Lake District where he died in 1900. Friar's Crag now has a memorial to Ruskin. He was a published poet by the age of 15, one of his first poems being *Iteriad*, an account of a journey from Windermere to Hawkshead. He gained an MA at Oxford where he later became Slade Professor of Fine Art. He became a friend of J.M.W. Turner whom he defended in *Modern Painters* and supported the Pre-Raphaelites in their return to naturalistic styles of painting. He described great art as 'the expression of a mind of a God-made man'. He advocated medieval styles of architecture, regarding the Gothic style as the supreme expression of artistic achievement. His publications *The Stones of Venice* and *The Seven Lamps of Architecture*, exercised a profound influence on attitudes to architecture and painting as did his monthly *Letters to the Workmen and Labourers of Great Britain*. His ideas inspired the Arts and Crafts Movement and the founders of the National Trust whose first acquisitions were made in the Lake District. He also inspired William Morris's Society for the Protection of Ancient Buildings. With his friend Ruskin's encouragement, Morris created many church windows in the Lake District.[30] He shared Wordsworth's misgivings about industrialisation and devoted the last years of his life to protecting Lakeland from it as Wordsworth had done, advocating smoke-free zones and green belts. He attacked the effects of industrialisation on the working classes for whom he actively promoted art education and public museums. He believed that the superiority of medieval architecture arose from the pleasure the workman took in the act of creation, a quality that he believed was lost by the process of industrialisation. He criticised the efforts of others to apply the principles of good design to mass production. A particular object of his wrath was Sir Henry Cole, first director of the Victoria and Albert Museum, writing that 'Sir Henry Cole at Kensington has corrupted the teaching of art-education all over England into a state of abortion and falsehood from which it will take twenty years to recover.' If his precepts had been followed then well-designed products, produced by hand, would presumably have been available only to wealthy people who could afford them, like Ruskin himself.

When he died in 1900 Ruskin was buried at St Andrew's church, Coniston, and his secretary, William Collingwood (1854–1932), established the Ruskin Museum at Coniston. Collingwood himself was another notable Lakeland writer and artist who settled in a home beside Coniston Water and founded the Lake Artists' Society in 1904. It still flourishes, with an exhibition at Grasmere each summer. He also wrote a guide to the area, *The Lake Counties* which was described by another literary resident, Sir Hugh Walpole, as 'the grandest prose writing about the Lake District in existence'.[31]

A further connection with Ruskin who was unrivalled in his activities in defence of the Lake District was Canon Hardwicke Rawnsley (1851–1920). He was born near Henley and educated at Oxford, where he met Ruskin, whose biography he wrote and who became a lifelong friend and influence.

Sir Hugh Walpole (1884–1941) Hugh Walpole was born in New Zealand, the son of a bishop but he came to England at the age of five and lived in the Lake District from 1924 until his death in 1941. By that date he was already a reasonably well-established novelist but his most popular and memorable works were his Cumberland family saga, the *Herries Chronicle*, consisting of four novels written in the 1930s and set in the Cumbrian village of Watendlath, in Borrowdale. They were written while Walpole was living at a house nearby called Brackenburn, overlooking Derwentwater. It was built of local Honister slate and enlarged by Walpole to include his library of 30,000 books and his collection of paintings. Arthur Ransome was among the many well-known writers who visited Brackenburn at a time when Walpole was at the height of his fame. He never fully recovered from Somerset Maugham's cruel caricature of him as the egregiously pushy and ingratiating popular novelist Alroy Kear in Maugham's *Cakes and Ale*. He retained his deep affection for the Lake District where he died in 1941 and was buried in Keswick. His diaries and the manuscripts of many of his now largely forgotten novels are housed in the Keswick Museum and Art Gallery.

In 1877 Rawnsley became vicar of Wray church near Ambleside and soon became involved in campaigns to protect the distinctive character of the Lake District against the railways and gentrified bungalows that had aroused Wordsworth's hostility. Rawnsley formed the Lake District Defence Society (later called the Friends of the Lake District) which numbered Tennyson, Ruskin and Browning among its members. He also campaigned against the growing practice of sending 'improper' postcards! His early writings were concerned with this cause though he also wrote 30,000 sonnets. He spent the rest of his life in the Lake District. In 1884 he formed the School of Industrial Art in Keswick which encouraged traditional local craftsmanship and in 1895 he was one of the founders of the National Trust. Beatrix Potter's father was the Trust's first life member and Rawnsley, as the Trust's first Honorary Secretary, raised the money to buy the Trust's first purchase, Brandlehow Wood, Derwentwater. He erected a monument to Wordsworth in Cockermouth, the poet's birthplace, and the monument to Ruskin at Friar's Crag, Keswick. In 1909 he bought Greta Hall, the former home of Coleridge and Southey and in 1913 he bought the Neolithic Castlerigg stone circle, near Keswick, one of the earliest in Britain. In 1917 he retired to another of his properties, Allan Bank, in Grasmere, a former home of Wordsworth. He died there in 1920, leaving the property to the National Trust, having made an unsurpassed contribution to the preservation of the Lake District's natural and literary heritage.

BEATRIX POTTER (1866–1943)

Rawnsley's greatest contribution both to the literary standing of the Lake District and to its preservation was his role in encouraging the young Beatrix Potter in her writing. Born in Kensington to wealthy and excessively protective parents, Helen Beatrix Potter never went to school. Her loneliness was relieved by her collection of pets and by a developing interest in the natural world which expressed itself in collecting and drawing fungi. She also compiled a journal in such an elaborate code that it was not deciphered until twenty years after her death, when it was published as *The Journal of Beatrix Potter* (1966). In 1882, aged 16, her parents took her on holiday to the Lake District which the family regularly revisited over the following twenty years. The guests they entertained included the local vicar, Hardwicke Rawnsley, who admired Beatrix's drawings of the squirrels, rabbits and other flora and fauna that she saw in the Lake District. He made a deep impression on the lonely young girl with his writings and his commitment to preserving the beauties of the area which she had come to love. He encouraged Beatrix's writings and contributed to an early version of *The Tale of Peter Rabbit* with drawings by Beatrix. Back in London Beatrix made greetings cards of her drawings and in 1893 she began *The Tale of Peter Rabbit* in a letter to the small son of her former governess. Rawnsley encouraged Beatrix to seek a publisher for her stories and, after some initial setbacks, Frederick Warne began to publish them in 1902. Her first major success was *Squirrel Nutkin* in 1903 which featured drawings of the countryside around Derwentwater.

Beatrix Potter (Mrs Heelis). *(National Portrait Gallery)*

Hill Top Farm, Beatrix Potter's home. *(Stephen Halliday)*

Herdwick Sheep. (*Simon Halliday*)

The royalties she was now earning enabled her to buy a field at Near Sawrey, soon followed by further purchases of farms nearby. Hill Top Farm became her principal home after 1905 and she eventually owned fourteen farms and 4,000 acres of land. Many of her books were based around Hill Top Farm which she made the home of Tom Kitten, Jemima Puddleduck and Samuel Whiskers. In 1913, aged 47, she married a local solicitor, William Heelis. In the 1920s she became an expert in breeding the local Herdwick sheep, winning many prizes and helping to preserve this unique and hardy breed. In 1934 she gave many of her drawings to the Armitt library in Ambleside and on her death in 1943 she left her sheep and most of her property to the National Trust. Her husband's office in Hawkshead became the Trust's *Beatrix Potter Gallery* where her original drawings for her books are exhibited. At the time of her death in 1943 she had published more than forty books and she has acquired a worldwide following. Thousands of Japanese visitors, in particular, make the journey to Hill Top Farm which rivals Dove Cottage as the most visited literary shrine in the Lake District. Beatrix Potter made her own contribution to the local cult of Wordsworth when she identified the house in Colthouse in which the young Wordsworth had been the lodger of Ann Tyson during his schooldays at Hawkshead.

ARTHUR RANSOME

Another children's writer who made his home in the area and set his stories on its lakes was Arthur Ransome (1884–1967) who was born in Leeds. His father, a professor of history, carried him to the summit of the Old Man of Coniston when Arthur was only a few weeks old and his childhood holidays were spent at Nibthwaite on Coniston's shores. After his education at a preparatory school in Windermere and at Rugby he joined a London publisher and became friendly with W.G. Collingwood, Ruskin's secretary, who lived by Coniston Water. Ransome then became a foreign correspondent of the *Manchester Guardian* in which capacity he travelled to Russia to report on the events of the

Arthur Ransome. *(National Portrait Gallery)*

William Heelis's office, now the Beatrix Potter Gallery. *(Stephen Halliday)*

Russian Revolution of 1917. He became an admirer of Trotsky and married Trotsky's secretary, Evgenia, who returned with him to England. In 1925 he bought Low Ludderburn, an old farmhouse at Cartmel Fell, east of Lake Windermere, living in the Lake District for most of the rest of his life. In 1916 he had published his first work, *Old Peter's Russian Tales*, based on Russian folk stories but he returned to his beloved Lake District for his first, and most famous, children's books, the *Swallows and Amazons* tales which he began to publish in 1930. The stories reflect his love of camping, sailing, fishing and other water-borne activities. Many of the locations mentioned in his books may be identified with his childhood holidays on Coniston, including Peel Island which in his books became *Wildcat Island* and the steam yacht which sailed around the lake and features in several of his stories. The yacht, *The Esperance*, may be seen at the Windermere Steamboat Museum at Bowness. His last home was at Hill Top, Haverthwaite (not to be confused with Beatrix Potter's Hill Top Farm a few miles distant). On Arthur's death his widow, Evgenia, donated many of his belongings to the Museum of Lakeland Life and History in Kendal which has a Ransome Room. The museum is now the headquarters of the Arthur Ransome Society. His stories are also popular in Japan from which many visitors come each year to visit the Lake District haunts they describe.

LIVING WRITERS

The Lake District continues to attract more than its share of writers, many of whom place their stories in Lakeland. Melvyn Bragg was born in Wigton, Cumbria in 1939 and studied history at Wadham College, Oxford before embarking upon a productive career as writer and broadcaster. He is best known as the presenter of arts programmes on television, notably *The South Bank Show* and an account of the eventful history of the English language and for ten years he presented Radio Four's *Start the Week*. He is also a prolific author who has set many of his novels in his native Lake District. They include *The Maid of Buttermere* and *The Soldier's Return* which is set in his birthplace, Wigton. He has also written about the geology of the Lake District in *The Land of the Lakes*. In 1998 he was made a life peer and took the title 'Lord Bragg of Wigton'. He still has a home in the Lake District.

Hunter Davies was born in Scotland in 1936 but was brought up in Cumbria. As a journalist he has written for the *Sunday Times*, *Punch* and *New Statesman* and has written many books about the Lake District and its inhabitants, notably *The Good Guide to the Lakes* and *Beatrix Potter's Lakeland* as well as a biography of William Wordsworth. He is President of the Cumbria Wildlife Trust and has a home in Cumbria. He is married to the writer Margaret Forster who was herself born in Carlisle and who has set books in the area, notably *Precious Lives*, and *Rich Desserts and Captain's Thin: a family and their times, 1831–1931*, an account of a Quaker family called Carr who set up a biscuit-making factory in Carlisle which became a nationally known baking business.

LANDSCAPE AND LITERATURE

Why is it that this remote part of England, with its forbidding climate, has attracted a greater concentration of writers, both as residents and as settings for their work, than any comparable part of the kingdom? Why have writers as diverse as William Wordsworth, Beatrix Potter and Melvyn Bragg found inspiration in its mountains and its lakes and striven so hard to preserve them? Perhaps the final words on the matter should be left to Wordsworth, Lakeland's greatest son. In his autobiographical poem *The Prelude, or the Growth of a Poet's Mind* Wordsworth makes explicit references to the influence exerted upon his imagination by his native Lakeland. His poetry and prose are filled with references to lakes, rivers, clouds and the landscape of which they are part. The last few lines of his ode *Intimations of Immortality, from Recollections of Early Childhood* expresses better than could anyone else the depth of Wordsworth's feelings about the landscape and its influence on him:

> I love the Brooks which down their channels fret,
> Even more than when I tripped lightly as they;
> The innocent brightness of a new-born Day
> Is lovely yet;
> The Clouds that gather round the setting sun
> Do take a sober colouring from an eye
> That hath kept watch o'er man's mortality;
> Another race hath been, and other palms are won.
> Thanks to the human heart by which we live,
> Thanks to its tenderness, its joys, and fears,
> To me the meanest flower that blows can give
> Thoughts that do often lie too deep for tears.

POSTSCRIPT: 'DAFFODILS' (1804)

I wandered, lonely, as a cloud
That floats on high o'er vales and hills,
When all at once I saw a crowd,
A host, of golden daffodils;
Beside the lake, beneath the trees,
Fluttering and dancing in the breeze.

Continuous as the stars that shine
And twinkle on the milky way,
They stretched in never-ending line
Along the margin of a bay;
Ten thousand saw I at a glance,
Tossing their heads in sprightly dance.

The waves beside them danced; but they
Outdid the sparkling waves in glee:
A poet could not but be gay,
In such a jocund company:
I gazed and gazed but little thought
What wealth to me the show had brought.

For oft, when on my couch I lie
In vacant or in pensive mood,
They flash upon that inward eye
Which is the bliss of solitude;
And then my heart with pleasure fills,
And dances with the daffodils.

7

'TAKING THE WATERS'

Water, Health and Recreation

There is nothing at all in this boasted system. Medicated baths can be no better than warm water. Be sure that the steam be directed to thy *head*, for *that* is the *peccant* [defective] part.

> *Dr Samuel Johnson on the supposed effects of spas*

Nash is much caressed, and everyone seems to submit with delight, so much is he esteemed by the regulations he imposes with regard to decorum and the economy of the place.

> *Daniel Defoe, writing of the impact of Beau Nash on Bath*

The water contains an aetherial essence which is lost when transported elsewhere; it cannot be contained in bottles as it will pass through the corks.

> *Dr William Oliver, inventor of the Bath Oliver biscuit, on the impossibility of retaining the unique qualities of Bath water when bottled*

ENTREPRENEURS, QUACKS AND CHARLATANS

In 1850 there were about 250 'spas' in Great Britain where Victorian citizens, in search of a cure for a real or imaginary illness, could 'take the waters'. They ranged from major spas which underpinned the local economy, like those at Bath and Cheltenham, to very small concerns like that in the Saxon hamlet of Dorton, in Buckinghamshire, which struggled for decades to attract visitors before falling into disuse in the nineteenth century. Visitors could take the waters either by drinking them or by immersing their bodies in liquids of sometimes doubtful quality whose temperature could vary from very warm to near freezing. There was some scientific basis for the cures offered by many spas but these came to be overlaid by extravagant claims, some of which continued to be made well into the twentieth century. The spa at Clifton, for example, claimed to be able to cure diabetes, while some of the 'cures' were of illnesses unknown to medical science. The spa fraternity attracted a remarkable gallery of entrepreneurs, quacks and charlatans while drawing patrons as sophisticated as Charles Darwin and as sceptical as Charles Dickens. Given the rudimentary state of medical knowledge at the time and the astounding claims that were made for many spas, it is surprising that there were not more casualties in a process that often depended more upon credulity than medical science. Nor were the treatments cheap. Water could cost as much as 6*d* a glass, cold baths 1*s* and warm baths twice as much when 5*s* was a day's wage for a skilled bricklayer. In the twentieth century, as medical knowledge advanced and the popularity of spa treatments declined, the seaside took over as the principal means by which the population took to the water for reasons of health and recreation. Blackpool, Southend and Broadstairs took over from Bath, Harrogate and Leamington, and with a very different clientele. Mr Pooter went to Broadstairs in search of diversions which were quite distinct from those for which Mr Pickwick visited Bath.[1]

BY ROYAL APPOINTMENT

Some of the myths went back a very long way. Bath claimed to have been founded in *c.* 850 BC by King Bladud[2] who was supposedly cured of leprosy by the waters into which his pigs wandered - the leprous pigs themselves being cleansed of this human affliction at the same time. Bladud is also credited with learning to fly with wings he made from feathers, and with founding a university at Stamford which later migrated to Cambridge. This busy king was succeeded by his son, King Lear, when his wings failed him and he crashed on New Troy. The Romans, who discovered the warm springs and called the city *Aqua Sulis*, were thus comparative latecomers to Bath according to this tale. The departure of the Romans did not mark the end of Bath's reputation as a centre for cures. In the following centuries it was known by the Saxons as *Akemanceaster*, 'Sick man's town'.

The Bladud story, with its royal connections, was prescient of much of the mythology that came to surround some of the spas in the years of their ascendancy. In the sixteenth century Mary, Queen of Scots, was allowed brief respites from her imprisonment at Wingfield Manor, in Derbyshire, to visit the spa at Buxton which the Romans had called *Aquae Arnemetia*. Other royal patrons followed, in a pattern that was to become familiar. Charles II took his Portuguese wife, Catherine of Braganza, to Tunbridge Wells in the 1660s in the hope that it would cure her infertility, having previously entertained the undoubtedly fertile Nell Gwynn at the same spa. Queen Anne, his niece, took the waters at the salt springs at Droitwich in Worcestershire for the same reason. The Droitwich waters were ten times as salty as sea water and four times as dense as the waters of the Dead Sea. Anne duly gave birth to seventeen children but sadly, none survived her.

The word 'spa' derives from the small Belgian town of that name in the Ardennes which was home to a Roman spa whose waters had been bottled and exported since 1583. Spa waters may broadly be divided into four categories, each with its own applications. The first group, the 'saline' waters include such minerals as magnesium sulphate, or Epsom salts, and are used as purgatives. The second group, originally known as 'Chalybeate' (pronounced Kali–bee–att) are rich in iron compounds and can be used as restoratives for conditions such as anaemia. The third group are the 'sulphur' waters which are recommended for skin conditions and are often found in areas affected by volcanic activity. Modern prescriptions for acne sometimes contain sulphur. Finally there are the waters which contain very few 'foreign' minerals. Malvern water, when analysed in the nineteenth century, was found to be in this category, to the great consternation of the entrepreneur, Dr John Wall, who had made the analysis. He had hoped to place the reputed medicinal powers of Malvern's Holy Well in one of the recognised categories. The hardness of the surrounding rocks was such that they did not dissolve in the water. Undaunted, Dr Wall marketed the water for its purity.[3]

Further misunderstandings arose over the beneficial effects of seawater. Ozone, a pungent form of oxygen which was identified in 1839, was believed to have properties beneficial to health. This was mistaken. Ozone is beneficial as a filter in the stratosphere against solar radiation but can cause serious respiratory problems at ground level. It was further mistakenly believed that ozone was given off by sea air because it bore a similar smell to that of decomposing seaweed. Thus was born a powerful myth.

In his new enterprise at Malvern the resourceful Dr Wall was assisted by the work of some predecessors who had helped to establish the new practice of hydrotherapy. One of the earliest was Dr James Currie (1756–1805) who studied medicine at Edinburgh and Glasgow, practised as a physician in Liverpool from 1780 and became a Fellow of the Royal Society in 1792. He was a pioneer in the use of the clinical thermometer and in the treatment of fevers, on which subject he had published *Medical Reports on the Effects of Water, Cold and Warm, as a Remedy in Fever*.[4] He advocated the consumption of copious amounts of water for people suffering from fevers. A later and more ardent advocate of hydrotherapy was Vincenz Priessnitz (1799–1851). The son of a farmer from Jesenik in Austrian Silesia (now in the Czech Republic), Priessnitz had little schooling and was probably illiterate. As a result of early experience with sick animals he came to believe that water, applied in a variety of ways, could be used as a remedy for many, if not most illnesses. It could be drunk, used for bathing (especially if cold), used as a cold compress, administered as a jet or used to soak sheets in which the hapless patient would be wrapped. His theories appear to have been based upon the four 'humours' of Hippocrates upon which ancient medicine was based – blood, phlegm, black bile and yellow bile – and a belief that water could cause them to assume the right balance. He founded a

Southend Kursaal is not used for cures, rather for entertainment. *(Stephen Halliday)*

hydrotherapeutic establishment in his home town, Jesenik, which apparently effected a number of cures. These may have owed much to nourishing food and exercise applied to reasonably healthy patients since sick people would probably have wilted in the face of Priessnitz's Spartan regime but his reputation was established and the spa he founded still flourishes.

The popularity of spas on the continent, especially in Germany, led to the adoption not only of Priessnitz's theories but also to the entry of German vocabulary into the practice of hydrotherapy. The word '*Kursaal*' in German means a room in which people take cures but many English establishments used the word to signify a place of ancillary entertainment. Thus Harrogate had its Kursaal where a brass band was required to play in all weathers, sometimes wearing mittens, their noses blue from the cold.[5] In Southend, where Londoners were encouraged to take to the sewage and salt water of the Thames estuary, the Kursaal soon became a rival to the beaches as a funfair and survives as a shopping precinct and housing development.

THE ENTREPRENEURS

In the early nineteenth century the rapid development of spas may be attributed to two factors. The first was the rudimentary state of medical science. Doctors could do little more for their patients than put them to bed, feed them beef broth or, in extreme cases, cut bits off them. At that time drugs were almost unknown. The most widely used, as painkillers, were various forms of opium. The most common of these was laudanum, a form of opium mixed with alcohol or sugar and water that was readily available from chemists. It was used for almost any condition including headaches, the sedation of peevish infants and tuberculosis. It was also, of course, addictive as Thomas De Quincey and Samuel Taylor Coleridge discovered to their cost.[6] In the circumstances it is not surprising that patients suffering from real or imaginary illnesses were susceptible to the blandishments of medical entrepreneurs who were prepared to offer alternative 'cures' for a wide variety of conditions in attractive and comfortable surroundings. Not everyone was convinced. Dr Samuel Johnson declared that 'There is nothing at all in this boasted system. Medicated baths can be no better than warm water' and when his listener doubted the advice, Johnson added 'Be sure that the steam be directed to thy *head*, for *that* is the *peccant* [defective] part' (his italics).[7]

The second factor which promoted the rise of the spas was the ruthless enterprise of the entrepreneurs who owned them. Endorsements from reputable

A view of the Beulah spa, Norwood. *(Corporation of London)*

authorities and, where possible, a royal connection, were eagerly sought and where necessary they could be fabricated. Thus the proprietor of the spa at Bishopston, near Stratford-upon-Avon, persuaded a professor of chemistry to write a favourable report on its waters and then arranged to open the facility on Princess (soon to be Queen) Victoria's 18th birthday on 24 May 1837. This gave him the excuse to name the enterprise 'The Victoria Spa'. The name survives as a small hotel though the spa itself failed to flourish. The proprietor of Beulah Spa, near Norwood in south London, sent a sample of its water to the eminent scientist Michael Faraday who confirmed that it contained magnesium sulphate (Epsom Salts) and declared it 'distinguished for the quantity of magnesia in it, resembling but far surpassing in this respect the Cheltenham waters'. The proprietor, John Davidson Smith, engaged the architect Decimus Burton, designer of the Palm House at Kew, the Wellington Arch at Hyde Park Corner and London Zoo's Giraffe House to build some elegant buildings to accommodate visitors and covered the well itself with a structure like a Red Indian Wigwam. The normal entrance fee was 1s or 2s and 6*d* on gala occasions. For the opening of the 1838 season Smith organised a horticultural exhibition and engaged the services of Johann Strauss's orchestra to entertain the visitors and charged 5*s*: a day's wage for a skilled worker.[8] In other places more ruthless methods were employed to promote the interests of individual proprietors. The 'Old Well' at Epsom had long been known for its purgative water, containing Epsom Salts, so in 1706 an apothecary called Levingtone bored a new well some distance from the old, advertised its curative properties and laid on an inn, shops and gambling rooms. When the enterprise flourished he bought and closed the old well and added cock-fighting and horse-racing to the entertainments. The new well did not outlive its founder but the horse-racing thrived, on Epsom Downs.[9]

BEAU NASH AND BATH

Others were more imaginative, and more successful, in the promotion of their spas. Bath's original Roman Baths lay mostly hidden until 1879 but the spa had enjoyed a modest prosperity since the reign of Elizabeth I when there were three baths in use. They later enjoyed the patronage of Queen Anne who took the waters there in hope of a cure for dropsy and gout. Its fortunes were transformed after 1705 when Beau Nash became Master of Ceremonies. Born in 1674 in Swansea, Richard 'Beau' Nash had studied at Oxford, briefly served in the army and dallied with the law though he earned his living mostly by gambling. The previous Master of Ceremonies, Captain Webster was an early example of a local authority entertainments manager. He organised spectacles and activities for the (mostly perfectly healthy) visitors who came to immerse themselves in Bath's pools before spending their days gambling, drinking chocolate or dancing. Webster lost his job when he became involved in a duel and Nash, his assistant, was invited by the civic fathers to take over. He persuaded the royal physician to recommend Bath's waters for drinking as well as bathing, thus opening up a market for new visitors at 6*d* a glass.

Nash banned swearing and the wearing of swords in public, to discourage aristocratic quarrels and the duelling that had dislodged his predecessor. He engaged the services of musicians from London to play at the baths and at dances in the evenings where his own rules of dress and decorum were imposed. He inspected lodging houses, regulated their prices and threatened to close them down if their standards fell. In the seventeenth century 'taking the waters' had been primarily an aristocratic pursuit of people like Lord Chesterfield who visited Bath to cure his deafness but many of Bath's

Richard 'Beau' Nash. *(National Portrait Gallery)*

newcomers were middle class, attracted by the leisure facilities that the town offered and by the opportunity to learn the social graces under Nash's expert tutelage. In 1708 Nash engaged Thomas Harrison to build assembly rooms for dancing and gambling. Bath was now the most fashionable watering place in Britain and attracted visitors from the continent. In his *Tour Through the Whole Island of Great Britain* Daniel Defoe recorded that Nash 'is much caressed, and everyone seems to submit with delight, so much is he esteemed by the regulations he imposes with regard to decorum and the economy of the place'. Like others, Nash was alert to the advantages of royal patronage. When the Prince of Orange visited Bath in 1734 Nash was quick to name the 'Orange Grove' after him as a permanent reminder of the royal visit. His success at Bath was such that, in 1735, he accepted an invitation to add to his responsibilities the post of Master of Ceremonies at Tunbridge Wells.

Nash was not without a conscience. He promoted the building of the Mineral Water Hospital for the poor, one of whose first physicians was Dr William Oliver (1695–1764), inventor of the 'Bath Oliver' biscuit. Dr Oliver's income depended upon paying customers coming to the town so he opposed the practice of bottling Bath's water for sale elsewhere, explaining that 'The water contains an aetherial essence which is lost when transported elsewhere; it cannot be contained in bottles as it will pass through the corks'. The hospital later became the 'Royal National Hospital for Rheumatic Diseases' which continues to serve the population of Bath. The spa treatment centre itself closed in 1976 though a hydrotherapy pool is now a prominent feature of the hospital's facilities.

Nash died in 1762, having been rendered destitute by prohibitions on gambling but he was buried with great ceremony in Bath Abbey. Bath itself continued to flourish and attracted celebrity architects as well as distinguished visitors. A new bathhouse was built by Decimus Burton.[10] Middle-class families were further encouraged by the introduction of cheaper 'family tickets' for the facilities at Bath and elsewhere and the town appears in the work of Jane Austen who herself lived in Bath for a while. The range of entertainments continued to expand under the rule of Nash's successors. Cricket and archery contests were arranged, German (i.e. brass) bands played, puppet shows and circuses came to town and in 1832 they were visited by Madame Tussaud and her waxworks, on tour from her London base. More exotic attractions included ascents by hot-air balloon and the town must have rejoiced when it was visited by Mr Pickwick and friends in Charles Dickens's *Pickwick Papers*. The character of the town may be judged from the 1801 census, in which 34 per cent of the population were described as servants and its success is evident from the fact that, in 1811, it was the twelfth town in England measured by the size of its population.

MALVERN AND DR GULLY

Malvern was almost equally adept at exploiting its waters though its most successful medical entrepreneurs fell out among themselves, one of them becoming involved in a notorious scandal. The waters of its Holy Well had claimed healing properties since medieval times and had been granted by Elizabeth I to John Hornyoed in 1558.[11] The water was bottled from about 1622. There was little further development until John Wall (1708–76), an enterprising physician from Worcester Infirmary analysed the water in 1745, probably expecting to find that it contained sulphur, iron or salts. Upon finding that the water contained no mineral deposits and was in fact remarkably pure he decided to market the product accordingly. In the words of a contemporary rhyme:

> The Malvern Water, says Dr John Wall,
> Is famous for containing just nothing at all.

In 1757 he built a bathhouse close to the Holy Well which was quickly followed by dwellings and lodging houses in the nearby village of Little Malvern. The water's healing powers were held to work both by drinking it and by immersion of afflicted limbs in its healing embrace. However, almost a century had passed before Malvern's moment arrived, just as the principal phase of spa openings was drawing to a close. In 1842 Dr James Wilson, who had studied with Priessnitz in Silesia[12] arrived in Malvern with his colleague Dr James Gully and proceeded to advertise the benefits of the full range of hydrotherapeutic treatments advocated by his mentor. The fact that the water was pure and lacking in mineral content was of no importance given the diverse methods by which the cold liquid was applied to the hapless patient. He demonstrated the effectiveness of the process by curing of gout a notorious local drunkard, using water from St Ann's Well in Great Malvern, though the means by which this was done is a mystery to medical science. By 1845 the two men, now partners, had built 'Priessnitz House' where the full range of water cures was available in a routine from which Spartan warriors would have shrunk in horror.[13] At 5 a.m. the patient was awoken and wrapped in cold, wet sheets for an hour. Upon release he was placed in a bath in which state a pitcher of cold water was poured on him. Sometimes the cold water issued from a 3in pipe positioned 20ft above the bath. After this the patient was required to walk to St Ann's Well where he would find a German band playing to revive his spirits while he drank copiously of the healing fluid. Upon return to Priessnitz House breakfast was served, consisting of bread, butter, treacle and yet more water. Further baths and exercise followed before dinner was served, at the unusual hour of 3 p.m. This invariably included boiled mutton and fish and was followed by further walks and yet more baths. Supper, at eight, consisted of bread, butter, milk and, of course, water, after which the patient retired, no doubt with a strong virtuous feeling.

Dr Gully was the author of a book called *The Water Cure in Chronic Disease* which attained such celebrity that it attracted patients as diverse as Florence Nightingale, Charles Dickens and Charles Darwin. The last, who was not noted for his gullibility in scientific matters, read Gully's book on the recommendation of an old companion from his *Beagle* voyage, on which he probably caught the chronic disease that afflicted him for the rest of his life. It has never been diagnosed with certainty. Darwin remained sceptical about many of Gully's enthusiasms, notably the doctor's beliefs in homeopathy and mesmerism, observing that Gully's 'sad flaw' was that he 'believes in everything'. Darwin subjected himself to the treatment described above for sixteen weeks and was sufficiently convinced of the efficacy of Gully's cure to continue with it after returning to his home, Down House in Kent. The village carpenter built a hut with a huge cistern containing 640 gallons of cold water. The carpenter's son, John Lewis, recalled that Darwin would 'pull the string, and all the water fell on him through a two-inch pipe'.[14] On other occasions Darwin would be wrapped in blankets 'till the sweat poured off him. . . . Then he'd get into the ice cold bath in the open air.' Fortunately for the cause of science Darwin survived this treatment so his health was presumably, in some senses, extremely robust.

Darwin returned to Malvern on more than one occasion, notably in March 1851 when his beloved daughter Annie became ill. A course of sea bathing at Ramsgate near the Darwins' Kent home had not helped her and Dr Gully's cure at Malvern, after appearing to revive her, proved ineffective. She died in April 1851 and is buried in Malvern Priory churchyard. It is a testimony to contemporary confidence in the water cure that a man as intelligent and well informed as Charles Darwin would seek the treatment for himself and his daughter.

By this time the town of Great Malvern was equipped with a library, billiard rooms, assembly rooms and souvenir shops but Drs Wilson and Gully had fallen out and Gully found himself locked out of Priessnitz House. Undismayed, Gully struck out on his own and became chairman of the Malvern Hotel Company, with an income estimated at £10,000 per annum – the equivalent of £10,000,000 in twenty-first-century values. However, his downfall was more newsworthy and spectacular than his rise. In April 1876 a barrister called Charles Bravo died. The post-mortem showed that he had been poisoned by antimony, a particularly painful and unpleasant death. His wife, Florence, was accused but never convicted of poisoning him though she had a motive in his bullying behaviour. During the inquiry into Bravo's death it emerged that Dr James Gully had been Florence's lover before and, in all probability, during her marriage. Following the scandal Gully was removed from the membership of medical societies and his reputation never recovered. *The Times* lamented in an obituary that Dr Gully 'will be remembered in connection with the Bravo case'.[15]

Dr Gully was finished but Malvern was not. In 1851 an ambitious little company called Schweppes gained the concession to supply refreshments to the Great Exhibition. One of the products they chose was Malvern water which had been bottled for over two hundred years. It was marketed as 'Malvern Seltzer' meaning 'sparkling water' and the enterprise was so successful that Schweppes later built a bottling plant themselves, close to the Great Western Railway, so that the product could be easily distributed throughout the country. Over 12 million litres are now bottled annually, both still and sparkling. Lea and Perrins secured the concession to sell larger, quart bottles. Dr John Wall would be delighted.

STEAM CARRIAGES AND HORSE RACES

Other spas flourished with the help of aristocratic money and patronage. Leamington Priors was little more than a village in 1784 when William Abbotts, an innkeeper, created a drinking well around the town's saline springs. The water was promoted, for drinking or bathing, as a remedy for 'dyspepsia, or indigestion, sluggish liver and affections of the digestive apparatus generally'.[16] Further springs were discovered in 1810, by which time the town had become Leamington Spa and the growing number of (presumably constipated) visitors to the town attracted the attention of a local landowner, the Duke of Bedford, who opened the Bedford Hotel in 1811. In 1814 the 'Royal Pump Room and Baths' were opened and in 1838 the town became Royal Leamington Spa on the authority of the new queen who, as Princess Victoria, had visited the baths eight years earlier. By this time 'gout, stiffness of tendons, rigidity of the joints, rheumatism and various paralytic conditions' had been added to the roster of complaints for which the town's waters were recommended. The location of the town in hunting country, in the vicinity of the Quorn and Pytchley hunts, was a piece of good fortune since the hunting fraternity had the money and the leisure time to take advantage of the facilities to repair their damaged and aching limbs. The usual collection of disparate attractions followed the visitors. They included archery and tennis tournaments, a picture gallery and a 'Museum of Curiosities' which contained exhibits including, it was claimed, the coronation gloves of Edward I and Mary, Queen of Scots. At the height of its fortunes, in the 1820s and 1830s, Leamington attracted many foreign visitors drawn by Dr Henry Jephson (1798–1878) whose cures involved brisk walks and the consumption of copious amounts of water. This brought him an income twice that of Dr Gully, amounting to the enormous sum of £20,000 per annum.[17] By 1831 the population of the town had risen to over 6,000 and John Nash's name had been added to the list of architects who had contributed to its development. By the middle of the century the number of visitors had begun to decline though hydrotherapy treatments continued until well into the twentieth century. In 1889 the Royal Pump Room became the home of the town's swimming pool for the next hundred years. In 1999, after extensive redevelopment, this fine building became home to the town's art gallery, museum and library.

One of the spas whose competition drew visitors away from Leamington was Cheltenham, whose fortunes were advanced when George III drank the town's waters in 1788 in an attempt to cure the abdominal spasms which were an early symptom of the porphyria to which he succumbed in that year. By 1815 the town contained seven spa centres and the population grew from 3,000 at the beginning of the century to 15,000 by 1825.[18] Jenny Lind, Jane Austen and Sir Walter Scott were among the visitors, as was Marshal Blucher whose timely aid to Wellington in 1815 had turned the battle of Waterloo. Less well known at the time was Dr Edward Jenner

(1749–1823) the Gloucestershire doctor who discovered the efficacy of vaccination and who formed a Literary and Scientific Institution in the town. The spa's attractions also accounted for the foundation there of Cheltenham College (1841) and Cheltenham Ladies' College (1854) though the tone of the community was reflected in the exclusion of the children of 'retail traders' from both establishments.

William Cobbett, in his *Rural Rides*, delivered a typically astringent verdict on Cheltenham which he classified as a 'Wen', a term he reserved for communities that uselessly consumed the product of the honest labour of others. London, of course, was the greatest Wen of all. Arriving in Cheltenham in September, 1826, he wrote:[19]

> here we come to one of the devouring Wens: namely Cheltenham, which is what they call a 'watering-place'; that is to say, a place to which East India plunderers, West India floggers, English tax-gorgers, together with gluttons, drunkards, and debauchees of all descriptions, female as well as male, resort, at the suggestion of silently laughing quacks, in the hope of getting rid of the bodily consequences of their manifold sins and iniquities. When I enter a place like this, I always feel disposed to squeeze up my nose with my fingers.

He did not like them! Despite Cobbett's disapproval the 'silently laughing' (and very prosperous) 'quacks' continued to thrive and the town offered other

---

Sir Goldsworthy Gurney (1793–1885) A Cornishman by birth, Goldsworthy Gurney practised as a surgeon in Wadebridge before moving to London in 1820 where he delivered lectures on chemistry which impressed the young Michael Faraday. Gurney developed the process for producing limelight, the very bright light which is used in theatrical productions; the blowtorch; and a steam jet which was used by the Stephensons in *The Rocket*. Gurney also patented a steam carriage which he exercised near his home in Regent's Park before travelling in it from London to Bath and back in 1829 at an average speed of 15mph, following which he introduced the Cheltenham–Gloucester service. He was given responsibility for installing the lighting and heating system in the Palace of Westminster, a task which caused great anxiety to himself and to the increasingly harassed architect, Charles Barry.

facilities that Leamington could not match. Among these was a steam carriage service between Cheltenham and Gloucester using a machine devised by Sir Goldsworthy Gurney. This early form of automobile transport covered the 9-mile distance in 50 minutes but had to be withdrawn when the local coach proprietors, alarmed at the competition from the hissing, steaming monster, placed large stones on the road to impede its progress.

A more lasting institution began in 1814 when some local entrepreneurs organised Cheltenham's first horse races as an entertainment for visitors. This gathering in due course would develop into one of the world's most famous national hunt meetings featuring one of its most celebrated races, the Cheltenham Gold Cup.

Pennine Springs

The Pennine springs in Derbyshire, like those at Leamington, attracted the attention of the local landowner, in this case the 6th Duke of Devonshire who, when he was not commissioning new and exotic additions from his gardener at nearby Chatsworth, Joseph Paxton, was promoting investment in the spas at Buxton and Matlock. His predecessor, the 5th Duke, had recognised the potential of Buxton in 1818 when he installed hot baths and built the Crescent and the Great Stables which have survived into the twenty-first century as part of the Royal Devonshire hospital. These improvements were evidently needed. In the seventeenth century the intrepid chronicler of spas, Lady Celia Fiennes, who seems to have spent much of her life and fortune visiting spas and describing their facilities, had recorded a very unfavourable verdict on the accommodation at Buxton, of which she wrote 'we stayed two nights by reason one of our company was ill but it was sore against our wills'. The resort did not really prosper until the nineteenth century when the Duke's investments upgraded the town's facilities.

Matlock's warm springs (28°C) had been known since medieval times but it was the enterprise of John Smedley (1803–74) which was decisive in the development of the town's reputation for hydrotherapy. Having evidently benefited from hydrotherapy himself, Smedley, a successful local mill-owner whose name is commemorated in the company which bears his name in the twenty-first century, became its ardent advocate. He opened an establishment which became known as 'Smedley's Hydro' in 1851. Strict rules of temperance were imposed by this devout Methodist, together with penalties

Sir Joseph Paxton (1801–65) Son of a farmer, apprenticed to a gardener, Paxton so impressed the 6th Duke of Devonshire with his enthusiasm and ingenuity that the Duke appointed Paxton head gardener at Chatsworth and took him on a tour of Europe to gather ideas. Paxton created the famous Chatsworth fountain, 267ft high, and a 300ft glass conservatory which he based on the structure of a lily brought home from South America by a botanist. The success of the conservatory inspired him to design, on similar principles, the 23-acre 'Crystal Palace' (the name coined by *Punch*) for the Great Exhibition of 1851 after 233 other designs had been rejected by the organising committee. He completed the design, based on prefabricated inter-changeable panels, in nine days. It held 14,000 exhibits, was visited by 6 million visitors and generated enough profit to start building the South Kensington museums. The structure was dismantled and re-erected at Sydenham, south London, by navvies whose work so impressed the authorities that they used them as a model for the 'Work Corps' employed in the Crimean War. They later developed into the Pioneer Corps. The Crystal Palace was destroyed by fire in 1936. Paxton also designed a pavilion for the spa at Scarborough.

for discussing illnesses during meals. One of the consequences of Smedley's prohibition on the serving of alcohol in his establishment was an impressive gathering of licensed premises in the surrounding streets! Eventually a score of hydropathic establishments settled in the town, offering such treatments as douches, cold baths and 'steam boxes', these last being primitive saunas. It was claimed that these applications were 'particularly valuable as curatives in rheumatism, consumption [tuberculosis], gout and pulmonary and nervous disorders' – a reasonably comprehensive list of common Victorian ailments which made the spa attractive to a wide variety of users. Once again the attractions included a multitude of entertainments including fireworks, circuses and sports events.

Matlock attracted many visitors and prospered throughout the nineteenth century. Lord Byron, Charles Dickens and Sir Walter Scott were among its patrons and it even featured in Jane Austen's *Pride and Prejudice* as being close to the home of Mr Darcy. In the twentieth century the advance of medical science led to the decline of Matlock as a treatment centre but it re-established itself as a fashionable holiday resort, attracting visitors like the

writers Noel Coward and John Wyndham and the *Coronation Street* actress
Violet Carson (Ena Sharples). It continues to prosper as a centre for the
Peak District.

LONDON'S SPAS

It would be a mistake to assume that spa resorts were confined to rural areas
and country towns. London contained several spas which have left memories
of their names long after the spas themselves were swallowed up by buildings.
Two of them were neighbours in the vicinity of the present site of Sadler's
Wells theatre. The first, which began to prosper in the late seventeenth
century, was Islington Spa, now occupied by Spa Fields Green, close to the
theatre. Its owner, a businessman called John Langley, changed its name to
New Tunbridge Wells in the hope of cashing in on the reputation of that more
celebrated resort. There is no record of the reaction of the burghers of
Tunbridge Wells to this appropriation of their name at a time when laws
governing such matters were less well developed than they are now. In 1733
the fortunes of Islington spa were advanced when it was visited by the
daughters of George II, each arrival of the royal pair being greeted by a
twenty-one gun salute to remind others of the spa's distinction and thereby
encourage further visitors. It failed to thrive even though it had already seen

Spa Fields Green, Islington, former site of Islington spa. *(Stephen Halliday)*

White Conduit House, a modest spa whose adjacent cricket field evolved into a more celebrated institution. (*Corporation of London*)

off competition from its neighbour, a well which had been located in 1683 in the garden of Thomas Sadler, an inspector of highways. Sadler's Wells never really thrived as a spa but the wooden shed known as the 'Musicke House' prospered with its musical entertainments and a more ambitious new owner, Thomas Rosoman,[20] replaced it with a more durable brick theatre which took the name 'Sadler's Wells'. When a new theatre was built on the site in 1931 the well was covered with a trap door, situated behind the stalls. Charles Dickens, in his *Dictionary of London*, reported that Rosoman's theatre had a connection with the nearby New River Head[21] which enabled it to stage nautical spectacles.

At a short distance, at White Conduit House, was another watering place which would evolve into an even more venerable institution. White Conduit Fields[22] just north of the Pentonville Road was favoured by the aristocracy for games of cricket. Their team took the name the 'White Conduit Club'. Since the fields were a public place, the teams of earls, honourables and colonels had to share them with more plebeian players. They therefore asked one of their bowlers, a businessman called Thomas Lord, to acquire some ground where they could play in private. This he did in Dorset Square but when he was offered a good price for the land he sold it and moved the ground to the site of a duck pond at St John's Wood. In the meantime, in recognition of its new home, the White Conduit Club took the name the 'Marylebone Cricket Club' or MCC. The new cricket ground, of course, took the name of its owner Thomas Lord.

THE DECLINE OF THE SPAS

Malvern was the last of the spas to attract significant investment, in the 1840s, and no major spas opened after 1850. The Public Baths and Wash-houses Act of 1846 had encouraged local authorities to provide baths and swimming pools which were much cheaper, and usually more conveniently situated, than the privately owned spas. Nevertheless many survived until well into the twentieth century despite the gradual advance of medical knowledge which produced effective treatments for conditions like gout, tuberculosis and diabetes which the more assertive spas had claimed as their own. The First World War gave some stimulus to their fortunes, many of the spas being used as hospitals for over fifty thousand wounded or convalescent servicemen. Evidence of the confidence which medical practitioners felt in spa treatments may be found in a booklet published under the auspices of the Royal Society of Medicine. It was entitled *Notes on Hydrological Treatment for Wounded and Invalid Soldiers and Sailors*, with a list of the British spas and health resorts and of the disorders which they benefit.[23] The booklet, published in 1915, explains that 'The condition of *nervous shock*, resulting from traumatism, mental strain, or operation, can be treated at most of the British health resorts, the choice of locality depending upon the requirements of the case.' The words 'nervous shock' are in bold in the original text and, although the sentence fails to make any clear recommendation as to the suitability of individual spas, it is interesting in recognising nervous shock as a medical condition at a time when the military authorities were reluctant to recognise 'shell shock' as anything better than cowardice. Harrogate and Leamington were especially recommended for 'melancholia' (depression) and Cheltenham for 'chronic gout' though it is not clear why servicemen would be suffering from this condition at all. Most of the spas claimed to be able to relieve this painful affliction, presumably because it was common and therefore a source of many customers.

In the years between the wars the spas made a determined effort to revive their fortunes by forming the British Health Resorts Association. The purpose of this organisation may be detected in the original name under which it was formed in 1931. It was first called the 'Wintering in England Movement' which, in the words of its own handbook 'came into existence at a time of great national financial difficulty because it was felt that a great deal of money was being spent abroad in pursuit of health which might be spent at home'.[24] The organisation, based at 199 Piccadilly, one of London's most expensive addresses, promoted the publication of guides to the facilities of the various spas which were prepared 'with the assistance of the Medical Officer of Health and the Medical Committees in the localities',[25] a clear endorsement from the medical authorities. It made the confident claim that: 'Scientific Research has proved that *Gout, Rheumatism, Sciatica* etc. [bold in original text] can be effectively cured by the Radio-active thermal waters of Buxton.' In 1924, when the work was first published, the term 'radioactive' did not have the sinister associations that it later acquired so this highly dubious claim presumably carried some weight. It went on to make the more ambitious assertion that 'British spas are best suited for the disorders and breakdowns of middle life' including especially 'persons who are not perhaps ill, but feel that they are in danger of illness'.[26] To this general appeal to affluent middle-aged hypochondriacs were added recommendations for more specific disorders, many of which will not be found in any modern medical dictionary. Thus 'All cases of chronic toxaemia should be considered for spa treatment' while cures for 'hyperpiesia, gastro-hepatic catarrh, catarrhal dyspepsia, obesity and advancing age' were also offered. The publication itself must have been enormously profitable because two-thirds of its 160 pages were filled with advertisements from watering places.

Despite the efforts of the descendant of the 'Wintering in England Movement' the use of spas continued to decline, though the National Health Service, whose services supplanted those of the spas, continued to make use of spa facilities for many years. Bath continued to supply spa treatments until 1976. Two years later its waters were found to include some harmful toxins which were eliminated at considerable expense. Treatments continued at Leamington until 1990. In more recent years the buildings, if not the spas themselves, have benefited from renewed investment, much of it from the national lottery. Reference has already been made to the conversion of Leamington's Royal Pump Room into a museum, art gallery and library and £22 million has been invested in Bath. In Buxton, lottery money is being invested in the Pump Room and St Ann's Well in Malvern and the Royal Devonshire Hospital, formerly the Duke of Devonshire's 'Great Stables', are also being refurbished.

BESIDE THE SEASIDE

The practice of sea bathing around the coasts of Britain developed later than that of taking to the waters of inland spas and reached its zenith a century later, before foreign holidays posed a serious challenge to the seaside. It was less concerned with the niceties of etiquette. There was no Beau Nash to conduct proceedings and seaside holidays were more classless from an early stage. Nevertheless some resorts like Brighton owed their development to royal patronage while Torquay, on the 'English Riviera' claimed in its own publicity to have been the choice of the royal families of Britain, France and Russia.

Scarborough, in Yorkshire, has a sound (if sometimes disputed) claim to have become the world's first seaside resort owing to the enterprise of a Mrs Farrow who, in 1626, declared that a stream of water running from the cliffs to the south of the town had medicinal properties. The little town could thus offer both spa water *and* the novel practice of bathing in the chilly waters of the North Sea. An enterprising local doctor, Robert Wittie, declared that Scarborough's spa water was 'good against diseases of the head, as the Apoplexy, Epilepsie, Catalepsie, Vertigo, Jaundice both yellow and black, Leprosie, Hypochondrical Melancholy and Windiness'.[27] Given such a comprehensive list of real and imaginary complaints, it is not surprising that within fifty years many fashionable people were visiting the town in search of cures and before the end of the century Scarborough had its first spa building to which Sir Joseph Paxton later made his own additions.[28]

Scarborough's sea bathing accounts for the town's claim to have witnessed the first use of bathing machines, a print of 1735 showing such a machine in use there. These cumbersome devices, which survived into the twentieth century, were designed to protect the modesty of female bathers, and not only from the prying eyes of onlookers. It was naturally to be expected that ladies would not wish to be observed disporting themselves in the sea while partially clothed. However, the more elaborate machines also protected the lady bathers themselves from shocking sights, namely the spectacle of male bathers. Benjamin Beale (1717–75) of Margate is credited with the invention of a bathing machine which served this purpose and was in use in Margate from about 1750. This was a structure which resembled a small shed mounted on a cart which was attached to a horse. At the back of the 'shed' was a canvas screen mounted on a hoop. The bather entered the shed on dry land via a small ladder and was then drawn by the horse into the sea. Within the shed the bather would change into bathing clothes, leaving her clothes and personal belongings on hooks and shelves that were supplied for the purpose. When a suitable depth of water was reached the hooped canvas screen was lowered, forming a structure like a tent at the back of the shed. The bather, who had changed into bathing clothes, could then enter the sea beneath the 'tent' where she remained, unable to see or be seen by other bathers. Modesty was more important than exercise, which must have been severely limited by the narrow radius in which the bather could move about in the water. The Margate guide books of the day included directories of dozens of local enterprises from which such a bathing machine could be hired, of which it was claimed that 'by means of this very useful contrivance both sexes may enjoy the renovating waters of the ocean, the one without any violation of public decency and the other safe from the gaze of idle or vulgar curiosity'.[29] Beach huts eventually took over from bathing machines though the latter were still in use in Blackpool until the outbreak of the Second World War.

Nude bathing, often associated with the French Riviera and with Brighton in the late twentieth century, was a feature of the English seaside from an early date. In 1809 a Margate tailor was fined for 'daily exposing himself on the beach'[30] and sixty-five years later the Revd Francis Kilvert wrote of the pleasures of contemplating an attractive naked female on a beach in the Isle of Wight while complaining that 'At Shanklin one has to adopt the detestable custom of bathing in drawers. If ladies don't like to see naked men why don't they keep away from the sight?'[31] The development of bathing costumes which were comfortable to wear and could be put on and taken off beneath the simple modesty of a towel began in the late nineteenth century and the practice of nude bathing ceased for almost a century. Nevertheless as late as 1927 a Member of Parliament, Colonel Day, asked the Home Secretary for general legislation to prohibit the unseemly practice of undressing on beaches, as Southwold and Margate had done through local bylaws. He was refused. Those who did not wish to bathe took to the new pastime of paddling, fortified by the belief that seawater was good for corns.

The Rational Dress Society

The practice of sea bathing, and of the hydrotherapy which preceded it, must take some credit for the rise of the Rational Dress Movement which flourished in the later nineteenth century in reaction to the cumbersome and even dangerous couture which had been inflicted upon women from the 1820s. Corsets had become fashionable in the 1820s for both sexes. The Prince Regent had adopted them in an attempt to disguise his ever-expanding girth but as the century unfolded it was socially ambitious women who were subjected to an ever-tighter regime of whalebone stays which could damage their ribs, liver and lungs. In 1859 a young woman was reported to have died as a result of her liver being pierced by her ribs.[32] From the 1830s women adopted the practice of wearing multiple petticoats and, later, crinolines, so the unnaturally narrow corseted waist, which restricted breathing, was now joined by several pounds of horsehair, whalebone, wire and wooden framework which offset the narrow waist and no doubt helped the wearers to acquire the pale, sickly appearance which was temporarily *de rigueur* in the upper reaches of society. It was not unknown for a woman's knees to be tied together in the belief that this would enable her to execute a more graceful walk.

Such practices were incompatible with sea bathing or hydrotherapy, both of which were popular with the aspiring middle classes. The movement towards more comfortable dress for women may be traced to the United States in the 1850s when the editor of a temperance magazine, Amelia Bloomer, gave her name to loose-fitting trousers which were worn under a skirt. The rigorous exercise associated with Dr Gully's cures at Malvern and the frequent need to disrobe in order to suffer his cold douches[33] encouraged the adoption of looser, more comfortable clothing, especially for women. The spa at Ilkley encouraged its visitors to play croquet and lawn tennis, neither of which was suited to corsets and crinolines.[34] Likewise sea bathing, with or without a bathing machine, did not lend itself to the complicated procedures involved in removing or donning the cumbersome mechanism of such garments. In 1881 Viscountess Harberton founded the 'Rational Dress Society' which aimed 'to promote the adoption of a style of dress based upon considerations of health, comfort and beauty' and whose publication, *The Gazette*, opposed any designs which constricted or distorted the female form. 'Emancipation waists' gradually replaced corsets among more active women. These were short-sleeved high-waisted dresses without stays which enabled women to exercise in comfort. The society also advocated the adoption of divided skirts (in effect disguised trousers) for bicycling, the passion for which among the middle classes ended the reign of the corset.

Brighton: by royal appointment

The development of Brighton as a seaside resort is usually associated with the Prince Regent, later George IV. Indeed the novelist Thackeray wrote that 'It is the fashion to run down George IV, but what myriads of Londoners ought to thank him for inventing Brighton.' Yet the town was established as a centre for therapeutic treatments a century earlier. Dr Richard Russell was born in the nearby town of Lewes in 1687, studied medicine in Holland and later worked in London at St Thomas's Hospital. In 1750, by which time he had married a wealthy heiress, he returned to practise medicine in his native Sussex and visited Brighton at an opportune moment for the town. In the 1720s much of this little fishing village had been destroyed in storms, the damage being so great that money was collected in churches throughout the kingdom for the relief of its stricken inhabitants. Richard Russell decided that seawater (for drinking as well as bathing) had curative properties, especially in the relief of pain. He wrote an influential 'Dissertation concerning the use of Seawater in Diseases of the Glands particularly the Scurvy, Jaundice, King's Evil, Leprosy and the Glandular Consumption'. His work earned him election to a Fellowship of the Royal Society and King Lear's father would no doubt have been pleased to hear that another cure for leprosy had been found.[35] However, it was the prospect of a cure for his unsightly swollen glands that drew the Prince Regent to Brighton in 1783 and turned Brighton, for the first time, into a fashionable resort. By this time the town was prospering and the Prince's enormous expenditure (over £500,000) on the Royal Pavilion and his frequent visits quickly turned the town into the most fashionable resort of the time. The town's transformation was completed by the construction of a pump room in 1830 and a further royal visit by Queen Adelaide, wife of William IV, in 1830. Brighton was noted for its use of 'Dippers', men or, more often, burly women, who would forcefully plunge the shivering, reluctant patient into the chilly depths for as long as the doctor ordered. Mrs Martha Gunn and a male 'dipper' called 'Old Smokey' were the Prince Regent's favourites, neither of them noted for deference to rank, however exalted.[36]

'*George IV and Old England, the People and Pier*'

Brighton, like other seaside resorts, copied the inland spas in creating entertainment for the visitors who came in search of cures. In addition to the usual repertory of concerts, gambling and dances, Brighton was one of the first resorts to have a pier which provided entertainment. The early piers had been built to enable visitors arriving by sea, before railways reached the resorts, to disembark dryshod. Brighton's first pier was built as a 'chain pier' (a series of short suspension bridges) to receive visitors from the Dieppe packet boat, opening in 1823. It soon became popular as a promenade in its own right and was used by George IV for this purpose. Its novelty inspired the following verses:[37]

> But of all the sweet pleasures that Brighton can boast
> A walk on the chain pier delighteth me most,
> That elegant structure light, airy and free,
> Like a work of enchantment hangs over the sea,
> The hey derry derry – be this the toast here,
> George IV and Old England, the People and Pier.

In the 1950s the longest pier of all, that of Southend with its railway over a mile in length, was still used as an embarkation point for passengers on the steamers *Royal Sovereign* and *Royal Daffodil*. These continued to take holiday-makers between Southend and London long after the railways had reached the town. Few passengers realised that in 1940 these steamers had assumed a more heroic role when they took part in the Dunkirk evacuation, bringing battle-weary troops back to safety from those perilous beaches. Forty-six thousand evacuated troops were landed at Margate pier alone.

Southend Pier, the world's longest, with its own train. (*Stephen Halliday*)

Brighton's chain pier was washed away in a storm in 1896 but earlier (in 1866) it had been relegated by the much grander West Pier, designed by Eugenius Birch and now a Grade I listed building. It was the subject of a major restoration project before becoming the victim of a disastrous fire on 28 March 2003. Its future is uncertain. Birch's piers were more concerned with entertainment than transport. Born in 1818, Birch trained as an engineer and worked on railway projects during the boom years of the 1840s before turning to the design of piers, for which he devised a number of novel techniques. Prominent among these was the cast-iron 'threaded' column which was screwed into the seabed to support the decking of the pier. He later built fourteen such piers in resorts which included Blackpool, Margate, Scarborough and Bournemouth. His piers featured theatres, concert halls and games rooms as well as landing stages for the passengers who used the piers to join and leave the pleasure craft which became such a feature of seaside resorts. Some towns were not content with one pier. Brighton built two and Blackpool three, the North Pier, by Eugenius Birch, opening in May 1863, on an occasion which the normally restrained *Guardian* described as 'a great gala day' when 'the appearance of the town itself was as gay as any holiday could make it'.[38] By the end of the century there were over ninety sea piers on the coasts of England and Wales.

During the Second World War many south coast piers were deliberately damaged for fear that they might be used by invaders, though any such force landing on a pier would have been very vulnerable to attack in such a confined space. Many piers had central sections removed, leaving a stump on the shore and an isolated platform out to sea. Southend's pier was taken over by the Admiralty, temporarily named HMS *Leigh* and used as an assembly point for 3,367 convoys of 84,297 ships.[39] The piers' best days were now behind them and many suffered neglect and worse indignities from the 1960s onwards. Southend pier was severely damaged in a fire in 1976 and the decaying railway closed in 1978 but in 1986 it was reopened, fully restored, with a locomotive named after Sir John Betjeman. The popular Poet Laureate had made known his admiration for the pier as a fine example of the Victorian enterprise that he frequently celebrated in his writings.

'*Sea Bathing for the Working Classes*'

Like the spas, the early visitors to the seaside, in the eighteenth century, had been the genteel classes. Weymouth was favoured by George III whose visits were recorded by a lady-in-waiting to the Queen, the novelist Fanny Burney. In

1789, during the King's early struggles with porphyria, she recorded 'The king bathes, and with great success', the event being accompanied by a band who, up to their knees in seawater, struck up *God Save the King*. Jane Austen visited Lyme Regis in 1804 and later used the town for some important passages in her novel *Persuasion*. Blackpool was a paradigm of the democratisation of the British holiday resort in the century that followed. The town had earned its name from the peaty lakes, or 'black pools' on this section of the Fylde coast but in the eighteenth century some early drainage works brought improvements which attracted gentry from Lancashire to its bracing seaside air, so by the end of the century four small hotels were recorded. In 1801 the first census recorded the population as 473 inhabitants. The advent of the railway in 1840 attracted working people from the mill towns of Lancashire and from Glasgow and the town's attractions were designed with their needs in mind.

The railways were at first hesitant about running excursions to the seaside towns on the workers' only day off, Sunday, because of objections from protectors of the Sabbath. As late as 1895 the Anti-Sunday Travelling Union had over 20,000 members and led to a movement to end work at lunchtime on Saturdays so that factory workers could enjoy a trip to the coast without compromising their religious duties. Professor James Millar, of Edinburgh, argued that 'Early closing is the key to the Sabbath. Saturday afternoon is the time for recreation, that is the time for the steamboat trips and cheap railway trains.'[40] Commercial self-interest quickly overcame sabbatarian reservations but an advertisement for the Lancashire and Yorkshire Railway's excursion trains to Blackpool in about 1850 still struck a cautious note and urged passengers to avoid profaning the Sabbath by buying their tickets on Saturday. It read:

ON AND AFTER SUNDAY MORNING NEXT

and on each succeeding Sunday until further notice
with a view of affording the benefit of

Sea Bathing for the Working Classes

a train will leave the following stations for Fleetwood and Blackpool

Buy tickets on Saturday evening to avoid any unnecessary confusion of

BUSINESS ON THE SUNDAY

The Lancashire 'Wakes Weeks' when all the mills in a town closed down for maintenance, contributed to the development of Blackpool as did the similar Scottish 'Fairs'. The slow development of paid annual holidays by enlightened employers like Lever Brothers of Birkenhead gave further impetus to the seaside holiday but it was Sir James Lubbock's Bank Holiday Act of 1871 which imparted the greatest momentum to the day out at the seaside. In the words of the *News of the World*, on the first August Bank Holiday in 1871: 'From 8 a.m. the cry at every railway station was "Still they come!" and the supply of passengers far exceeded the supply of accommodation. At Fenchurch Street Station there was a crowd of hundreds of passengers struggling for tickets to Margate and Southend.'[41]

'*Vulgarians turn their backs on the town*'

Many seaside resorts sought to develop their own distinctive style. The opening of Blackpool's first pier, already noted, was soon followed by two more piers, the Tower, the Grand Theatre (both 1894), and the Winter Gardens, all designed to attract working families. The North Pier's admission fee of 2*d* was intended to secure a degree of exclusivity to the promenaders but the demotic character of Blackpool was now so firmly established that, in the words of a contemporary writer, 'Respectable visitors would not go upon the pier during the time that the excursionists were there.' The distinctly classless Pleasure Beach followed in 1905, to which the American inventor Hiram Maxim, better know for the Maxim gun, contributed a 'flying machine' which still swings giddy passengers around a whirligig a century and a half later. By the time the Pleasure Beach opened the town's population had passed 50,000 and the town was still a pioneer in the development of inexpensive, popular attractions. Having been the first town in the world to install an extensive system of electric street lighting[42] it was appropriate that Blackpool should lead the way with its illuminations in 1912, enabling it to extend the holiday season by two months.

At the other extreme Frinton in Essex became the butt of music hall comedians because it declined to permit the opening of any fish and chip shops, while Thorpeness, in Suffolk, with its boating lake, golf course and mock period architecture received the imprimatur of the arch-Victorian John Betjeman. Torquay was somewhere in between. In its *Official Guide* for 1932 it announced that: 'Vulgarians, whose idea of a holiday is compounded of paper caps, donkeys and tin whistles turn their backs on the town. The residue, the thoroughly normal, healthy and educated people who are the backbone of the nation, love Torquay as few other towns are loved.'

Medical values and uses in the prevention and cure of disease

Despite their more populist character the seaside resorts did not forget their therapeutic origins. They joined with their cousins, the inland spas, to publish *British Spas and Seaside Resorts: an appreciation of their medical values and uses in the prevention and cure of disease*[43] which made for the seaside claims of the kind already associated with the spas. From the 1850s research in Germany had suggested that seaside air was beneficial to victims of tuberculosis, a claim made for Torquay as early as 1841. In an authoritative guide to watering places it asserted that its air's 'genial and beneficial influence is to cure consumption, or at all events to prolong the existence of its victims'.[44] The creation of the 'Sunlight League' after the First World War to encourage sunbathing as a means of combating rickets added another therapeutic claim to the resorts' repertoire of cures.

Thus Margate informed potential visitors that 'for more than a hundred years admirable results have been obtained in children with tuberculous [sic] diseases' while Blackpool was recommended for 'chronic catarrhs of the *upper* respiratory passage' the italics presumably being designed to impart a degree of medical authenticity to the claim.[45] Those suffering from malaria were directed to Bournemouth (!) which was also suited to 'delicate and debilitated subjects, semi-invalids and elderly people' on account of its 'aromatic emanations of pine trees'. This aroma presumably masked that of the sewage which, it was acknowledged, was discharged offshore. It is a testimony to the confidence that many felt in water cures that the foreword to the 1936 edition was written by Sir Kingsley Wood, Minister of Health. He urged local authorities and their medical officers to continue their cooperation with the British Health Resorts Association in order to promote the nation's health. His endorsement of the association is, perhaps, a reminder of how recent is our understanding of the real causes of many common illnesses.

A final impetus to the popularity of the seaside holiday was given by the opening of holiday camps. The first was that of the Civil Service Clerical Association at Lowestoft in 1924, and Billy Butlin opened his first camp at Skegness in 1937. In the years after the Second World War the resorts benefited from legislation granting holidays with pay to most workers. In the 1950s 30 million people took seaside holidays, Blackpool alone attracting

7 million visitors. Thereafter, as increasingly affluent consumers sought more assured sunshine abroad, the fortnight at the seaside went into decline. Their fortunes were not advanced by the revelation that their seawater, the original reason for their popularity, was polluted by sewage. In 1993 the European Court ruled that all of Blackpool's beaches were excessively polluted by harmful bacteria, a decision that prompted the local MP to declare that 'People don't come here to swim.' True perhaps, but rather missing the point.

New roles for old waters

Both the seaside resorts and the spas have had to reinvent themselves to find new roles for the better-informed, more affluent and more fastidious customers of the twenty-first century. The seaside resorts have become more dependent on short breaks, day trippers and conferences to fill their hotels, restaurants and theatres while seaside towns like Eastbourne, Lyme Regis and Shanklin on the Isle of Wight have attracted large populations of retired residents. Spas, like Buxton, have benefited from the enormous growth in the demand for mineral water. This market was slow to develop in Britain, probably because our homes received clean tap water before such supplies were available on the continent. Average per capita consumption of bottled water in Britain is still barely one-tenth that of Italy, for example. However, in the twenty-first century more than £½ billion per annum is spent on bottled water in Britain and some £7 million on advertising it. Buxton, the leading British brand, accounts for about 8 per cent of the market, while the success of Malvern water has already been noted.[46]

PAIN MANAGEMENT – A NEW APPLICATION

Hydrotherapy has itself undergone a revival within recognised medical practice. Birthing pools are an increasingly common feature of maternity units to ease the processes of childbirth. The Pain Society promotes the use of a number of techniques in the management of chronic pain through almost a hundred pain management centres in England. Prominent among the techniques recommended is the use of hydrotherapy and at the time of writing, the society is campaigning for the establishment of a hydrotherapy pool at Brighton, where Dr Richard Russell first recognised the benefits of exercise in water to relieve pain. One fund-raising venture, carried out in Russell's name, raised £19,000 for the pain management programme of St Thomas's Hospital,

London, Russell's former employer. One of the most successful applications of hydrotherapy in the management of pain is to be found in Bath, where it all began in 850 BC. One of England's leading pain management units has been established at the Royal National Hospital for Rheumatic Diseases in Bath (still referred to locally as 'the mineral water hospital'), in association with the University of Bath. King Bladud would be pleased.

A computer-generated picture of the new Spa at Bath. *(Thermae Bath Spa)*

Epilogue
Water in the Twenty-First Century

Water or Ice Cream?

In May 2003, leaders of the world's wealthiest industrial powers gathered at Evian, France for the G8 summit. The agenda included a discussion of aid to the developing world. Evian is the home of one of the world's most celebrated mineral waters so it would be pleasing to report that the twenty world leaders and five thousand officials who gathered there devoted some of their time to considering ways of achieving the previously agreed goal of halving the number of people who lack access to clean water by the year 2015. Unfortunately politics dictated that the need for clean water was only briefly mentioned in one of the closing communiqués. Far more energy and ingenuity was devoted to manoeuvring around the issues arising from the recent war on Iraq than to reaffirming commitments to increase levels of aid to developing countries. None of the G8 countries has achieved the United Nations target of raising aid to 0.7 per cent of the national income and less than a twentieth of that is devoted to water and sanitation projects. The G8 countries spend more on ice cream and on bottled water than they do on aid.[1]

By some measures the problem is becoming worse. World population growth is concentrated in developing countries where the availability of clean water is most problematical. In some areas the destruction of forests, which hold together the soil, has resulted in the loss of beneficial microbes which consume harmful waste in river water.[2] WaterAid reports that in Ethiopia only 24 per cent of the population has access to safe water and 15 per cent to adequate sanitation. Infant mortality exceeds 10 per cent. Similar problems are found in neighbouring countries like Tanzania, Uganda, Malawi and Mozambique. In these countries diseases like dysentery and cholera remain a threat to human life, helping to ensure that life expectancy is in some cases half that of Britain, remaining at levels that Britons experienced in the nineteenth century.[3]

ICEBERGS OR DESALINATION?

Considerable ingenuity has been devoted to developing techniques to deliver safe water to areas of need, some of them eccentric. Plans to tow icebergs from the Arctic to the African coast are out of favour at present but desalination processes remain on the agenda. A method of desalinating seawater was the subject of a patent issued in Great Britain as early as 1852 but it was 1928 before the first working plant was established in Curaçao, off the coast of Venezuela. Ten years later Saudi Arabia received its first plant. This was an ideal location since the country has plenty of sunshine to promote the evaporation processes associated with many desalination plants and also has the money available to pay the heavy capital costs involved. In April 1961 President John F. Kennedy suggested that the development of an economical method of desalinating seawater would 'dwarf any other scientific accomplishments' and desalination plants now exist in 120 countries. More than half are to be found in the hot, arid areas of the Middle East and North Africa, though one-sixth are in the USA. Between them they produce enough drinking water in a year to supply the world's needs for about half a day.[4] More recent proposals for improving water supplies in developing countries have emphasised household-based systems: devices for filtering and purifying water for small groups of dwellings and for treating and using their waste on a similar scale. Such methods would not require the huge infrastructure projects whose cost has been an obstacle to progress in the past.[5]

PUBLIC OR PRIVATE?

The problem is not confined to developing countries. By some estimates the river systems which will manifest increasing problems in safe water supply in the next quarter-century include the Volta, the Nile and also the Colorado River in the USA.[6] Even the capital city of the most prosperous nation on earth has its problems. By 1990 Washington DC's nineteenth-century water supply and sanitation system had deteriorated to a point where laws on safe drinking water were in danger of being breached. After a long debate it was decided that the systems would remain in public ownership and that the cost of raising them to the required standards would be met by the sale of bonds rather than by handing them over to the private sector. In Great Britain the opposite view was taken. Water and sewage systems have been privatised, though subject to a carefully contrived regulatory apparatus. This combination has helped to ensure that river water, beaches and the seas around Britain are cleaner than they were under the former regime of public ownership and inadequate investment. The number of 'Blue Flag' beaches has been steadily growing.

The issue of private sector involvement in provision of water and sanitation services in developing countries is itself controversial.[7] Is access to water a human right, like access to air, or is it an economic good with a value attached to it? If, as most people agree, the cost of delivering clean water and good sanitation is so great that economic considerations have to be taken into account, should the resources of private capital be admitted to this sensitive area? If so, how will these essential services be delivered to shanty towns where the need is particularly great but from which it is hard to collect revenue? It is, perhaps, worth reflecting that most of the investment in the development of facilities in Great Britain for drinking water, drainage and canals came from private sources. Sir Hugh Myddleton's New River would have recognised the problems experienced in the supply of drinking water to cities in developing countries where illegal connections are commonplace. The problem is so pronounced in Dar es Salaam, the capital of Tanzania, that one writer compared the water supply pipes with a porcupine.[8]

Many people in developing countries are worse off than the citizens served by Sir Hugh Myddleton's New River in the reign of James I and by Sir Joseph Bazalgette in the reign of Victoria. WaterAid, founded in 1981, works with fifteen developing countries in Africa and Asia to improve water supplies and sanitation. Its work is uncontroversial, involving installing sewage disposal systems, drilling wells and providing piped water to communities that lack these essential services. Larger, politically driven projects, however, arouse the sort of opposition that would have been familiar to Hugh Myddleton, though on a much greater and more threatening scale.

DAMS OR PEOPLE?

The most controversial schemes involve building huge dams to provide drinking water, irrigation or hydroelectric power but whose environmental and political consequences are unacceptable. In the 1960s the construction of the Aswan High Dam on the Nile in Egypt threatened to submerge the 3,000-year-old temples of Abu Simbel. With the help of UNESCO these priceless monuments were dismantled and reassembled 60m above their original site. Twenty years later a greater controversy surrounded the Pergau Dam in Malaysia. Supposedly designed to improve electricity supplies to neglected communities in Malaysia, it emerged that the great majority of the power generated would go to the prosperous financial centre of Kuala Lumpur. Moreover, the British government's substantial contribution to the cost of the project was found to be linked to purchases of armaments from British suppliers.

That scandal was financial but worse was to follow. The Rivers Tigris and Euphrates both rise in south-eastern Turkey before flowing through Syria and Iraq. For twenty years the Turkish government has been building dams on the headwaters of the Tigris and Euphrates to supply power, drinking water and irrigation for their own citizens. These developments, reasonable in themselves, have provoked loud protests from the governments of Syria and Iraq that Turkey's effective control over the flow of the rivers represents a threat to the security of the water supply to these two nations. It is now suggested that, in this highly sensitive region, Turkey's control of water resources could become a source of conflict, perhaps even of war. The situation has been made worse by the proposed Ilisu Dam, the largest project so far, on the Tigris. Besides the additional alarm caused to the people of Syria and Iraq, it threatens to submerge Kurdish villages which, as well as being home to more than 30,000 Kurds, are of archaeological importance. The huge reservoir could trap up to half the annual flow of the Tigris and affect the seasonal flooding in Syria and Iraq which helped to make the 'Fertile Crescent' of Mesopotamia the cradle of civilisation. For these reasons the World Bank declined to finance the project. When the British government offered to provide finance they were severely criticised by the International Development Select Committee who made some menacing noises about the government's supposedly 'ethical' foreign policy. Government backing for the project was withdrawn and, to the relief of many, there are now doubts about whether the project will proceed. China, like Turkey, has declined to sign the 1997 United Nations Convention on the Non-Navigational Use of Transboundary Waterways and is proceeding with its own controversial 'Three Gorges Dam Project'. This involves damming the Yangtse River in a scheme which, by some estimates, is the most expensive construction project in history. The reservoir will flood over a thousand archaeological sites, create a reservoir approximately 300 miles long and require the resettlement of over a million people. The effects on the ecology of the area are a subject of controversy.

WATER WARS?

However, the greatest source of conflict over water may well exacerbate the bitterest dispute of all: that between Israel and the Palestinians. The principal supplies of fresh water in the lands that these two peoples uneasily share come from the River Jordan and the streams and aquifers that lie in the occupied territories of the West Bank. Chaim Weizmann, the first President of Israel, declared that it was 'of vital importance not only to secure all water resources already feeding the country but also to be able to conserve and control them *at their sources*'.[9] This last aim was not achieved until Israel's victory in the war of 1967. At present, therefore, Israel effectively controls most of these sources and fears that any settlement which leads to the creation of a Palestinian state will hand over control of the country's water supplies to an enemy. This neglected feature of the Israel–Palestinian problem may prove to be the most intractable of all. Conflicts over Middle Eastern oil were a familiar source of anxiety in the twentieth century. It is to be hoped that, in the twenty-first century, they are not overtaken by water wars.

NOTES

Prologue

1. *The World's Water, 2000–1* by P.H. Gleick, Washington DC, 2000, p. 23.
2. *Australian Capital Territory Future Water Supply Strategy*, Canberra, 1994.
3. *Watershed* by S. Lonergan and D. Brooks, Ottawa, 1994, is a valuable source of information on water problems in developing countries.
4. *World Resources 2000–1*, World Resources Institute, Washington DC, 2000, p. 110.
5. *New Rules, New Roles: Does PSP Benefit the Poor?*, WaterAid and Tearfund, 2003, p. 20; a synthesis of the report may be seen on the WaterAid website.

1. Water for Drinking

1. Sometimes spelt Middleton; the 'y' spelling will be used throughout the present work.
2. *Water Supply of Greater London* by H.W. Dickinson, Newcomen Society, 1954, p. 7.
3. *London under London* by R. Trench and E. Hillman, John Murray, 1984, p. 83 describes the construction of the Great Conduit.
4. *Water Supply of Greater London* by H.W. Dickinson, Newcomen Society, 1954, p. 20.
5. *London Water Supply* by H. Richards and W. Payne, London, 1899, p. 5.
6. The wording of the Act was unclear so the following year, 1606, another Act was passed 'for explanation of the Statute made in the third year of the reign of King James I . . .'.
7. *Sir Hugh Myddleton and the New River*: Transactions of the Honourable Society of Cymnrodorion, 1957, London Guildhall library, describes this episode.
8. *Lives of the Engineers* by Samuel Smiles, John Murray, 1874, vol. 1, p. 62.
9. For example the failure to raise money to bring water from Hampstead despite the passage of the London Water Act, described above.
10. *Metropolitan Water Board 50 years Review*, Staples Press, 1953, p. 303.
11. *Exploring the New River* by Michael Essex-Lopresti, Studley Brewin, 1986, p. 5.

12. The Metropolitan Water Board estimated that, at the time of opening, the enterprise had cost £18,525; *Metropolitan Water Board 50 years Review*, Staples Press, 1953, p. 223.

13. *The New River: a Legal History* by B. Rudden, Clarendon Press, 1985, p. 23, is the source of these figures and those that follow.

14. *Lives of the Engineers* by Samuel Smiles, John Murray, 1874, vol. 1, p. 79.

15. *Diary of John Evelyn*, Oxford University Press, 1955, vol. IV, p. 365, 4 February 1684.

16. *The New River: a Legal History* by B. Rudden, Clarendon Press, 1985, p. 134.

17. *Londinopolis*, ed. by P. Griffiths and M. Jenner, Manchester University Press, 2000, p. 260.

18. But not a limited liability company. This concept was not created until 1855.

19. *The New River: a Legal History* by B. Rudden, Clarendon Press, 1985, p. 19, makes this estimate.

20. *Ibid.*, p. 35.

21. *Ibid.*, appendix I.

22. See ch. 4, p. 109, for an account of Newcomen's work.

23. *The New River: a Legal History* by B. Rudden, Clarendon Press, 1985, p. 139.

24. *An Answer to the Report on the Alleged Combination of the New River and East London Waterworks Companies* by Richard Bigg, 1818, Guildhall pamphlet 4186.

25. This issue is dealt with in full in ch. 5.

26. *The Dolphin*, T. Butcher (publisher), London, 1828, p. 61.

27. *Early Victorian Water Engineers* by G.M. Binnie, 1981, Thomas Telford Press, p. 71.

28. *Early Victorian Water Engineers* by G.M. Binnie, 1981, Thomas Telford Press, gives an account of the dispute.

29. *The Architect and Contract Reporter*, 29 September 1893.

30. See ch. 5 for an account of Bazalgette's work in London.

2. Too Much Water

1. *The History of Imbanking and drayning of divers Fennes and Marshes* by Sir William Dugdale, 1662, p. 375.

2. See p. 49 for an account of Vermuyden's work at Canvey Island.

3. *History of the Commonwealth and Protectorate* by S.R. Gardiner, 1897, pp. 349–51, describes this episode.

4. *The History of the Drainage of the Great Level of the Fens* by Samuel Wells, secretary to the Bedford Level Corporation, 1830, London, p. 161.

5. See p. 26 above for this reference.

6. *Sir Cornelius Vermuyden: the Lifework of a Great Anglo-Dutchman* by J. Korthals-Altes, Williams and Northgate, 1925, p. 21.

7. The contract is printed in *Sir Cornelius Vermuyden: the Lifework of a Great Anglo-Dutchman* by J. Korthals-Altes, Williams and Northgate, 1925, appendix II, p. 6.

8. *The History of Imbanking and Drayning of divers Fennes and Marshes* by Sir William Dugdale, 1662, p. 145.

9. *Vermuyden and the Fens* by L.E. Harris, Cleaver-Hume Press, 1953, p. 52.

10. *Sir Cornelius Vermuyden: the Lifework of a Great Anglo-Dutchman* by J. Korthals-Altes, Williams and Northgate, 1925, p. 53.

11. *The History of Imbanking and Drayning of divers Fennes and Marshes* by Sir William Dugdale, 1662, p. 146.

12. *Lives of the Engineers*, vol. 1, by Samuel Smiles, John Murray, 1874, pp. 26–7 describes this incident.

13. *Huguenot Heritage* by R.D. Gwynn, Routledge & Kegan Paul, 1985, p. 35, identifies this community.

14. *The River Makers* by Trevor Bevis, 1999, p. 43, quoting a document of 1752.

15. *Lives of the Engineers* by Samuel Smiles, John Murray, 1874, p. 29.

16. *Sir Cornelius Vermuyden: the Lifework of a Great Anglo-Dutchman* by J. Korthals-Altes, Williams and Northgate, 1925, p. 128.

17. See p. 28 above for this reference.

18. *The Great Level* by Dorothy Summers, David & Charles, 1976, p. 64. This book is the definitive account of the drainage of the East Anglian fens.

19. *The History of the Drainage of the Great Level of the Fens* by Samuel Wells, secretary to the Bedford Level Corporation, 1830, London, p. 161.

20. *Lives of the Engineers*, vol. 1, by Samuel Smiles, John Murray, 1874, p. 33.

21. See p. 32 above for this reference.

22. *The River Makers* by Trevor Bevis, 1999, p. 32, recounts this incident.

23. *Sir Cornelius Vermuyden: the Lifework of a Great Anglo-Dutchman* by J. Korthals-Altes, Williams and Northgate, 1925, preface, quotes the poem in full.

24. *The History of Imbanking and Drayning of divers Fennes and Marshes* by Sir William Dugdale, 1662, p. 414.

25. *The Black Fens* by H.J. Mason, Providence Press, 1984, p. 11.

26. *Journal of the House of Commons*, vol. 2, 1641, p. 394.

27. See p. 29 above for these references.

28. Printed in full in *The History of the Drainage of the Great Level of the Fennes* by Samuel Wells, secretary to the Bedford Level Corporation, London, 1830, appendix 17, p. 339.

29. *Ibid.*, appendix 17, p. 346.

30. See p. 33 above for this reference.

31. His name as an Adventurer is registered as 'Andrew Burrell' rather than 'Andrewes' but it is surely the same person.

32. Originally printed in 1642; British Library catalogue no. 725.c.36.

33. *The River Makers* by Trevor Bevis, 1999, p. 39, describes Corporal Foster's exploits.

34. *The Great Level* by Dorothy Summers, David & Charles, 1976, p. 77.

35. *History of the University of Cambridge* by Thomas Fuller, 1665, section V.

36. *Vermuyden and the Fens* by L.E. Harris, Cleaver-Hume Press, 1953, ch. 10.

37. *The Urgent Hour: the Drainage of the Burnt Fen District* by J. Beckett, Ely Local History Publications Board, 1983, p. 15.

38. A particularly remarkable example of such a house may be seen at Thorney.

39. *The Urgent Hour: the Drainage of the Burnt Fen District* by J. Beckett, Ely

Local History Publications Board, 1983, pp. 34–5.

40. *Lord Orford's Voyage round the Fens in 1774*, Cambridgeshire libraries publication, 1988, p. 42.

41. *Ibid.*, p. 11.

42. *Ibid.*, p. 50.

43. *Ibid.* p. 18.

44. *The Great Level* by Dorothy Summers, David & Charles, 1976, p. 94.

45. *The Black Fens* by H.J. Mason, Providence Press, 1984, p. 30, describes a fen blow.

46. *Sir Cornelius Vermuyden: the Lifework of a Great Anglo-Dutchman* by J. Korthals-Altes, Williams and Northgate, 1925, p. 131.

47. *Lives of the Engineers*, vol. 1, by Samuel Smiles, John Murray, 1874, p. 47.

48. *Concise Dictionary of National Biography*, Oxford University Press, 1993, vol. 3, p. 3187.

49. *Water, Water, Everywhere* by T. Bevis, March, 1992, p. 38.

50. See p. 34 above.

51. *The Black Fens* by H.J. Mason, Providence Press, 1984, p. 19, describes this procedure.

52. *The Great Level* by Dorothy Summers, David & Charles, 1976, p. 195.

53. See the website at *www.greatfen.org.uk*

54. *A History of Canvey Island* by F. McCave, Ian Henry publications, 1985, contains an account of the early history of the island.

55. The honour of giving his name to 'Big Ben' has also been assigned to Sir Benjamin Hall, Chief Commissioner of Works. Nothing is certain.

56. See ch. 5 for an account of Bazalgette's work.

57. *Pall Mall Gazette*, 7 January 1886, p. 11.

58. *A History of Canvey Island* by F. McCave, Ian Henry publications, 1985, displays the advertisement.

59. *Hansard*, 2 February 1953, vol. 511, cols 2292–4.

60. *The Times*, 2 February 1953, pp. 8 and 9, gave a full account of the disaster.

61. *Hansard*, 2 February 1953, vol. 511, col. 1484.

62. The gifts were duly acknowledged; see *Hansard*, February–March 1953, vol. 511, cols 1731 and 2296; vol. 513, col. 1220.

63. See www.greenwichengland.com for an account of the Thames Barrier project and www.corrosion-doctors.org.

3. The Inland Waterways

1. *Bridgewater, the Canal Duke* by Hugh Malet, Manchester University Press, 1977, ch. 3.

2. *Ibid.*, p. 12.

3. *Ibid.*, p. 13.

4. Letter dated 7 June 1753, quoted in *Bridgewater, the Canal Duke*, p. 13.

5. Letter dated 18 May 1754, from Lyons, quoted in *Bridgewater, the Canal Duke*, p. 16.

6. See ch. 2 for an account of these waterways.

7. *A Tour of the Grand Junction Canal in 1819* by John Hassell, London, 1968, p. 1.

8. See pp. 111–13 for an account of the lives of Matthew Boulton and James Watt.

9. *Bridgewater, the Canal Duke* by Hugh Malet, Manchester University

Press, 1977, ch. 4, describes the role of John Gilbert (and his brother Thomas) in the Duke's canal projects.

10. *Bridgewater, the Canal Duke* by Hugh Malet, Manchester University Press, 1977, p. 60, contains a compelling account of this incident.

11. See ch. 1 for an account of the construction of the New River.

12. *A Description of Manchester* by James Ogden, 1783.

13. *A General History of Inland Navigation . . .* by John Phillips, surveyor, London, 1792, p. 78.

14. *The History of Inland Navigation, particularly those of the Duke of Bridgwater*, London, 1766, available in the British Library.

15. *The Canals of England* by E. De Mare, Architectural Press, 1950, p. 63.

16. *Bridgewater, the Canal Duke* by Hugh Malet, Manchester University Press, 1977, p. 121, describes the service.

17. *The Canals of England* by M.M. Evans, Weidenfeld & Nicolson, 1994, p. 64.

18. *Bridgewater, the Canal Duke* by Hugh Malet, Manchester University Press, 1977, appendix F, gives the details in full. Comparisons with twenty-first-century values are notoriously hard to calculate but a multiple of over a thousand would be indicative.

19. See ch. 4, pp. 111–13 for details of the careers of Boulton and Watt.

20. *The History of Inland Navigation, particularly those of the Duke of Bridgwater*, London, 1766, available in the British Library.

21. *Observations on the Proposed Grand Union Canal*, *c.* 1800, London, British Library.

22. Now part of Milton Keynes.

23. William Praed is commemorated by the street named after him at Paddington, one of the canal's termini.

24. *Hadfield's British Canals*, 8th edition, by J. Boughey, Sutton Publishing, 1994, p. 83; *Canal Mania* by Anthony Burton, Aurum Press, 1993, describes this frantic period of canal construction.

25. *Canal Mania* by Anthony Burton, Aurum Press, 1993, p. 14.

26. In 2004 plans are well advanced to reopen the Wendover branch.

27. Other arms were constructed to Slough, Paddington, Aylesbury, Northampton and Buckingham of which all but the last remain in use.

28. The longest canal on the system is the Standedge tunnel on the Huddersfield narrow canal beneath the Pennines; over 3 miles long, it opened in 1811 after much tribulation, closed in 1944 and reopened in 2001.

29. *Waterways of Northamptonshire* by D. Blagrove, Northants Libraries, 1990, p. vi.

30. *History of Canal and River Navigations* by E. Paget-Tomlinson, Sheffield, 1993, p. 292.

31. See pp. 91ff for an account of the Royal Military Canal.

32. *T. Payne Defended or, a Reprimand for the Grand Junction Canal Company* by Augustus Cove, London, 1908, British Library.

33. *Ibid.*, p. 54.

34. *The Tocsin sounded* etc., London, 1813, British Library.

35. See ch. 1 for an account of the New River Company.

36. The first inclined plane was built at Ketley, Shropshire, in 1788.

37. *A History of Inland Navigation*, 1779, quoted in *The Canal Builders* by A. Burton, Baldwin, 1993, p. 156.

38. *The Times*, 11 April 1793, p. 2, reported Courtenay's remarks.

39. *The Railway Navvies* by T. Coleman, Penguin edn, 1981, p. 25.

40. *The History of the Railway Connecting London and Birmingham* by P. Lecount, 1839, London, quoted in *The Canal Builders* by A. Burton, Baldwin, 1993, p. 165.

41. *The Carlisle Patriot*, 27 February 1846, quoted in *The Railway Navvies* by T. Coleman, Penguin edn, 1981, p. 29.

42. The Truck Acts, passed between 1831 and 1896, required that wages be paid in the currency of the realm, not in employers' tokens, but they were frequently ignored by contractors.

43. *The Canal Builders* by A. Burton, Baldwin, 1993, p. 167.

44. See panel on pp. 71–2 for details of John Rennie's career.

45. *Canals and Inland Navigation*, ed. by G. Crompton, Scolar Publications, 1996, p. 18.

46. *The Canals of England* by E. de Mare, Architectural Press, 1950, p. 68.

47. *Canals and Inland Navigation*, ed. by G. Crompton, Scolar Publications, 1996, p. 107.

48. *History of Canal and River Navigations* by E. Paget-Tomlinson, Sheffield, 1993, p. 302.

49. *Rural Rides* by William Cobbett, 1830, Everyman edn, vol. 2, p. 93.

50. *Canals and Inland Navigation*, ed. by G. Crompton, Scolar Publications, 1996, p. 107.

51. *Hadfield's British Canals* by C. Hadfield, ed. by J. Boughey, Sutton Publishing, 1998, p. 203.

52. *Bradshaw's Canals and Navigable Rivers of England and Wales* by H. De Salis, Blacklock, 1904.

53. *The Canal Boatmen 1760–1914* by H. Hanson, Manchester University Press, 1975, p. 42.

54. *Women and Children of the Cut* by Wendy Freer, Railway & Canal Historical Society, 1995, p. 14.

55. *Women and Children of the Cut* by Wendy Freer, Railway & Canal Historical Society, 1995, pp. 30ff. is the source of this and other information about the lives of boating families.

56. Vintage edn, 1999, p. 13.

57. *The Canals of England* by E. De Mare, Architectural Press, 1950, p. 15; there is little evidence to back the suggestion, however.

58. *Troubled Waters: Memoirs of a Canal Boatwoman* by Margaret Cornish, Baldwin, 1994, p. 13.

59. *Idle Women* by Susan Woolfitt, Benn, 1947. Sir Donald changed the spelling of his stage name to Wolfit from the original form which his wife used in her book.

60. Edith Cavell was shot by the Germans in 1915 for helping escaping allied servicemen.

61. *Waterways of Northamptonshire*, D. Blagrove, Northants Libraries, 1990, p. 196.

62. Lander Westall & Co., London 1908, and J. Murby & Co., London 1916, respectively.

63. *The Canals of England* by E. De Mare, Architectural Press, 1950, p. 112, with introduction by A.P. Herbert.
64. Though the network narrowly avoided wholesale closures in the 1950s and 1960s. See *Race Against Time* by David Bolton, Mandarin, 1991 for an account of the struggle to save the canals.
65. See British Waterways website for further details: www.britishwaterways.co.uk.
66. See www.romneymarsh.org website for this and other details.
67. *The Royal Military Canal* by Paul Vine, David & Charles, 1972, p. 9.
68. Undeserved target of the derisory rhyme 'The Grand Old Duke of York' etc.
69. *The Royal Military Canal* by Paul Vine, David & Charles, 1972, p. 27, describes this episode.
70. See pp. 71–2 for an account of the career of John Rennie.
71. The *Kentish Gazette* covered the story regularly throughout October and November 1804.
72. *Sussex Weekly Advertiser*, 22 October 1804, p. 3.
73. *Lives of the Engineers* by Samuel Smiles, London, 1861, vol. 2, p. 283.
74. *The Royal Military Canal* by Paul Vine, David & Charles, 1972, quotes Brown's account.
75. See pp. 83ff above for similar effects when navigational canals were being built.
76. *Kentish Gazette*, 8 January 1805, p. 4.
77. *Kentish Gazette*, 15 March 1805, p. 4.
78. See p. 9 above for an explanation of this process.
79. *The Royal Military Canal* by Paul Vine, David & Charles, 1972, p. 195.
80. *Ibid.*, p. 189.
81. *The Royal Military Canal, a Brief History* by G. Hutchinson, Brede Publications, 1995, pp. 20ff.
82. Immensely wealthy cousin of the poet Siegfried Sassoon, later military secretary to Sir Douglas Haig and political secretary to Lloyd George.

4. Water as Power

1. *Stronger than a Hundred Men: a History of the Vertical Waterwheel* by T.S. Reynolds, Johns Hopkins University Press, 1983, is the source of this early account of water power.
2. *Britannia* by William Camden, trans. by E. Gibson, 2nd edn, 1722, vol. 1, col. 196.
3. *Stronger than a Hundred Men: a History of the Vertical Waterwheel* by T.S. Reynolds, Johns Hopkins University Press, 1983, p. 139.
4. See ch. 1, p. 6 above for a description of this mechanism.
5. See p. 59 above for an account of this incident.
6. *Stronger than a Hundred Men: a History of the Vertical Waterwheel* by T.S. Reynolds, Johns Hopkins University Press, 1983, p. 123.
7. Presented to the Royal Society in 1759, published in London in 1794.
8. See panel on pp. 71–2 for an account of Rennie's career.
9. See www.cottontimes.co.uk and www.sabchurchill.com for a brief account of Arkwright's career.

10. *Abstract of British Historical Statistics* by B.R. Mitchell and P. Deane, Cambridge University Press, 1976, pp. 177–9.

11. See ch. 6, pp. 181ff. above for an account of the poet's views on this matter.

12. *The Lady Isabella Waterwheel of the Great Laxey Mining Company* by A. Jespersen, 1970; British Library ref. X.615/612 gives a good account of the origins of the wheel.

13. *The Manx Sun*, 30 September 1854, described the event.

14. Hero of Alexandria is credited with making a steam-operated device in the first century BC but if it was ever made, it was for entertainment, with no practical application.

15. See p. 205 for an account of Goldsworthy Gurney's career.

16. The world's oldest surviving steam locomotive, now in the Science Museum.

17. *Durham County Advertiser*, 1 October 1825.

18. See p. 62 above for reference to the Duke of Bridgewater's encounter with this feature.

19. *Mechanics Magazine*, 10, 17, 24 and 31 October 1829.

20. *Mechanics Magazine*, 24 October 1829.

21. *The Times*, 14 June 1879, p. 8.

22. *Parliamentary Papers*, 1898, vol. 45 contain the evidence given to the inquiry.

23. *British Road Steam Vehicles* by Brown, Riley & Thomas, Bramley Books, 1999, p. 5.

24. *Annual Abstract of Statistics, 2003*, Office of National Statistics, table 21.8.

25. A megawatt is 1 million watts; 25 megawatts would provide electricity for the homes of about 170,000 people: roughly the resident population of the city of York.

26. See website www.aboutbritain.com/Cragside.

27. See p. 102 above for this reference.

5. *Water as Deadly Danger*

1. See ch. 3 for an account of the Grand Junction Canal Company.

2. *Household Words*, 13 April 1850.

3. *Parliamentary Papers*, 1828, vol. 9, p. 149, Dr Pearson's evidence.

4. *Edinburgh Review*, April 1850, vol. 91, pp. 381–2.

5. The cause of Albert's death is not certain: cancer has also been suggested.

6. *Parliamentary Papers*, 1828, vol. 9, pp. 61–2, 122–3 and 168 describe medieval London's sewage problems.

7. Now the more decorously named Sherborne Lane, off King William Street, EC4.

8. *Memorials of London Life*, ed. by H.T. Riley, Metropolitan Archives, pp. 295–9.

9. *Leigh's New Picture of London*, London, 1818, p. 33.

10. *The Builder*, 18 July 1844, pp. 350–1; the origin of the professor's title is lost to history.

11. *Parliamentary Papers*, 1844, vol. 18, question 181.

12. *Parliamentary Papers*, 1840, vol. 11, question 3452.

13. *A History of Epidemics in Britain* by C. Creighton, Cambridge University Press, 1894, p. 858.

14. See p. 21 for an account of Liverpool's enterprise in this respect.

15. Liverpool City Archives ref. Hq.050 KAL.

16. *Parliamentary Papers*, 1844, vol. 17, contains Holme's and Duncan's testimony.

17. See p. 20 for an account of the work of Thomas Hawksley.

18. *Duncan of Liverpool* by W.M. Frazer, Hamish Hamilton, 1947, p. 98.

19. *Liverpool Daily Post*, 26 May 1863.

20. The abolition of Duncan's post was eventually announced on 10 September 2001, as a result of the reorganisation of health care in Merseyside and Cheshire.

21. *The Times*, 16 March 1850, p. 7 described the schemes.

22. *Civil Engineer and Architect's Journal*, 1852, vol. 15, p. 160.

23. The engineer, Isambard Kingdom Brunel, and London's first medical officer, Sir John Simon, are two other examples.

24. The Royal Archives, which the present author was allowed to consult by gracious permission of Her Majesty the Queen, contains details of Jean-Louis's attempts to recover his money: Royal Archives boxes 7/32 and 7/34.

25. See p. 72 above for an account of the work of Thomas Telford.

26. *Quarterly Review* (1850), vol. 88, p. 455.

27. Metropolitan Board of Works, printed papers, vol. 1, no. 10, Metropolitan Archives.

28. *The Main Drainage of London* by Sir George Humphreys, LCC, 1930, Metropolitan Archives.

29. A verdict that invariably has been repeated by the many Thames Water employees with whom the author has discussed the matter.

30. *Cassell's Saturday Journal*, 30 August 1890, p. 1160.

31. See ch. 1 for an account of Simpson's work.

32. *Parliamentary Papers*, 1884, vol. 41 contains a blow-by-blow account of the arguments.

33. Metropolitan Board of Works *Annual Report*, 1857–8, pp. 5–6 gives the estimates.

34. *Hansard*, 1857–8, vol. 51, col. 23.

35. Enough bricks to build 64,000 modern semis, for which information I am indebted to Mr E. Keane, builder by trade.

36. Metropolitan Board of Works *Annual Report*, 1860–1, engineer's report, p. 23.

37. Metropolitan Board of Works contract document 2431/1, Thames Embankment, 27 October 1863.

38. *The Observer*, 14 April 1861, p. 5.

39. *The City Press*, 14 September 1861, p. 4.

40. *Marylebone Mercury*, 12 October 1861, p. 2.

41. *The Times*, 14 July 1870, p. 10.

42. *A History of Epidemics in Britain* by C. Creighton, Cambridge University Press, 1894, p. 858.

43. *Endangered Lives: Public Health in Victorian Britain* by A.S. Wohl, Methuen, 1984, p. 119.

44. *The Lancet*, 12 November 1831, p. 216.

45. See pp. 134–5 above for an account of Dr W.H. Duncan's work in Liverpool.

46. *Report of the General Board of Health on the Epidemic Cholera of 1848 and 1849*, HMSO, 1850, p. 10.

47. *Parliamentary Papers*, 1846, vol. 10, p. 651.

48. *The Builder*, 1 February 1890, p. 79.

49. *Notes on Nursing*, Florence Nightingale, Harrison 1859 facsimile reprint, p. 16.

50. *Parliamentary Papers*, 1850, vol. 21, p. 543, contains Snow's evidence.

51. *Medical Times and Gazette*, 1858, p. 191.

52. *On Cholera* by John Snow, Wade Hampton Frost New York, 1936, pp. 110, 125.

53. See pp. 19–20 for the events surrounding these changes.

54. *The Great Stink of London: Sir Joseph Bazalgette and the Cleansing of the Victorian Metropolis* by Stephen Halliday, Sutton Publishing, 2001, ch. 6, gives a full account of this episode.

55. *Parliamentary Papers*, 1867–8, vol. 37, p. 117.

56. *Ibid*, pp. 79–80.

57. The restoration is being carried out by the Crossness Engines Trust; see their website www.crossness.org.uk for details of opportunities to visit the site.

58. 10, 17 and 14 September 1892.

59. *Minutes of Proceedings*, Institution of Civil Engineers, 1864–5, vol. 24, p. 285.

60. Institution of Civil Engineers Archives B867 BAZ RDT, pp. 454–9.

61. *Parliamentary Papers*, 1896, vol. 37, Supplement to 24th report of the Local Government Board, 1894–5, p. v.

62. *The Times*, 16 March 1891, p. 4.

6. *Water, Landscape and Literature*

1. *The Lake Poets* by Gavin Smith, Dalesman Publications, 1998, p. 7.

2. *The Wordsmiths at Gorsemere* by Sue Limb, Bantam, 1987.

3. *Oxford Companion to English Literature*, ed. by Margaret Drabble, OUP, 6th edn, 2000, 'Romanticism'.

4. Not to be confused with the other Seathwaite further south in the valley of the River Duddon.

5. For example, the picture taken from a satellite which is featured in *Land of the Lakes* by Melvyn Bragg, Hodder & Stoughton, 1990, p. 4.

6. The period of glaciation ended as recently as *c.* 10,000 years ago.

7. Thirlmere and Haweswater are both reservoirs for Manchester.

8. *Recollections of the Lake Poets* by Thomas De Quincey, Penguin edn, 1970, p. 216.

9. *The Prelude*, Book 12, lines 102ff., from which the quoted passage is an extract.

10. *Recollections of the Lake Poets* by Thomas De Quincey, Penguin edn, 1970, p. 135.

11. The *Journal* entry relates to 15 April and David McCracken has identified the site as south of Glencoyne Beck on the western shore of Ullswater; see *Wordsworth and the Lake District* by David McCracken, Oxford University Press, 1984, p. 143.

12. *Wordsworth and the Lake District* by David McCracken, Oxford University Press, 1984, p. 146, discusses the process by which

Dorothy's journal entry was transformed into William's magical poem. The poem is printed in full at the end of this chapter.

13. *The Prelude*, Book 1, lines 270–4.

14. *Ibid*, lines 288–91.

15. *The Prelude*, Book 5, lines 364–9.

16. *The Illustrated Wordsworth's Guide to the Lakes*, ed. by P. Bicknell, Webb and Bower, 1984, p. 90.

17. *The Illustrated Wordsworth's Guide to the Lakes*, ed. by P. Bicknell, Webb and Bower, 1984, p. 159.

18. *The Prelude*, Book 4, lines 50–4.

19. Duddon Sonnets numbers 2, 9 and 32 respectively.

20. *The Illustrated Wordsworth's Guide to the Lakes*, ed. by P. Bicknell, Webb and Bower, 1984, pp. 192ff.; extracts from Wordsworth's letter to the *Morning Post*, December 1844

21. Sonnet, 1844, *Proud were Ye, Mountains, When in Times of Old*.

22. *The Illustrated Wordsworth's Guide to the Lakes*, ed. by P. Bicknell, Webb and Bower, 1984, p. 116.

23. *Ibid*, pp. 129 and 133.

24. See the mill's website at www.britainexpress.com/History/stott-park.

25. *The Excursion*, Book 9, lines 113–17.

26. *Ibid.*, lines 267–71.

27. *Wordsworth and the Lake District* by David McCracken, Oxford University Press, 1984, p. 3.

28. *The Illustrated Wordsworth's Guide to the Lakes*, ed. by P. Bicknell, Webb and Bower, 1984, p. 25.

29. The Lake District now attracts about 15 million visitors each year: equal to a quarter of the UK population.

30. Notably the east window at Jesus Church, Troutbeck, designed by the Pre-Raphaelite Edward Burne-Jones and made by Morris's company. See website at www.visitcumbria.com/wmorris.

31. See the website www.visitcumbria.com/wgcoll for information about Collingwood.

7. 'Taking the Waters'

1. See Dickens's *Pickwick Papers* and the Grossmiths' *Diary of a Nobody* for the accounts of these very different Victorian holidays.

2. Geoffrey of Monmouth's myth-ridden twelfth-century *History of the Kings of Britain* refers to Bladud.

3. See pp. 201ff for an account of Dr John Wall's activities.

4. British Library catalogue, shelfmark 1509/1286.

5. *British Spas from 1815 to the Present, a Social History* by Phyllis Hembry, 1997, p. 166.

6. See ch. 6 for an account of the addictive problems of these two members of the Lake School.

7. *Beside the Seaside: a Social History of the Popular Seaside Holiday* by J. Walvin, Allen Lane, 1978, p. 15.

8. See www.fullerswood.fsnet.co.uk/norwood for these and other details of the Beulah spa.

9. *A Hundred British Spas* by Kathleen Denbigh, London, 1981, p. 190.

10. See p. 198 above for further details of Decimus Burton's career.

11. *A Hundred British Spas* by Kathleen Denbigh, London, 1981, p. 175.

12. See p. 196 above for an account of Priessnitz's career.

13. *A Hundred British Spas* by Kathleen Denbigh, London, 1981, p. 182, describes the routine.

14. *Darwin* by Adrian Desmond and James Moore, Michael Joseph, 1991, p. 366.

15. *The Times*, 5 April 1883, p. 5.

16. *British Spas from 1815 to the Present, a Social History* by Phyllis Hembry, 1997, p. 9.

17. *Ibid.*, p. 13.

18. *Ibid.*, p. 33.

19. *Rural Rides* by William Cobbett, Everyman edn, 1973, Book 2, p. 126.

20. Now commemorated by Rosoman Street, nearby.

21. See ch. 1 for an account of the New River.

22. The site is marked by White Conduit Street off Chapel Market, N1.

23. British Library catalogue, shelfmark 7462.cc.21.

24. *British Spas and Seaside Resorts*, 1936 handbook, preface, British Library catalogue, shelfmark P.P.2487.fcl.

25. *A Medical Guide to the Principal British Spas and Climatic Health Resorts*, British Library catalogue, shelfmark P.P.2487.fck.

26. *Ibid.*, pp. 3, 6.

27. *Beside the Seaside: a Social History of the Popular Seaside Holiday* by J. Walvin, Allen Lane, 1978, p. 17.

28. See p. 207 above for an account of Sir Joseph Paxton's career.

29. Website of Margate Charter Trustees: www.margate-kent.freeserve.co.uk/bathing-machine.

30. *Beside the Seaside: a Social History of the Popular Seaside Holiday* by J. Walvin, Allen Lane, 1978, p. 23.

31. *Ibid.*, p. 70.

32. www.mpmbooks.com contains an account of the movement towards more comfortable clothing.

33. See pp. 201ff above for an account of Gully's cures at Malvern.

34. *British Spas from 1815 to the Present, a Social History* by Phyllis Hembry, 1997 p. 174.

35. See p. 194 above for the reference to Bladud and Bath.

36. *Beside the Sea: Victorian Resorts in the Nineteenth Century* by Andrea Inglis, Melbourne, 1962.

37. *Guide to British Piers* by T.J. Mickleburgh, Atherstone, England, 1980, p. 4.

38. *The Guardian*, 22 May 1863.

39. See Southend pier's website www.theheritagetrail.co.uk/piers/southend for these and other details.

40. *Beside the Seaside: a Social History of the Popular Seaside Holiday* by J. Walvin, Allen Lane, 1978, p. 43, is the source of this quotation and pl. 6 in the same book shows the advertisement which follows.

41. *Ibid.*, p. 61.

42. Sir Joseph Bazalgette had installed electric lighting on his Victoria Embankment, London, in 1878 but this was on a smaller scale and was discontinued in 1884 when the electricity supplier went bankrupt.

43. *British Spas and Seaside Resorts*, British Library catalogue, shelfmark P.P.2487.fcl.

44. *Spas of England and Principal Sea-Bathing Places* by Dr A.B. Granville, London, 1841, vol. 1, p. 488.
45. *British Spas and Seaside Resorts*, British Library catalogue, shelfmark P.P.2487.fcl.
46. See p. 203 above.

Epilogue: Water in the Twenty-first Century

1. See WaterAid's website: www.wateraid.org.uk
2. *World Resources 2000–1*, World Resource Institute, Washington DC, 2000, pp. 12ff.
3. For these facts quoted I am indebted to WaterAid's factsheets. The charity's address is 27–9, Albert Embankment, London SE1 7UB.
4. *The World's Water* by P.H. Gleick, Washington DC, 2000, pp. 93ff.
5. These ideas were discussed at a conference at the World Health Organisation's HQ in Geneva in February 2003, involving engineers, academics, companies, charities and others.
6. *World Resources 2000–1*, World Resource Institute, Washington DC, 2000, pp. 110ff.
7. *New Rules, New Roles: Does PSP Benefit the Poor?* WaterAid and Tearfund report, 2003, available from the WaterAid website discusses these issues in a synthesis of a report which may be seen on the WaterAid website.
8. See reference on p. 12 above to the problems of the New River in this respect; *New Rules, New Roles: Does PSP Benefit the Poor?* WaterAid and Tearfund report, 2003, p. 24, contains the Dar es Salaam reference.
9. *Watershed* by S. Lonergan and D. Brooks, Ottawa, 1994, pp. 121–2.

INDEX